A Handbook of Test Construction

PAUL KLINE

A Handbook of Test Construction

Introduction to psychometric design

Methuen

First published in 1986 by
Methuen & Co. Ltd
11 New Fetter Lane, London EC4P 4EE

Published in the USA by
Methuen & Co.
in association with Methuen, Inc.
29 West 35th Street, New York NY 10001

Typeset by MC Typeset, Chatham, Kent
Printed in Great Britain
at the University Press, Cambridge

British Library Cataloguing in Publication Data

Kline, Paul
    A handbook of test construction: introduction to psychometric design.
    1. Psychological tests
    I. Title
    150'.28'7   BF176

    ISBN 0-416-39420-5
    ISBN 0-416-39430-2 Pbk

Library of Congress Cataloging in Publication Data

Kline, Paul
    A handbook of test construction.
    Bibliography: p.
    Includes index.
    1. Psychological tests—Design and construction.
    2. Educational tests—Design and construction.
    3. Employment tests—Design and construction.   I. Title.
    BF176.K578   1986   150'.28'7   86-12878
    ISBN 0-416-39420-5
    ISBN 0-416-39430-2 (pbk.)

Contents

Preface

This book has been given the title *A Handbook of Test Construction* to indicate its essentially practical aim. It is intended to be a guide, a vade-mecum for anybody who needs to construct a psychological test.

It contains an introductory theoretical chapter explicating the statistical rationale of the methods of test construction which are described in the text. This is to ensure that there is understanding, not blind obedience to dogma. Such understanding should also enable, it is hoped, the user of the handbook to modify sensibly any of the procedures in the light of his particular needs.

This book seeks to help the test constructor not only to execute the psychometric techniques necessary for adequate test construction but also to stimulate his production of test items. This is really an art, even though there are useful rules and guidelines, but it is one well worth cultivating since in the end the quality of a test is bounded by the quality of its items.

Finally I want to say a word about the computer programs included in this book. First I want to thank my colleague Dr Colin Cooper, who has worked with me on many research projects, for especially writing these programs. He is an expert programmer and statistician, and has produced a suite of programs which allow the user to carry out most of the statistical techniques described in this handbook. These have been rendered as foolproof as is reasonable (it is doubtful whether a truly foolproof program could ever be written), and they are capable of handling quite large data sets. Thus, armed with the handbook and the programs, a reader can construct and validate a test. In addition, the programs are useful for readers who want to try out the techniques described with a little trial data.

I have also set out the computational steps for many of the psychometric techniques in an effort to curb the frightening dependence on computer programs that many social scientists have developed. In examining PhDs at many universities, I find complex and outlandish statistical techniques used by students with only minimal insight. This can only be a bad development for psychology – hence the often laborious explanations of what has to be done, as well as the computer program.

Paul Kline
Department of Psychology
University of Exeter
April 1986

Glossary of terms

Biserial correlation This is the coefficient suitable for a continuous variable to be correlated with a dichotomized variable (e.g. pass–fail where the distribution is essentially continuous).

Communality The proportion of variance accounted for by a set of factors.

Concurrent validity This is measured by the correlation of a test with other tests purporting to measure the same variable.

Construct validity The more the results of a test fit the hypotheses that can be made about them, from the nature of the variable (i.e. the construct), the higher the construct validity of that test.

Correlation An index of the degree of relationship between two variables. It runs from -1 to $+1$. A correlation of 0 indicates no relationship; $+1$ shows perfect agreement.

Correlation matrix A set of correlations between variables. The resulting rows and columns of correlation coefficients contribute to the matrix.

Degrees of freedom An indication of the number of observations which are free to vary.

Face validity The more a test appears to measure what it claims to measure, the higher is its face validity.

Facility-value In item analysis, this refers to the proportion giving the correct response or putting the keyed response in a personality inventory.

Factors (factor analysis) Factors can be thought of as dimensions, constructs or vectors which can mathematically account for the covariance between variables.

Factor analysis This is a statistical technique which uncovers the determinants of correlations and thus helps to account for them.

Factor loadings These are the correlations of the factors with the variables. Thus a factor can be defined by or identified from its factor loadings.

Factor rotation If factors are conceived as vectors, then it is possible to rotate one factor relative to another. In so doing, the loadings change but are mathematically equivalent and thus there is an infinity of equivalent factor-analytic solutions.

Frequency distribution The number of persons obtaining each score on, for example, a test.

Hyperplane A plane in the spatial representation of factors, formed by all those variables with zero loadings on the factor perpendicular to the hyperplane.

Ipsative scoring The standardization of a subject's score in terms of that subject's own performance on similar items.

Item analysis A procedure for evaluating the effectiveness of an item in a test. This can involve correlating items with the total score on the test, factor-analysing items, Rasch scaling the items or subjecting the items to other estimations of their characteristic curves.

Mean The average of a set of scores.

Multiple regression A statistical method for computing the correlation between a set of variables and a criterion variable. Each variable is weighted optimally to maximize this correlation – the beta weights.

Norms The scores from different groups of subjects obtained during test standardization.

Objective test A test which can be objectively scored (i.e. the scorers are required to make no judgements) and whose purpose is almost impossible to guess.

Oblique rotation If the vectors or factors are rotated so that they are in the oblique position (i.e. are less than 90°), the factors are correlated, the correlation being the cosine of the angle between them.

Orthogonal rotation If factors are rotated orthogonally, the vectors remain at right angles to each other, and the correlation between them is zero.

Pearson product-moment correlation The coefficient of correlation suitable for continuous variables.

Phi coefficient This is the correlation coefficient suited to the case where both variables are dichotomous.

Point-biserial correlation This is suited to the case where one variable is continuous and the other is a true dichotomy (e.g. dead or alive).

Power test In a power test there is no time limit. Items are so graded that only a few subjects could get all correct, however long they tried.

Predictive validity The better a test is able to predict a criterion or criteria, the higher is its predictive validity.

Projective tests These are tests in which subjects are expected, generally, to respond to ambiguous stimuli. It is assumed that the responses are the result of subjects projecting their own inner feelings and conflicts into their descriptions, hence the name.

Q analysis A factor analysis in which people, rather than tests or measures, are the variables.

Rank-order correlation (Spearman's rho) This is the coefficient where the two variables are ranked.

Rasch scaling An item-scaling method developed by Rasch which assumes that the probability of a correct response is determined by two parameters: the extent to which the item elicits the latent trait and the position of the subject on this trait. These can be estimated independently.

Reliability The consistency of a test (a) internally and (b) over time.

Response sets These are patterns of responding to test items, which tend to distort validity. Acquiescence, agreeing with items regardless of content, and social desirability, the tendency to endorse items because it is socially desirable so to do, are common response sets.

Simple structure This is rotation of the set of factors which produces the most simple position, simple being defined as factors with each a few high loadings and the rest zero.

Standard error of measurement This is the range of scores within which the true score (*q.v.*) falls, given the obtained score, at various degrees of probability.

Standard deviation This is the square root of the variance (*q.v.*) and is thus an index of variability.

Standard score This reflects the position of a subject relative to a normative group.

T score A standard score which has a distribution with a mean of 50 and a standard deviation of 10.

T score (normalized) A standard score with a normal distribution, a mean of 50 and a standard deviation of 10.

Test standardization The collection of scores from representative groups of subjects thus making any obtained score meaningful in comparative terms.

True score A hypothetical score – the one a subject would have if he had taken the whole universe of items of which the test items are a sample.

Variance An index of variability around the mean of a set of measurements, the average of the squared deviations from the mean, the squared standard deviation.

Z score A standard score (*q.v.*) with a mean of 0 and standard deviation of 1.

1

The characteristics of good tests in psychology

A psychological test may be described justly as a good test if it has certain characteristics. It should be at least an interval scale, be further reliable, valid and discriminating, and either have good norms or fit a Rasch or similar model with high precision, or be expertly tailored to its subjects.

In this handbook I intend to demonstrate how these characteristics can be built into tests by sound and creative test construction. Before this can be done, however, it will be necessary to discuss and define all those terms which must be thoroughly understood if tests are not only to be properly constructed but properly used.

However, there is, as it were, a prior reason for requiring psychological tests to possess these characteristics. This is to improve the precision and accuracy of measurement. These qualities are themselves desirable because such measurement is a *sine qua non* of science. In the natural sciences progress has depended upon the development of good measures and, in my view, psychology is no exception to this rule. In brief, each of the characteristics which I shall describe below contributes to psychometric efficiency.

Types of scale

There are a number of levels of scales, hierarchically ordered. These are, beginning with the simplest, as follows:

(1) *Nominal*. This simply classifies subjects: male/female is a nominal scaling classification.
(2) *Ordinal*. Here subjects are ranked, as by weight or height. This is clearly crude because differences between ranks are ignored.
(3) *Interval*. Here the differences between scale points at all points of

the scale are equal. Equal interval scales can be linearly transformed, thus allowing transformation of scores to common scales and thus comparison of scores. Further, many statistical procedures assume an interval scale of measurement.

(4) *Ratio scale*. Ratio scales in addition have a meaningful zero point. This is clearly a problem for most psychological variables, although there are methods of test construction which allow for this possibility.

An examination of these four types of scale reveals clearly that, ideally, psychological test constructors should aim to produce ratio scales. Failing that, interval scales are desirable if the results are to be subjected to any form of statistical analysis. Since the study of the validity of tests almost inevitably involves such analysis, and since it is from the quantification of scores that psychological tests derive their advantages over other forms of assessment, the conclusion is obvious: nothing less than interval scales will do. In fact, as Brown (1976) points out, most psychometric tests approximate interval scales, and treating test scores as if they were interval scales produces useful results.

Reliability

In psychometrics, reliability has two meanings. A test is said to be reliable if it is self-consistent. It is also said to be reliable if it yields the same score for each subject (given that subjects have not changed) on retesting. This reliability over time is known as test–retest reliability.

The meaning and importance of the internal-consistency reliability

Psychometrists are eager to develop tests which are highly self-consistent, for the obvious reason that if part of a test is measuring a variable, then the other parts, if not consistent with it, cannot be measuring that variable. Thus it would appear that for a test to be valid (i.e. measure what it claims to measure), it *must* be consistent; hence the psychometric emphasis on internal-consistency reliability. Indeed, the general psychometric view is exactly this, that high reliability is a prerequisite of validity (e.g. Guilford, 1956; Nunnally, 1978). The only dissenting voice of any note is that of Cattell (e.g. Cattell and Kline, 1977). Cattell argues that high internal consistency is actually antithetical to validity on the grounds that any item must cover less ground or be narrower than the criterion we are trying to measure. Thus, if all items are highly consistent, they are also highly correlated, and hence a reliable test will only measure a narrow variable of little variance. As support for this argument it must be noted (1) that it is true that Cronbach's alpha increases with the item intercorrelations, and (2) that in any multivariate predictive study, the maximum multiple correlation between tests and the criterion (in the case of tests items and the total score) is obtained when the variables are uncorrelated. This is obviously the case, for if two variables were perfectly correlated, one would be providing no new information. Thus maximum validity, in Cattell's argument, is obtained where test items do not all correlate with each other, but where each correlates positively with the criterion. Such a test would have only low internal-consistency reliability. In my view, Cattell is theoretically correct. However, to my knowledge no test constructor has managed to write items that, while correlating with the criterion, do not correlate with each other. Barrett and Kline (1982) have examined Cattell's own personality test, the 16 PF test, where such an attempt has been made, but it appears not to be entirely successful. Despite these comments, generally the psychometric claim holds: in practice valid tests are highly consistent.

Test–retest reliability

Test–retest reliability is obviously essential. If a test fails to yield the same score for a subject (given that they have not changed) on different occasions, all cannot be well. The measurement of test–retest reliability is essentially simple. The scores from a set of subjects tested on two occasions are correlated. The minimum satisfying figure for test reliability is 0.7. Below this, as Guilford (1956) points out, a test becomes unsatisfactory for use with individuals because the standard error of an obtained score becomes so large that interpretation of scores is dubious. The meaning and implications of this standard error of score are discussed later in this chapter when I examine what has been called the classical model of test error (Nunnally, 1978), which is implicit in this discussion of reliability.

Although test–retest reliability is simple to compute, care must be taken not to raise it artefactually by having the sessions close together, and samples must be representative of the population for whom the test is intended.

Finally, in this connection I must mention parallel-form reliability. Here equivalent or parallel sets of items are constructed. Thus subjects take an entirely different test on subsequent occasions. However, there are difficulties here in demonstrating that the two forms are truly equivalent. Nevertheless, in practice parallel forms of test are found to be useful.

Validity

I shall now briefly examine the nature of validity, the second major characteristic of good tests. As with the treatment of relaibility, the aim in this chapter is to enable readers to grasp the concept sufficiently to understand the problems of test construction with validity as the target. The actual methods of establishing validity will be fully presented later in the book.

A test is valid if it measures what it claims to measure. However, this does not sufficiently explicate the meaning of validity. Instead it raises the new question of how we know whether a test measures what it claims. In fact, there is a variety of ways of demonstrating test validity, and each contributes facets of its meaning. These are set out below:

Face validity

A test is said to be face valid if it appears to measure what it purports to measure, especially to subjects. Face validity bears no relation to true validity and is important only in so far as adults will generally not co-operate on tests that lack face validity, regarding them as silly and insulting. Children, used to school, are not quite so fussy. Face validity, then, is simply to aid co-operation of subjects.

Concurrent validity

This is assessed by correlating the test with other tests. Thus, if we are trying to establish the concurrent validity of an intelligence test, we would correlate it with other tests known to be valid measures. This example clearly illustrates the horns of the dilemma of concurrent validity. If there is already another valid test, good enough to act as a criterion, the new test, to be validated, may be somewhat otiose. Indeed, it will be so unless it has some valuable feature not possessed by other valid tests. Thus, if it were very short, easy to administer, quick to score, or particularly enjoyed by subjects, this would certainly justify the creation of a new test where other criterion tests exist. On the other hand, where no good criterion tests exist, where the new test breaks fresh ground, then clearly concurrent validity studies become difficult.

Sometimes, where no criterion tests exist, we can attempt to use ratings. Here, however, there are severe problems. The validity of the ratings may well be questioned and, in addition, if ratings are possible, there may be little need for a test.

Generally, concurrent validity is useful in that often there are poor tests of the same variable which the new test attempts to improve on. In cases such as these, concurrent validity studies would expect significant but modest correlations. Clearly though, concurrent validity is not an entirely satisfactory aspect of validity. To accept a test as valid we would need further and different evidence in addition to studies of concurrent validity. It is also useful to establish what the test does not measure. The test should have no correlation with tests measuring quite different variables.

Predictive validity

To establish the predictive validity of a test, correlations are obtained between the test given on one occasion and some later criterion. The predictive validity of an intelligence test can be demonstrated, for example, by correlating scores at age 11 with performance at 16 years of age at 'O' level or even university degree classes. Many psychometrists (e.g. Cronbach, 1970) regard predictive validity as the most convincing evidence for the efficiency of a test.

A major difficulty with this approach to test validity lies in establishing a meaningful criterion. In the case of intelligence tests it makes sense, given our concept of intelligence, to use future academic success or even money earned in jobs. However, since there are clearly other variables than intelligence related to these criteria, such as persistence, the ability to get on with people, together with more random factors – good teaching and vacancies for jobs at the right time – correlations with intelligence test scores could be expected only to be moderate. Furthermore, intelligence is perhaps the easiest variable for which predictive validity studies can be designed. Neuroticism or anxiety also lend themselves to predictive-validity research because scores can be related to incidence of psychiatric morbidity and treatment, although even here there may be gross inaccuracy since cases may go untreated and undetected.

However, many variables are difficult to investigate in respect of their predictive validity. For example, Cattell's factor C – ego strength (Cattell *et al.*, 1970) – would undoubtedly provide a severe test even for the most imaginative investigator. In addition, there are further difficulties of a statistical nature, the most severe being the attenuation of correlations due to homogeneity of variance, but these technical problems will be discussed in chapter 7.

Incremental and differential validity

These two terms (discussed by Vernon, 1950) deserve brief mention. Incremental validity refers to the case where one test of a test battery may have a low correlation with the criterion but have no overlap with the other tests in the battery. This test then has incremental validity for selection in respect of the criterion. In occupational psychology this can be useful. Differential validity is best illustrated perhaps by interest tests. These correlate only moderately with university success but differentially for different subjects. Hence they may be said to possess differential validity for academic performance. IQ tests, on the other hand, have higher correlations with university degree classifications but cannot differentiate between subjects.

In summary, incremental and differential validity are useful indices of test efficiency for tests which are to be used in selection procedures.

Content validity

This is a term applicable in the main to attainment scores, and one which I shall simply describe. If the items of a test can be shown to reflect all aspects of the subject being tested, then it is *per se* valid, given that the instructions are clear. This is not simply face validity, which is related to the appearance of the test items. After all, if, in a test of mathematics, we want to test the ability to multiply terms in brackets and we have items such as $(y + 2k)(2y - 3x) = ?$, then it is difficult to argue that the item is not valid. Obviously, content validity is only useful for tests where, as in mathematics, the subject matter is clear.

Construct validity

Construct validity was a concept first introduced by Cronbach and Meehl (1955). To demonstrate the construct validity of a test it is necessary to delineate as fully as possible the variable (construct) which the test purports to measure. This is done by setting up hypotheses about scores on the test in the light of all that is known about the variable. Thus construct validity embraces all the approaches to validity which I have discussed so far. Construct validity is probably best explained using an illustration. I set out below the hypotheses to be tested in establishing the construct validity of a test of oral personality traits, – the Oral Pessimism Questionnaire (OPQ) – developed by the author (Kline, 1978).

(1) The OPQ should correlate positively but moderately (for they are not good tests) with other oral tests.

(2) From the description of the oral pessimistic syndrome, there should be a moderate correlation with neuroticism.

(3) Since the Cattell 16 PF factors contain no measures similar to that of the oral pessimistic syndrome, there should be no correlations with them.

(4) Since OPQ is a personality test, there should be no significant correlations with ability or motivational variables. Notice that this hypothesis exemplifies the need, in the study of construct validity, to show what the test does *not* measure as well as what it does measure.

If all these hypotheses were supported, then it would appear reasonable to argue that the construct validity of OPQ, as a measure of the personality constellation labelled 'oral pessimistic', was demonstrated. A further, more direct, approach to demonstrating test validity could constitute a fifth hypothesis, namely that subjects rated high on oral pessimistic traits would score more highly on OPQ than subjects rated low.

Thus construct validity is a powerful method of demonstrating the validity of tests for which the establishment of a single criterion is difficult. Rather than a single result, we have to consider simultaneously a whole set of results.

There is one problem with construct validity that must be raised. This concerns the subjective element involved in the interpretation of construct validity results. When, as is usually the case in practice, they are not clear-cut much depends on the interpretative skill of the test constructor.

Summary

I have described a variety of techniques for demonstrating the validity of tests; some of these are radically different from others. Thus construct validity is closely tied to our definition of a valid test as one measuring what it purports to measure. For this reason it is perhaps the most important aspect of validity, especially if tests are to be used to extend psychological knowledge. Differential validity, on the other hand, is aimed at demonstrating the validity of a test for a particular purpose. This is a different use of the term validity and one which approximates utility. Nevertheless, in the practical application of tests this aspect of validity is highly important.

From the discussion it should also be clear that there can be no one figure demonstrating the validity of a test. To assess it fully, a set of findings has to be taken into account. Nevertheless, many tests (although only a small proportion of the total number) have been shown to be highly valid both conceptually, as in construct validity, and for practical purposes. Furthermore, as will become clear in the course of this book, test validity can be virtually guaranteed by sound logical methods of test construction.

Discriminatory power

Another characteristic of good tests is discriminatory power. Indeed, this is one of the aims of the test constructor, to achieve a good spread of scores. There is little need to stress this point, which becomes self-evident if we think of the value of a psychological test on which all subjects scored the same. It is possible by careful test construction to ensure good discriminatory power, and this is where tests gain considerably over other forms of assessment. Generally, it has been found that about nine categories can be held in mind by markers or raters (see Vernon, 1950) and that in interviews it is perhaps most efficient to use three categories: below average, average and above average. Similarly, rating scales rarely contain more than nine categories. This means that subjects are put into nine groups at best. This ill compares with a psychometric test of some length where scores can range extremely widely and can yield standard scores running effectively from 20 to 80, with extreme scorers beyond these limits. Discriminatory power is measured by Ferguson's delta and is at its highest in a rectangular distribution of scores ($\delta=1$).

Before leaving the topic of reliability, validity and discriminatory power, I shall briefly outline the model of measurement implicit in all the above discussion. Even a slight acquaintance with the model will illuminate insight into the nature of test construction. It will also provide a rational statistical basis for the computations and procedures in test construction which are set out in this handbook.

Classical theory of error in measurement

Note: This section on the classical model of error measurement is the only one in the book with any mathematics in it, and the mathematics embrace less than is done for 'O' level in the subject. As I indicated, they are included to provide a rationale for the statistical procedures of test construction. Should they prove too fiercesome, the section can be omitted, or referred to, as the test constructor actually deals with the procedures in practice. So faint-hearted readers may proceed to p. 24.

The theory of errors in measurements which I shall outline has been called the classical theory because it has been developed from the most simple assumptions that have been made by psychological testers since the inception of testing. Both Guilford (1958) and Nunnally (1978) stress the fact that although more sophisticated models have been produced recently, the main principles of the classical theory still hold. Furthermore, these principles are easy to build into tests and are thus particularly valuable in the practice of test construction.

The true score

In this theory it is assumed that for any trait (e.g. fluid intelligence, extraversion, mechanical interests), each individual has a true score. Any score on a test for an individual on any occasion differs from his true score on account of random error. If we were to test an individual on many occasions, a distribution of scores would be obtained around his true score. The mean of this distribution, which is assumed to be normal, approximates the true score.

The standard error of measurement

The true score is the basis of the standard error of measurement. Thus, if we find that there is a large variance of obtained scores for an individual, there is clearly considerable error of measurement. The standard deviation of this error distribution is in fact an index of error. Indeed, since it is reasonable to assume that the error is the same for all individuals, the standard deviation of errors becomes the standard error of measurement. Since the test–retest reliability is the correlation between the obtained scores on two occasions, it is obvious that the higher the test–retest reliability, the smaller the standard error of measurement, on this model. This is indicated by the formula for the standard error of measurement (σ meas):

$$\sigma \text{ meas} = \sigma t / \sqrt{1 - rtt} \qquad (1.1)$$

where σt = the standard deviation of the test and rtt = the test–retest reliability.

The universe, population or domain of items

The classical theory of error assumes that any test consists of a random sample of items from the universe, population or domain of items relevant to the trait. Thus, if we are constructing a test of obsessional traits, it is assumed that our items are a random sample of all possible obsessional-trait items. Of course, this universe of items is hypothetical, apart from in spelling tests, where a full dictionary must constitute, if we include grammatical variants, the population.

In most cases, items are not thus randomly selected. However, as Nunnally (1978) points out, the fact that test constructors deliberately aim to create a diversity of items has the same effect. To the extent that items do not reflect the universe of items, the test will be errorful.

Relation of true score to the universe of items

In this model the true score is the score an individual would obtain if he were to be given all possible items. Hence the error of tests reflects the extent to which the actual sample items embrace the universe of items. It is to be noted that this model therefore leaves out other contributions to error of measurement such as how subjects feel, the temperature of the testing room and the adequacy of the tester.

Statistical basis of the classical model

The statistical basis for the classical model is fully set out by Nunnally (1978). I shall present the main essentials. As we have argued, the true score is the score of a subject on the hypothetical universe of items. This universe of items produces a correlation matrix (infinitely large) of inter-item correlations. The average inter-item correlation of this matrix, $\bar{r}_{ij}$, indicates the extent of a common core among the items. Thus, if, for example, we inserted into a test one item from a diversity of unrelated tests, the average inter-item correlation would be 0.00, indicating, quite rightly, that no common core ran through the items. Similarly, the variance of the correlations around $\bar{r}_{ij}$ indicates the extent to which items vary in sharing the common core. In the model it is assumed that all items have an equal amount of the common core, meaning that the average correlation of each item with all others is the same for all items. This is the basic assumption of the model.

From this classical model it can be shown that the *correlation of an item with the true score equals the square root of its average correlation with all other items.* Nunnally (1978) contains the fully worked derivation:

$$r_{it} = \sqrt{\bar{r}_{ij}} \qquad (1.2)$$

Strictly this is so only when the number of items approaches infinity, but even when only 100 items are used, there is little effect on the correlation coefficients.

From the viewpoint of the test constructor, this formula (1.2) is obviously of great importance, because if he develops a large pool of items and selects those the square root of whose average correlations with the other items is high, then by definition his test must be highly correlated with the true score; that is, highly reliable and free from measurement error. Formula 1.2 is clearly the statistical basis for item selection from a pool of items. This does not apply to speeded tests where unattempted items artificially correlate.

The same arguments, relating items to items, are exactly applicable to parallel tests of the same variable, each test being regarded as a random sample of items from the universe of items. The means and variances of such random samples of items differ from true scores only through chance. Hence, if, in all the equations we have examined, the standard scores for items are replaced by standard scores for tests (i.e. collections of items), the whole reduction process can be again utilized, and thus formula 1.2 can be written $r_{it} = \sqrt{\bar{r}_{ij}}$, where r_{it} = the correlation of scores on test 1 and the true score, and $\bar{r}_{ij}$ is the average correlation of test 1 with all tests in the universe.

Reliability coefficient

The average correlation of one test or item with all tests or items in the universe is the reliability coefficient. The square root of the reliability is the correlation of the test or item with the true score (as formula 1.2 indicates). However, this reliability $\bar{r}_{ii}$ cannot be known in practice, because the number of items and tests is not infinite, and tests are not randomly parallel. This means that the reliability of a test can only be estimated (r_{ii}).

Since, in practice, reliability coefficients are based upon the correlation of one test with one other, this estimate may not be highly accurate. This means, of course, that the more important correlation of test or item with the true score may also be an inaccurate estimate.

Fallible scores

These are the scores on any test, that is scores composed of true scores and measurement error. Any reliability coefficient that we obtain in practice, r_{ii}, for a test or item, will approximate $\bar{r}_{ii}$. If we assume that $r_{ii} = \bar{r}_{ii}$, then r_{it} (correlation of true and fallible score) $= \bar{r}_{ii}$. Thus r_{it} can be estimated. Given this, estimates of true standard scores can be obtained from fallible scores by the following formula:

$$Z't = r_{it}Z_i = \sqrt{r_{ii}}Z_i \qquad (1.3)$$

where $Z't$ = estimates of true standard scores, Z_i = standard scores on the fallible measure, r_{it} = the correlation of fallible scores and true scores and r_{ii} is the reliability of variable 1.

Since the square of the correlation coefficient equals the variance in one variable explicable in terms of the other, r_{it}^2 = the percentage of true score variance explicable by the fallible measure, but $r_{it} = r_{ii}$, hence *the reliability squared equals the percentage of true score variance in the fallible measure.*

Indeed, as Nunnally (1978) shows, if the test scores are deviation or raw scores (rather than standard scores), then:

$$r_{ii} = \frac{\sigma_t^2}{\sigma_i^2} \qquad (1.4)$$

where σ_i^2 = the variance of variable 1, and σ_t^2 = variance of variable 1 explained by true scores, and r_{ii} is the reliability. This is an easy estimate of σ_t^2 since r_{ii} and σ_i^2 are easily computed. Clearly, then, given the classical model of error variance, reliability is highly important.

Test homogeneity and reliability

The reliability of a test is related to the average correlation among the items, that is its homogeneity. However, since item correlations are obviously not identical, there must be a distribution of these around the mean. In the classical model of measurement it is assumed that this distribution is normal. Given this assumption, as Nunnally (1978) points out, it is possible to estimate the precision of the reliability coefficient by computing the standard error of the estimate of the average item intercorrelation in the whole universe of items.

$$\sigma \bar{r}_{ij} = \frac{\sigma r_{ij}}{\sqrt{\frac{1}{2}k\,(k-1)-1}} \qquad (1.5)$$

where $\sigma \bar{r}_{ij}$ = standard error of estimating r_{ij} in the universe, σr_{ij} = standard deviation of item correlations in a test, and k = the number of test items. Formula 1.5 indicates that the standard error of the estimate is obtained by dividing the standard deviation of the item correlations by the square root of the number of possible correlations among k items.

The minus one gives the correct degrees of freedom. From formula 1.5 it is clear that (a) as the standard error of this estimate rises the more the correlations differ among themselves and (b) as k increases, so the standard error falls, that is *the more items there are, the greater the precision of the estimate of the reliability coefficient.* Thus this formula shows that reliability increases with test homogeneity and test length, or strictly that the reliability of the estimate increases with test length.

These inferences from formula 1.5 are so useful for the practical test constructor that we shall discuss them further. First I must remind readers of the meaning of the standard error of the estimate of item correlations.

It means that 68 per cent of all sample average correlations fall between the mean plus or minus one standard error and that 95 per cent fall between plus or minus two standard errors of the mean. If we assume that the standard deviation of correlations on a test is 0.15 (a by no means unusual case) and apply formula 1.5 to tests of ten, twenty and thirty items we find the following standard errors:

ten-item test   0.02
twenty-item test   0.01
thirty-item test   0.007

Given these results it is clear that even with as few as ten items, the precision of the estimate of reliability is surprisingly high. This is due to the fact that the denominator of formula 1.5 increases rapidly as the number of items rises.

From the viewpoint of the test constructor, this precision is most encouraging. It means in practical terms that there is little error in the estimation of reliability due to random error in item selection. Another important inference as pointed out by Nunnally (1978) is that when apparently parallel tests have low correlations between them, this cannot be attributed to random errors in item selection. Either the items must represent different universes of items (i.e. they are measuring different variables) or else there is sampling error due to subjects.

Thus it can be seen that formula 1.5 gives the test constructor confidence that random errors are not likely to destroy his test construction analyses. Even with few items, reliability estimates can be precise.

Nunnally (1978) derives from this classical model a number of principles which are of value in practical test construction. The power of this classical model lies in the fact that so many useful derivations can be made. In fact, three important topics are covered: the relation of test length to reliability, the reliability of any sample of items and the estimation of true scores from obtained or fallible scores.

Reliability and test length

It should be clear that reliability increases with test length. Since true scores are defined as the scores on the universe or population of items, it must be the case that the longer the test, the higher the correlation with the true score, the extreme example being the hypothetical case where the test consists of all items in the universe except one.

From the viewpoint of the test constructor, what is important is the rate of increase of reliability with increasing numbers of items. It is often difficult to construct large numbers of valid items (i.e. those in the right universe of items); consequently if we can demonstrate that with, say, twenty-five items (of given average correlation) reliability is high, then this becomes a rational target. Nunnally (1978) shows how this can be done.

The result is the *Spearman–Brown Prophecy* formula (used in calculating the split-half reliability):

$$r_{kk} = \frac{k\bar{r}_{ij}}{1 + (k-1)\bar{r}_{ij}} \tag{1.6}$$

where r_{kk} = the reliability of the test, k = the number of items, and $\bar{r}_{ij}$ = the average intercorrelation of items. The Spearman–Brown formula is highly useful, as was indicated, in test construction. Suppose we had three sets of items: (a) ten items, (b) twenty items and (c) thirty items. Suppose the average correlation between items was 0.20:

$$\text{Set A} = r_{kk} = \frac{10 \times 0.20}{1 + (\ 9 \times 0.20)} = 0.667$$

$$\text{Set B} = r_{kk} = \frac{20 \times 0.20}{1 + (19 \times 0.20)} = 0.80$$

$$\text{Set C} = r_{kk} = \frac{30 \times 0.20}{1 + (29 \times 0.20)} = 0.959$$

r_{kk} is the reliability of the test, and its square root gives us estimated correlations of the items with the true score. Even a ten-item test yields a tolerable reliability, while with thirty items a very high figure is reached. Now these figures are obtained with items whose intercorrelations are low, only 0.20. In a test more homogeneous, where the average correlation is higher, 0.40, we find:

$$\text{Set D} = 30 \text{ items of } r_{ij} = 0.40$$

$$r_{kk} = \frac{30 \times 0.40}{1 + 29 \times 0.40} = \frac{12}{13} = 0.923$$

Thus a test constructor who can draw upon a large pool of homogeneous items is bound to construct a reliable test. It is to be noted, too, that if he split the thirty items into two parallel forms of fifteen items, these would both be satisfactorily reliable. Indeed, r_{kk} gives us the expected correlation of a test of k items with another k-item test from the same universe. r_{kk} *is the reliability calculated from the intercorrelations of test items*.

This Spearman–Brown Prophecy formula (1.6) is used in the calculation of the split-half reliability of a test (where the correlation between the halves is corrected for length). Here each half of the test is regarded as the sample from the universe. This enables the formula to be simplified for the special case ($k = 2$). The Spearman–Brown formula for use in split-half reliability is:

$$r_{kk} = \frac{2r_{12}}{1 + r_{12}}$$

where r_{12} = the correlation between the two halves of the test. Indeed, the basic formula (1.6) holds regardless of the size of the unit – items, or tests of any length.

Reliability and samples of items

The methods of calculating the reliability of tests which I shall set out in detail for the practice of test construction in chapter 5 have their statistical basis in this model of measurement error. Indeed, the Spearman–Brown Prophecy formula can be used to compute the reliability of a test. However, the computation of the correlation matrix is lengthy, and as a result other methods have been developed which are essentially the same, although they look different.

COEFFICIENT ALPHA
Cronbach (1971) and Nunnally (1978) both regard coefficient alpha as the most important index of test reliability and the formula is relatively simple. As Nunnally (1978) shows, it is derived from the classical model of error measurement. The alpha coefficient is the estimated correlation of the test with another test of the same length from the item universe. Its square root is the estimated correlation of the test with true scores. Thus:

$$\text{coefficient alpha} = \frac{k}{k-1}\left[1 - \frac{\Sigma\sigma_i^2}{\sigma_y^2}\right] \qquad (1.7)$$

where k = the number of items in the test, $\Sigma\sigma_i^2$ = the sum of the item variances, and σ_y^2 = the variance of the test.

This is the expected correlation of the test with a test of similar length from the same universe of items. The square root is the estimated correlation of the test with true scores.

Kuder–Richardson 20 (K–R20) is a special case of coefficient alpha for dichotomously scored items:

$$r_{kk} = \frac{k}{k-1} \left(1 - \frac{\Sigma PQ}{\sigma_y^2} \right)$$

(1.8)

where P = proportion putting the keyed response, $Q = 1 - P$, and σ_y^2 = variance of test. This is a simple coefficient to compute and naturally has the same characteristics as coefficient alpha, PQ being the equivalent of σ^2 in the dichotomous case.

It can also be derived from formula alpha that reliable tests have greater variance (and hence are more discriminating) than unreliable tests, an important practical corollary of this aspect of the model.

It is possible to estimate true scores from obtained scores utilizing the classical model of error measurement. However, this is not relevant to test construction, being of little practical value, and we shall not discuss this topic here.

One useful statistic can be derived from the model (mentioned at the beginning of this section) is *the standard error of measurement*. This is the expected standard deviation of scores for any person taking a large number of randomly parallel tests. It can be used to set confidence limits to obtained scores, although these zones are symmetrical about the true score not the obtained score, a point that is usually ignored in practice.

$$\sigma \text{ meas} = \sigma x \sqrt{1 - r_{xt}}$$

(1.1)

where x is a set of obtained scores and t is a set of true scores

$$= \sigma x \sqrt{1 - r_{xx}} \quad \text{(the reliability)}$$

Thus the standard error of measurement is the standard error of estimating true scores from obtained scores.

Enough has now been said about the classical model of measurement error. I hope that the rationale and statistical basis of the psychometric formulae used in test construction can now be understood. They are not simply the inventions of test constructors but follow logically from the assumptions of measurement error which are held in classical psychometrics. So let us leave this topic and turn to one of great simplicity, but one which is, nevertheless, highly useful in the application of psychological tests.

Standardization and norms

A further characteristic of good tests, which however is not intrinsic to
the test, is good norms. Norms are sets of scores from clearly defined
samples and the development and procedures of obtaining these scores
constitute the test standardization.

Norms enable the test user to interpret meaningfully the scores which
he obtains from individuals. They are, therefore, most valuable in the
practical application of tests rather than for research purposes, where
the original, raw test scores are used and where the norms add in little
useful information.

In chapter 8 I shall describe how norms should be set up for different
kinds of tests. Suffice it to say here that the sampling of groups must be
adequate and the numbers large. Otherwise the test norms can be worse
than useless, that is actually misleading. Nevertheless, if the standardization has been properly carried out, psychological test scores give us a
basis for comparison which no unstandardized procedure can provide.

It must also be realized that most methods of assessment other than
tests cannot be standardized, so that this capability is an important
characteristic of psychometric tests.

Some other models of test responses

I now want to discuss some different approaches to psychological testing
which make different assumptions about test responses. Some of these
are particularly important because they permit scales with a true zero to
be constructed and because they enable tests to be developed with
subsets of items that are truly equivalent, a property which has been
utilized in recent developments in psychological testing: tailored testing
and computer-based testing. Both of these methods are fully explicated
in chapter 10. In the present chapter I intend to discuss, albeit briefly,
the theoretical rationale of these methods.

Item-characteristic curves

Methods based on item-characteristic curves describe the relation of the
probability of responding Yes or No to dichotomous items to the
hypothetical attributes or latent traits which they measure. Their
statistical basis is fully described in Lord and Novick (1968).

There are various models of item responding based upon these
item-characteristic curves, which as Levy (1973) argues are broadly in
agreement. Birnbaum (1968) has a general latent-trait model where the

probability of a correct answer is a logistic function of item difficulty, tester's ability and a guessing parameter. The Rasch (1966) model is in effect a special case of the Birnbaum model, and is related to Guttman's (1950) scaling procedure where items are selected in order of difficulty such that any subject who fails item X will fail all items harder than X and pass all easier items. As Levy (1973) points out if Rasch scale items are distinct in terms of difficulty, a Guttman scale results, if this is not the case, and it rarely is, then a probabilistic version of a Guttman scale is produced. Similarly, Lazarsfeld's (1950) model is shown by Lord and Novick to be a special case of Birnbaum's model.

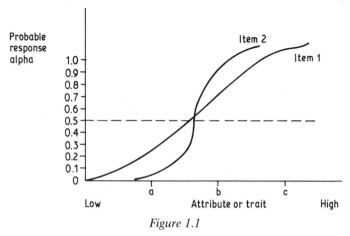

Figure 1.1

Figure 1.1 shows some hypothetical item-response curves for two items and helps to clarify the implications of item-response curves for the construction of psychological tests. First it should be noticed, as Nunnally (1978) emphasizes, that the latent trait or attribute is hypothetical and inferred from the items. In this respect, item-characteristic models are not different from the other kinds of tests which we have previously discussed. The general factor running through a set of items is, as we have seen, a construct to account for the item variance.

Let us suppose, for the sake of illustration, that the latent trait of the two items in figure 1.1 is intelligence. Subjects are distributed along a continuum – low to high intelligence. a, b and c represent three points on it. Subjects at point a have a probability of 0.015 of putting the correct response to item 2 and 0.15 of putting the correct response to item 1. Those at point c have a probability of 1 of putting the correct response to item 2 and of 0.95 to item 1.

The slope of the curves in figure 1.1 is not coincidental. Models based upon item-characteristic curves assume that these are normal ogives (cumulative normal distributions) or, for ease of computation, that they are logistic curves. This assumption is supported by the fact that, as Nunnally (1978) argues, psychophysical judgements closely fit this curve.

Item curves applied to testing

The item-characteristic curves in a pool of items are not expected to be or desired to be identical. If they were, each item would have identical qualities. Rather, the assumption is that each item tends to fit the logistic curve. The qualities of items reflected in the item-characteristic curve are partly shown in figure 1.1. These are:

(1) Difficulty (*d*)
This is reflected in how far to the right or left the curve is displaced, and is defined as the point on the attribute where the curve crosses the 0.5 probability value. Thus these items in figure 1.1 are almost equal in difficulty.

(2) Discriminability (*r*)
This is reflected in the steepness of the curve. The higher the value of r, the more sharply the item discriminates among people on the latent trait who are in the zone corresponding to a P value of 0.5.

Item subsets

Figure 1.1 shows that from item-characteristic curves it is possible to estimate the scores of subjects on items they did not take, given that their place on the latent trait continuum is known. This means that scores from subsets of items allow estimates of scores on the total test to be made, and item subsets can be drawn which are equivalent. Such indices of item difficulty tend to be more stable, being sample-independent, than the simple difficulty level estimated by the proportion of subjects getting the answer right, which is highly sample-dependent.

There are insufficient tests constructed by these methods to be confident about how efficiently, in practice, they might work. Nunnally (1978) has argued that the correlation between tests constructed by this method and by the conventional method is high. Nevertheless, one method, that of Rasch (1966), has had some strong advocates (e.g. Elliot *et al.*, 1978) and some critics (e.g. Mellenbergh, 1983) and as a particular version of the item-characteristic based method of test construction it must be briefly discussed.

The Rasch simple logistic response model

This simple logistic model (Rasch, 1960) can be expressed in a variety of ways. We present here the one that is the most easily interpreted. The point of the model is (1) to provide a procedure which can reveal whether a scale is internally consistent irrespective of the trait variance in populations, and (2) identify any item–population interactions (for within-population item variance may differ from between-population variance) which, of course, would render dubious any comparisons among populations as, for example, in cross-cultural studies.

When subject v encounters item k and responds Yes or No to it, a response variable x_{vk} is scored as 0 or 1, depending on whether the response points respectively to a low or high status on the trait being measured. The response is taken to depend both on the facility item k has for eliciting the trait status of all subjects as well as the status of a subject which governs his responses to all items. Let the trait status of subject v, which will be called the subject's trait measure, be represented by the parameter T_v, and let the facility that item k has for eliciting this status (in tests of ability called the item's difficulty) be represented by the parameter a_k. The response model which gives the probability of the score x_{vk} then takes the form:

$$P\{x_{vk} \mid a_k, T_v\} = \frac{\exp\left((T_v - a_k) x_{vk}\right)}{1 + \exp\left(T_v - a_k\right)} \qquad (1.9)$$

It is clear that the greater the measure T_v, the greater the probability that subject v will have a score of 1 for his response, and analogously, the lower the facility a_k of item k, the greater the probability that a subject will also have a score of 1 for his response. It is also clear that the subject and item parameters are considered unidimensional. If the responses of subjects to a set of items conform to the model, the evidence is that the items provide a unidimensional scale, or in traditional terminology, that the items are internally consistent or homogeneous.

The critical property of the response model defined by formula 1.9, which is clearly enunciated by Rasch (1960, 1961) and Wright (1968), is that the estimates of a_k are independent of the values of T_v and are therefore also independent of the distribution of the trait in any sample of subjects whose responses are analysed. As a consequence, evidence regarding the internal consistency of a scale within a population can be obtained without it being contaminated by the lack of variance in the sample measured. In addition, because the estimate of the value a_k for each item k should be equivalent irrespective of the measures of the subjects used to obtain responses, a check of scale consistency among populations can be made.

A number of procedures have been developed for estimating the parameters a_k and T_v and for identifying those items to which responses do not fit or accord with the model.

The parameter estimation involves maximizing the likelihood of the response matrix with respect to the item and subject parameters simultaneously, while the test of fit entails checking whether the observed data can be recovered by the model after the subject and item parameters have been estimated.

The check as to whether or not items are internally consistent relative to a single population will be called the within-population item-fit. The check as to whether or not items fit the model relative to a number of populations will be called the among-population item-fit. The procedure for making this check arises directly from the property that the item parameter estimates should be independent of which subjects have responded to the items. For each item the parameter values obtained from a sample from each population of subjects are compared statistically. For details of the complex estimation equations readers must be referred to Wright (1968) or Rasch (1961).

This Rasch model is mathematically far more complex than the classical model, and its computations demand a computer program. The advantage claimed for it as a basis of test construction is that the items may be used to obtain accurate scores for subjects regardless of the ability level of the subjects because item difficulty can be distinguished from subjects' ability (if we are measuring a variable in the ability sphere). As was pointed out above, this Rasch model is in fact a special case of the latent-trait model, and this may not be psychologically appropriate for many areas of measurement.

Various difficulties with the Rasch model are set out below, and these to some extent counterbalance the advantages of item-free and population-free measurement.

Some of the more detailed assumptions of the Rasch model are almost certainly wrong – that items are equally discriminating; that no guessing takes place; that only one trait runs through the items. Certainly an extra parameter to cope with guessing can be inserted into the Rasch model, but if this is done, then the procedures become too unwieldy for practical application.

Furthermore, as Lord (1974) points out, huge samples have to be tested if reliable, population-free calibration is to be successful. In addition, experience with attainment testing (e.g. Chopin, 1976) indicates that items often do not fit the model, and in any case there is considerable disagreement as to the statistical procedures to measure item-fit. To make matters worse, Wood (1978) showed that random data could be made to fit the Rasch model. Finally, Nunnally (1978) argues that in any case there is a very high correlation between Rasch scales and scales made to fit the classical model.

Barrett and Kline (1984) have shown that Rasch scaling can produce meaningless scales. Thus Rasch scaling of the Eysenck Personality Questionnaire (EPQ) produced a composite of N, E, P and L personality scales. Yet despite all these points, for some purposes, especially where testing is concerned with a clear population of items and where short forms of test or repeated testing are desirable, then Rasch scaling may be useful. Chapter 10 includes the practical procedures necessary for constructing such tests.

Finally, at this point, it is necessary to discuss briefly two other new approaches to testing which are not unrelated to Rasch scaling. I refer to tailored testing and computerized testing (described fully in chapter 10).

Tailored testing

Tailored testing involves, as the name suggests, bespoke tailoring tests to individual subjects. In essence an item of mid-range difficulty will be presented to a subject. If it is answered correctly, a more difficult one is presented; if wrong, an easier one. By such means a subject's precise level on a set of items can be accurately ascertained with only a relatively few items presented. All this involves computer presentation of items with Rasch or other scaled-difficulty indices stored in the memory and a computer program which presents items depending upon the response and item difficulties. Most tailored tests use items calibrated from item-characteristic curves so that accurate estimates can be drawn from subsets of items. Such tailored testing is indubitably valuable in practical testing where time is important.

Computer testing

Computer testing at its simplest involves presenting the items of a test on a computer screen and recording the response from the computer's keyboard or from a specially built response keyboard. At the end of the test the computer can display the subject's score and a simple interpretation based upon the norms of the handbook which have been inserted into the computer's memory. Each subject's scores on items and the total scores can be scored so that item analysis and factor analysis of items or any other psychometric technique is automatically available. Thus computer presentation of standard tests can be a highly efficient means of administration and psychometric analysis. In this sense the computer presentation resembles the binding of a book: it is good that this is beautiful and efficient but ultimately the content is more important.

Most standard tests, although there may be problems of identity with visual materials, can be presented on a microcomputer. When a conventional test is rehosted on a computer it should be revalidated and the norms should be checked. A more complex procedure, making more use of the computer's potential, is to devise tests that can only be presented on a computer. Examples of these could be items where the measure was reaction time, with the test items being varied according to the reaction speed. In this latter respect the test becomes a tailored test, and tailored tests, of course, are really computer-dependent. Generally, computerized testing, where items that are truly computer-dependent (as distinct from the presentation rules, as in tailored testing) is much in its infancy. However, in chapter 10 I shall describe how such tests can be developed.

Conclusions and summary

In this first chapter I have described the most important characteristics of psychological tests: their scale properties, reliability, validity, discriminatory power and standardization. I outlined the model of test error which underlies these psychometric notions and further described some different approaches to testing, including those based upon item characteristic curves, Rasch scaling, tailored testing and computerized testing.

In sum, it can be argued that the aim of test construction is to produce tests of high validity, reliability and discriminatory power. How this is to be done, for tests of various types, will be set out in the subsequent chapters of this handbook.

2

Making tests reliable I
Intelligence and ability tests. Item writing

We saw in chapter 1 that high reliability was a vital attribute of good tests. It was also evident that reliability was dependent to some extent on test length. Hence it is important in test construction to be able to draw on as large a pool of items as possible. Furthermore, a prime cause of unreliability in tests is marker unreliability, that is differences between the same scorer on two occasions and between different scorers. This can be virtually entirely eliminated if items can be written that do not require the scorers to make any judgements – that is objective items. For these reasons item writing is obviously crucial to the development of good tests. Indeed, a test can be no better than its items. However, it can be worse, if it is badly standardized or if the item trials and validation procedures are faulty (techniques which are fully explicated in later chapters of this handbook).

In this chapter I shall therefore concentrate upon the fundamental aspect of test construction: item writing. There are now huge numbers and varieties of psychological tests, and as a consequence there are enormous numbers and kinds of item. In this chapter I shall restrict myself to tests of ability, intelligence and aptitude – sometimes called cognitive tests. Even within this category it will be impossible to discuss every type of item that might be used. However, this is no disadvantage. When the general principles of item writing for cognitive tests are understood, specific item writing becomes easier. Thus I shall demonstrate the principles of item writing by illustration from the most commonly used types of item. By this means I hope to encourage creative item writing, the essence of good psychometry.

Before this explanation of item writing, some small but nevertheless important points in test construction must be mentioned. As I have indicated, to ignore these essentially trivial matters can ruin what would otherwise be good tests.

Instructions

The instructions for subjects taking the test must be as simple and clear as possible. If they are at all complex, some subjects will fail to understand them and this will adversely affect their scores. If this occurs, a general intelligence factor (accounting for the comprehension of instructions) will become compounded with the factor or factors tapped by the items.

In the test trials it would appear sensible to try out the instructions at some stage. I do not want to labour in detail this obvious point, but it is worth ensuring that the instructions are not sources of error for subjects who have failed items. This can often best be ascertained by interview, when we can find out what low scorers were trying to do. Such interviews also reveal inevitably the offending part of the instructions, which can then be changed.

The few rules for test instructions are: (1) be as brief as possible; (2) be as simple as possible, giving single sentences without qualifying clauses; and (3) examples should always help to clarify instructions. An attractive possibility is to write the test instructions as part of a pretesting procedure. This involves the test administrator, before the test starts, going over the instructions with the subjects, even to the extent of giving them trial questions and making sure the answers are understood. This not only results in all subjects understanding the instructions and becoming familiar with the kinds of item (both possible sources of measurement error – in terms of the classical model these aspects of the items are part of a different universe of items), but in addition it establishes a good rapport between subjects and testers, which is essential if the subjects are to show their best performance and is one of the claimed advantages of individual over group tests, as Nisbet (1972) points out. In fact, Alice Heim uses this method of presenting instructions for her AH series of intelligence tests (Heim *et al.*, 1970).

Indeed, I would advocate that test instructions be written separately from the test unless speed of administration is of prime importance or ease of administration by untrained testers. Since neither of these characteristics is desirable for tests, I suggest that test instructions should be separate from the test itself and should be such that the test administrator ensures their comprehension.

Items for intelligence tests

I would now like to examine the kinds of item suitable for intelligence tests, essentially following Spearman's (1927) definition of intelligence in terms of factor-analytic results. The most convincing factorial analysis of abilities, having regard to the technical problems of factor analysis, seems to be that of Hakstian and Cattell (1974). From this work, the basis of which is fully discussed in Cattell (1971), two factors of intelligence emerge: g_f fluid ability and g_c crystallized ability. Fluid ability closely resembles Spearman's g in that it involves the capacity to perceive relations and educe correlates but with materials which minimize individual differences in education and acculturation. Crystallized ability involves these same capacities but as they are realized within any given culture. Most efficient intelligence tests, devised before the factorial splitting of g into crystallized and fluid ability, in fact have items which load on both these factors. Since the crystallized ability represents the extent to which an individual's fluid ability has been utilized in a culturally viable way, it can be seen that the kind of items tapping each ability will be similar in principle but different in detail.

Analogies

The *analogy* is a type of item commonly found in most tests of intelligence. It is particularly useful because, first, the difficulty level is easily manipulated, in respect of the actual relationship and not just the obscurity of objects to be related, a feature making for items suitable for all age groups and levels of ability. Second, the materials with which the analogies are to be made can be almost limitless. This means that *analogies* is a suitable item form for both g_c and g_f tests.

There follows a number of examples of analogies items. All items are constructed by the present author. They have not been tried out (except where stated), and their only validity is face validity. It must be made clear that I am not claiming these to be good items. I am including them as examples of item types. The comments are designed to explicate their construction. Their quality would be judged by the item statistics and the subsequent validity of tests of which they formed a part. Each item involves a relationship which has to be educed, hence their importance for intelligence testing.

EXAMPLE 1

Wren is to bird as minnow is to . . .
(a) animal, (b) ant, (c) fish, (d) bird, (e) reptile

This is clearly an easy item, measuring g_c – the crystallized ability – as it is evinced in our culture. There are two points to note here. First, the relationship is easy to work out that *wren* is a member of a particular class. The solution therefore involves putting *minnow* into an analogous class. The item is also easy in that the knowledge required is elementary: most 9-year-olds should have sufficient information about natural history to solve it. However, it obviously does demand knowledge. For example, an African or Indian who did not know these species could not solve it, however bright he or she might be. The multiple choice distractors should always be tried out, to ensure that they do distract, since if they fail to do so, the item becomes absurdly easy. This aspect of test construction is dealt with on p. 36.

EXAMPLE 2

Vulture is to bird as cobra is to . . .
(a) animal, (b) ant, (c) fish, (d) bird, (e) reptile

This item is suggested as a possible equivalent in Africa or India. Whether in fact these classifications would be there as well known as the alternatives in the first item are in Britain would be determined in the test trials. This problem highlights the need in cross-cultural testing to know the culture for which the test is intended well.

EXAMPLE 3

Sampson Agonistes is to Comus as the Bacchae are to . . .
(a) Oedipus Rex, (b) Medaea, (c) Satyricon, (d) Prometheus Bound, (e) The Tempest

This is obviously an item tapping, if anything, g_c, in that it clearly demands knowledge of the sort that, in these barbarous times, is only (but not always) acquired in higher education. In our view it is probably a poor item because it demands esoteric and specialized knowledge, but the relationship to be educed is simple – one of authorship. It has been included because it resembles items found in a high-level intelligence test used to select for graduate education in America – that is Miller's Analogies (Miller, 1970) – and because its apparent difficulty resides not in the reasoning required, the essence of intelligence, but in the information necessary to solve it. Example 3 demonstrates that if we want to write difficult items for tests of crystallized ability, we need to construct items where the informational and the reasoning demands are high.

EXAMPLE 4

Television is to microscope as telephone is to . . .
(a) amplifier, (b) microprocessor, (c) microdot, (d) microphone, (e) loudspeaker

This would appear to be a difficult item, measuring g_c mainly but also g_f, far superior to example 3. This item requires a reasonable amount of knowledge of the function of modern high technology gadgets before it can be correctly answered. However, in addition, the analogy itself is not so glaringly obvious. Thus the correct solution demands that the subject sees that the relationship is one of distance to size magnification. Hence (a) is the correct response. Notice that the distractors have been cunningly worded so that the subject who has only worked out an imprecise relationship will probably plump for microphone. Of course, it must be stressed, these distractors would be tried out in the item trials to ensure that, first, they are distracting and, second, that they do not distract the best subjects (see p. 36). However, good distractor writing is important, and it is likely that the distractors here associated either with micros or sounds will in fact trap the poor reasoner. It is also noteworthy that difficult g_c items which demand deduction and information will load on both g_c and g_f which demand deduction alone.

One of the advantages of analogies as an item form is that various types of relationships can be woven into the items. In our examples so far we have seen class membership and opposition, but others are possible.

EXAMPLE 5

Molehill is to hummock as gorge is to . . .
(a) ditch, (b) valley, (c) chasm, (d) river, (e) mountain

This item again is an easy g_c item where the relationship is one of sequential increase in size. Mere geographic information would be insufficient to solve it since all the distractors are of this kind.

EXAMPLE 6

Fast is to celerity as slow is to . . .
(a) sloth, (b) speed, (c) haste, (d) tardiness, (e) lassitude

Here the relationship is one of abstraction – from noun to adjective. Obviously, the solution depends upon adequate vocabulary. This verbal item is important because verbal reasoning items are usually the best single predictors of crystallized ability. For subjects who have had equal opportunities to acquire a good vocabulary, such items, although not necessarily in analogous form, constitute powerful intelligence test items.

The analogies items which we have so far illustrated in our examples are tests of g_c and to some extent g_f because they demand knowledge and information as well as reasoning ability. However, as I have indicated, analogies are a useful type of item because they can be formulated in non-verbal terms, ideal for testing fluid ability. As Cattell (1971) has argued, fluid ability is best tested either by items which all members of a culture have overlearned, or by items with which all subjects, regardless of education and background, are equally unfamiliar. The analogies items set out below are those which would be expected to load almost entirely on g_f. Of the former, the most obvious examples are those using the alphabet and numbers (given that the reasoning in the case of numbers does not require mathematical ability). Of the latter there are numerous varieties of abstract shapes and patterns.

EXAMPLE 7

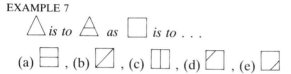

This is a typical spatial, non-verbal item, measuring g_f. There is almost no knowledge required to solve this easy item. Indeed, provided the subject is accustomed to two-dimensional drawings on paper – and in some African societies (e.g. Hudson, 1967) there is no such familiarity – this must be a relatively culture-fair item.

EXAMPLE 8

G is to J as M is to . . .
(a) P, (b) O, (c) N, (d) L, (e) K

This is a simple item based on the alphabetic sequence. The argument that G and J both can sound the same is not relevant since there is no other consonant which sounds like an M.

EXAMPLE 9

D is to W as L is to . . .
(a) O, (b) N, (c) T, (d), R, (e) H

This is a far more difficult item. The relation of D and W resides in their symmetrical position from the ends of the alphabet. The same principle has to be applied in the case of L.

EXAMPLE 10

25 is to 10 as 53 is to . . .
(a) 2, (b) 8, (c) 31, (d) 15, (e) 24

This is a medium-difficult numerical item: the relationship being the non-obvious one that 10 is a multiple of 2 and 5.

Examples 7 to 10 are difficult to judge: some test constructors might think the relationships to be educed are too trivial or too obscure to serve as tests of intelligence. This may well be correct. If I were constructing an intelligence test, I would try out these items but would feel no surprise if they turned out to be useless. I can, however, see them as being quite reasonable.

The analogies items are intended to illustrate how a variety of relationships may be encapsulated by this item format within a variety of materials, some requiring information, others not. There is almost no limit to how difficult such items may be rendered (difficult in respect of the relationship involved rather than the information). Test constructors who want examples of such items may examine with admiration the items in AH5 and AH6 (Heim *et al.*, 1970). In constructing analogies the art lies in hitting upon an interesting and, in the case of difficult items, non-obvious relationships between the components, thus allowing subjects to educe the relation – the essence of intelligence.

Although, as I hope is now clear, analogies are capable of yielding a wide variety of items, at various levels of difficulty, these alone would not be sufficient to compose a good intelligence test. This is because ability at analogies can be shown, by factor analysis, to involve not only the two g factors. In addition, there is the item-specific ability of analogy solving, although this accounts for less variance than do the g factors. Every type of test item has its own specific variance, so that to minimize the unwanted effects, good tests use as wide a variety of item types as possible.

I shall now scrutinize other types of item which are suitable for intelligence tests.

Odd-man-out items

A commonly used and useful form of items is the odd-man-out. In these a list of objects, words, shapes, numbers or whatever the ingenuity of the test constructor can manage, is presented, and the subject has to pick out the one that does not fit the list. To do this subjects have to find the relationships between the items to establish the grounds of similarity and distinction. Obviously here the eduction of relationships and correlates is necessary. As was the case with analogies, difficulty can be manipulated easily both in terms of the complexity of the relationship among the items in the list and in terms of esoteric knowledge required before the relationship could be discovered. Generally, as with analogies, except for highly educated subjects, informational demands should be as low as possible.

EXAMPLE 1

Sparrow, starling, goose, bat, swallow

This is a simple item depending upon the subject's ability to classify into birds or mammals. It is a test of g_c.

EXAMPLE 2

Goose, swallow, swift, duck, starling

This is a far more subtle item. Here the odd-man-out is starling, since all the other items are birds and have other meanings. Notice that duck was chosen rather than lark since if lark were substituted, goose would become an alternative response – being the only aquatic bird. With lark the item is simple – depending much on knowledge. With duck, although a good vocabulary is necessary, the item becomes a more severe test of g_c.

EXAMPLE 3

Early, greasy, messy, swiftly, furry

The odd-man-out here is the adverb. Given our subjects are acquainted with grammar, this is a simple item testing g_c.

EXAMPLE 4

24, 63, 10, 48, 35

This is an item probably loading both g_c and g_f. The relationship here is that four of these numbers are squares minus one. Provided that subjects are familiar with square roots and squares, the solution becomes one of defining the relationship. Clearly it is suited only for educated subjects.

EXAMPLE 5

This is a simple item loading on g_f. Four items have at least one straight line. Although easy, it requires subjects to find the common relationship between the majority of items. Knowledge, however, is not useful. This item is so obvious that it would only be suitable for primary school-children, and even amongst these it might not discriminate. It illustrates the principle, however.

These five examples illustrate that odd-man-out, as analogies, is an item form suited to the reasoning tasks needed in intelligence tests and one capable of being adapted to a wide variety of material. Our examples and their comments also illustrate that such items can be constructed using rules:

(1) Think of the relationship that the item is to deal with, for example opposites.
(2) Exemplify it in the item: black is to white as right is to . . .
(3) Check that the components of the item do not inadvertently form other relationships, thus allowing alternative solutions.
(4) Except with educated subjects, keep the material as simple as possible: difficulty should arise from the nature of the relationships to be found, not from esoteric material itself.

Sequences

These are an extremely useful item form in which relationships of various levels of difficulty can easily be encapsulated.

As with analogies and odd-man-out, examples of sequences and comments can be found below.

EXAMPLE 1

12, 15, 17, 20, 22 . . .

This is a relatively easy item where the sequence increases by 3 and 2, in turn. Numbers are particularly suitable for testing relationships since they are easy to manipulate and do not necessarily require mathematical knowledge for their eduction.

EXAMPLE 2

16, 4, 1, 0.25 . . .

This is a very simple item, although the knowledge of decimals necessary might render it invalid as a test of intelligence. This item has been included to illustrate this omnipresent danger with numerical materials – the demand for mathematical knowledge which is obviously different from intelligence.

EXAMPLE 3

Non-verbal materials such as these triangles are clearly useful for constructing sequences for the testing of g_f. This is an easy item. However, as in Raven's Matrices and the culture-fair tests, these can be made difficult.

EXAMPLE 4

To complete this sequence, we would offer a selection of multiple-choice items varying in size and relationship of circle to triangle. It must be noted that subjects need not be asked to complete the sequence: a sequence can be given, for example, with the central part needing completion.

EXAMPLE 5

Miniscule, minute, tiny . . . big, large

This is a verbal example of sequences which constitutes an easy test of g_c. Clearly, it will also load on verbal ability. Multiple-choice distractors are needed here: enormous, small, heavy, gigantic, prodigious.

Sequences are the item form of one entire test – Raven's Matrices (Raven, 1965) – which uses entirely non-verbal abstract patterns. These tests (for there are several versions for age groups ranging from 4½ years to superior adults) are superb illustrations of how this particular item form is equally suited to items of all difficulty levels. Indeed, the sole problem with the matrices test, from the viewpoint of test construction, is that the use of only one type of item puts undue weight on the specific factor associated with response to this type of item. Test constructors wishing to use sequences should carefully examine Raven's Matrices. Indeed, it can be said that the examination of good tests is an excellent method of learning to write items, just as it is helpful in music, for example, to hear the performances of the finest virtuosi; not for imitation but for insight.

In our view, with these three types of item – analogies, odd-man-out and sequences – it is possible to write a large number of items measuring fluid and crystallized ability with a variety of different materials and at all levels of difficulty. Although the form of these items as set out in our examples is fully satisfactory, for the avoidance of monotony (from the viewpoint of the subject), there can be variants of these forms.

Variants of sequences

(1) Subjects are required to find some mid term of the series.
(2) Subjects are required to complete not the next term but some yet later term.
(3) Subjects are required to rearrange items in sequence.

Variant of odd-man-out

Items are shown with common features. Subjects have to select from further items those that lack these features.

Variant of analogies

These are used by Alice Heim in her AH tests. Two words are given. From a further list subjects are required to pick out one which bears a similar relationship to both of the given words. This variant is a form of analogies which is capable of providing items of extreme difficulty in the sphere of verbal intelligence or reasoning and is thus particularly suited to high-level tests for educated subjects.

With these three basic item types and their variants, test constructors have a sound basis for developing tests of fluid and crystallized ability. This is obviously not to argue that these are the only types that have been and should be used. Nevertheless, these are the forms most readily available for good item writing.

Tests of ability and attainment

In most ability tests other than intelligence tests – for example, verbal aptitude or numerical aptitude, as well as the more simple attainment tests – there is a dual problem in writing items: that of form and content. In intelligence tests, the content consists of the relationship to be found by the subjects. The art of writing good intelligence test items resides, therefore, in finding the form of item which allows such relationships to be easily captured. As I have argued, this is best done by analogies, odd-man-out and sequences.

In tests of ability and attainment, with certain exceptions which I shall discuss later in the chapter, the critical variable is the content. The item types which I shall describe are designed mainly to ensure objectivity of marking. Furthermore, certain item types fit certain kinds of material better than others for reasons that are perfectly obvious from the nature of the item. Therefore, as test constructors we have to first find the ideal test content and, second, find the form of item which best contains the contents.

Content of items

Much has been written concerning ways of ensuring that test content is adequate. This involves arranging for a panel of subject experts to specify what precisely should be known by children at various ages in various subjects. Such experts should be able to weigh the importance in the test of one aspect of the subject matter relative to the others. The objectives of any courses should be stated so that the content of items can be seen to be relevant to these objectives. How such objectives can be best stated from the viewpoint of item writing has itself been subjected to considerable study. Bloom's *Taxonomy of Educational Objectives Handbook* (1956) provided a widely used and viable method of ensuring that, as far as possible, teachers conceived of their objectives in behavioural and thus essentially testable terms.

However, much of this aspect of testing belongs, as does the Rasch Calibration of item banks, to the sphere of education – edumetrics rather than psychometrics. Thus we do not intend here to discuss the means by which educators decide what the content of their tests must be. Thorndike and Hagen (1977) offer a simple but detailed description of these procedures.

Instead, we shall assume that we have been told what is required in terms of item content. We shall concentrate in our description on how this subject matter is turned into reasonable psychological tests.

The multiple-choice item

This is by far the most commonly used item type, and it is suited to a huge variety of subject matter. There are two parts: (1) the *stem*, which contains the question or problem, and (2) the *options*, which make up a set of possible answers from which subjects have to choose the correct one. It is usual to write four or five options. There are rules which help in writing good multiple-choice items (many of which apply to all the item types discussed in this section).

(1) *Simplicity*. The item should be written as simply as is consonant with formulating a precise item. We do not want to confound results with subject's vocabulary level or general ability.

(2) *All distractors (the incorrect options) should be capable of distracting subjects.* Thus in item trials, ideally, each distractor should be equally used by subjects failing the item. Obviously, as distractors in the options become useless, so an item becomes easier and easier. Thus, if all distractors could not be correct, then the item will have virtually a 100 per cent pass rate. A method of obtaining good distractors is to try out items informally as open-ended items and use the wrong answers that subjects actually write. It should be noted that care must be taken to ensure that distractors are not distracting the best subjects.

(3) *Only one option should be correct.* Sometimes a different way of looking at a problem could result in an unintended answer being correct.

(4) *The answer to one question should not give clues to the answer to another.* That is, the distractors to some questions are not useful in answering others.

(5) *Avoid testing the trivial because it is easy to test.* Thorndike and Hagen (1977) argue that each item should be independent. However, in our view this is an impossible demand. If items are drawn from a universe of items, they cannot be independent. Indeed, if they were, each would be testing a separate variable. Since most knowledge forms a structure of some kind, I regard this rule as best ignored.

All these rules, even including those related to the writing of distractors, are relevant to all item forms.

Thorndike and Hagen (1977) drawing on the instructions for writing items published by the Educational Testing Service (1963) list a number of other rules, most of which we have already discussed under our five more general headings.

The problem should be contained in the stem, rather than be carried over into the options, which should be as short as possible. Both these points relate to our rule 1 – simplicity – as does the claim that only what is necessary for clarity and precision in the statement of the problem should be included in the stem. Similarly, Thorndike and Hagen advise that the negative be only rarely used in stems both because it causes confusion (reading problems) and because, except in rare instances, negative knowledge is not as important as positive. To know that a bat is not a bird, beetle, fish or reptile is not necessarily to know what it is. Two of their other points are useful for practical test construction:

(1) The use of 'none of these' as a distractor should only be used when there is an unequivocal correct answer – as in, say, items concerned with spelling or mathematics.

(2) Similarly, the use of 'all of these' as a distractor tends to permit

sloppy item writing in which the distractors are not particularly discriminating because the item writer knows that any of them is correct.

Thus, bearing our main five points in mind, I shall now illustrate the art of multiple-choice item writing. Clearly, in a short series of examples I cannot produce items that effectively bear on point 4 – that clues to answers should not be given by other items. As with our typical intelligence test items, I shall set out the examples followed by comments. The items will be designed to test verbal and numerical ability and also psychometrics.

EXAMPLE 1

In the forest glade, the gorilla waited and suddenly uttered a scream of anguish.
In this sentence, the object is:
(a) gorilla, (b) glade, (c) anguish, (d) scream, (e) forest

This is a simple, clear item in which all information is contained in the stem. There is only one possible correct answer and all the distractors are nouns, that is the kind of words that could be objects, thus not allowing candidates who know that objects cannot be verbs or adverbs to eliminate options. It should be noted that the position of the correct option should be randomized over the test as a whole to prevent guessing.

EXAMPLE 2

Suddenly a scream of anguish was uttered by a gorilla who had been waiting in the forest glade.
In this sentence the subject is:
(a) gorilla, (b) scream, (c) forest, (d) glade, (e) anguish

This example is similarly clear, and all information is contained in the stem. It deliberately relates to item 1 because those candidates whose knowledge of object and subject is vague and believe that the subject is the 'doer' will be unable to answer this item. Similarly, the fact that a sentence with almost identical meaning now has subject and object reversed will cause difficulty to those whose grasp of grammar is incomplete. Note again that all options are possible subjects.

EXAMPLE 3

I do not like to think of you crossing the road all on your own at that time of day.

There is a grammatical error in this sentence. The incorrect word is:
(a) I, (b) crossing, (c) day, (d) of, (e) you

This is an example of a *poor item*. It is clear, all information is contained in the stem and there is an unequivocal, correct answer. Furthermore, the point of the item is not trivial. However, there is only one error in the sentence, hence subjects could arrive at the correct answer by eliminating the distractors which are obviously not incorrect.

In some way the item should be reworded; for example, 'If there is a grammatical error in this sentence, the incorrect word is: (a) I, (b) crossing, (c) you, (d) day, (e) none of these since there is no error'. This overcomes the problem, but it is somewhat clumsy. Probably the best solution is to use a different item form, such as, 'Which of these is grammatically correct: (a) I don't like to think of you crossing the road, or (b) I don't like to think of your crossing the road?' This example illustrates well the limitations of the multiple-choice item format. In certain conditions where the question is brief, the need to provide distractors makes the item too easy. Hence a different item form is to be preferred. General rules for this are difficult to formulate. Test constructors must keep their wits about them. This example indicates the kind of reasoning that test constructors must go through in considering their items. The question now arises: could we construct a multiple-choice item to test this point of grammar – the gerund?

EXAMPLE 4

I don't like to think of your crossing the road.
In this sentence crossing is a:
(a) gerund, (b) verb, (c) participle, (d) adjective, (e) gerundive

This item certainly tests more directly than the original item in example 3, the knowledge of gerunds. However, it does not test usage in the way that the former item did. The distractors have been chosen to trap the grammatically illiterate, especially (b) and (c).

EXAMPLE 5

Expand the term $(P+Q)^2$
The answer is:
(a) P^2+Q^2, (b) PQ^2, (c) $(2P+2Q)$, (d) $P^2+2PQ+Q^2$, (e) $2P+PQ+2Q$.

This item appears to obey all the criteria previously discussed in our section on item writing. Mathematics is a particularly suitable subject for objective testing since the right answer is not usually in doubt. To students uncertain of the expansion, the distractors are probably fairly efficient. Notice that the final distractor (e) was inserted to avoid giving a clue to the correct answer by its being longer than the others.

EXAMPLE 6

If apples are 5 pence per pound and a housewife buys 75 pence of apples (of average size, four to the pound), and if she discards three apples as bad, how many has she left?
(a) 75, (b) 72, (c) 57, (d) 17, (e) 50

This item is complex: the subject has to hold four pieces of information in his head to solve the problem. However, this complexity is an intrinsic part of the problem. Of course, no scrap paper should be allowed. The choice of distractors is difficult but use has been made of numbers in the problem itself.

One point to be noticed about these examples of multi-choice tests is that they do not fully exploit the format. Since there is only one correct answer, subjects could have been required simply to fill in a blank.

EXAMPLE 7

Which of the following reliability coefficients is not concerned with test homogeneity?
(a) test–retest, (b) Hoyt's analysis of variance, (c) alpha coefficient, (d) Kuder–Richardson coefficient, or (e) the split-half reliability

This item makes full use of the format. Five kinds of coefficient are presented, and unless subjects understand what these do, there is no way of arriving at the correct answer. This item could not be worded more simply, and it fits all the criteria suggested for writing good items. If a true–false type of item were used, five items would be needed to obtain the same information. This is therefore an ideal multi-choice item, except that guessing is a difficulty.

EXAMPLE 8

In classical test theory, the true score is defined as:
(a) The scoring of each item can be made perfectly reliable.
(b) The score on the population of items from which the test items are drawn.
(c) The test score corrected for guessing.
(d) The test score corrected for error.
(e) The average score of a subject after several tests.

This item again makes use of the multi-choice-item format, since the distractors all have an element of the true definition within them, thus confusing the candidate whose knowledge is but vague. Here a free-response format would not do since we would run into the difficulty of what constitutes an adequate definition. Notice here that all options grammatically fit the stem. Although obvious, care must be taken that this is so.

These eight items are probably sufficient, together with their comments, to indicate how multi-choice items should be constructed.

The advantages of multi-choice items

The multi-choice item is perhaps the most widely used type of item in tests of ability, attainment and aptitude because it has, compared with other types of item which we shall discuss below, a number of advantages in addition to sharing with them other good item qualities.

(1) Each item can be made perfectly reliable. Thus there is only one correct answer (in properly constructed items) and therefore no unreliability between different markers or the same markers on different occasions. This is true of other objective items, by definition, but it is no less important on that account.

(2) These items are easily scored. This is most important, especially in long tests, and tests are better long (as shown in chapter 1). Not only are they more reliable but for attainment and ability tests more ground can be covered than with tests of a few questions. In addition, easy scoring reduces clerical errors in marking.

It is usual to employ a separate score sheet with multi-choice items. The options for each item A to E being set out, the student indicates his choice. A cut-out key is then held over each answer sheet in which all correct answers are exposed. All marks are then counted. Computer scoring of tests on computer-markable scoring sheets is now possible. Similarly, the whole test can be administered and scored by computer (see chapter 10).

(3) Guessing is a major difficulty in tests, especially of ability and aptitude. The multi-choice items where the distractors are equally good reduces the positive effects of guessing to a one-in-five chance, compared with the 50 per cent chance of true–false items. Similarly, with matching items, if a subject knows three of the four matches to be made, guessing for that item is different as regards probability of success for the item where he knows none.

(4) Because the multi-choice item deals with a precise point, it is possible to have a precise estimate of test content. This is important in assessing its suitability for the subjects and for the purpose for which the test is designed.

The true–false item

This is an item form which generally consists of a sentence which the subject has to mark as true or false. However, there are some obvious problems with this item format such that its use will probably be highly restricted in tests of ability, aptitude and attainment.

PROBLEMS WITH TRUE–FALSE ITEMS

(1) Guessing is important since there is a 50 per cent probability of correctly guessing an item which can clearly affect scores unless the test is extremely long.

(2) It is difficult to write statements that are unequivocally true or false, and this is particularly important since it is likely, therefore, that the cleverest students will see the disconfirming cases and hence get the item wrong.

(3) Related to this need for precision of statement is the difficulty of using words such as 'all', 'every', 'always' and 'never', where a disconfirmatory instance can usually be found. Similarly, qualifying words such as 'sometimes', 'frequently', are so subjective that they hardly have a fixed meaning and hence cause unwanted variance in response.

(4) What is unequivocally true or false may be trivial. Hence items adequate in psychometric terms may be weak in respect of content.

Despite these problems, the true–false item format can be a useful and brief method of examining knowledge – useful, that is, more for attainment tests than tests of ability.

EXAMPLE 1

Squaring a correlation coefficient indicates how much variance in common there is between two sets of scores. True or false?

Notice that if we want to find out whether candidates know that common variance is indicated by the square of the correlation, the true–false item can do this. The mathematical component of the question makes it suitable (the answer being unequivocal) for the true–false item format. It is difficult to see how this could be tested briefly by a multi-choice item or an item requiring subjects to match two lists.

On the other hand, the subject with but a slight knowledge of correlations may dimly recall having seen the sentence before and hence get it correct, not a guess but a dim recollection of things past. Compare the above with this item: 'A correlation of 0.30 was observed between introversion and success in English in the GCE 'O' level. How much variance in common is there between these two variables?' This item is much more difficult, since there is no clue as to what the answer may be. Effective guessing is also difficult.

In this form the item may be given as a multi-choice item. All that would be needed would be to include the following options: (a) 30%, (b) 6%, (c) 9%, (d) 3%, (e) 33%. These options have been selected because they all involve simple and obvious transformations of the correlation. Thus the candidate who knows there is some relationship between a correlation and variance in common, but is not sure what, cannot eliminate any of the options as an aid to guessing.

This example illustrates that this true–false item can with careful test construction be replaced by a multi-choice item which reduces the effect of guessing and is considerably easier to mark. It also gives less clues to the correct response.

EXAMPLE 2

A correlation indicates the extent of agreement between two sets of scores. True or false?

This item is more suited than the former to the true–false format. First, it tests one piece of information which the candidate either knows or not. It is certainly not suited for an open-ended response, since there is no fixed answer and the adequacy of the statement of what correlations measure becomes a matter of subjective judgement which inevitably leads to poor reliability. In addition, such free-response formats involve verbal skills, which presumably in a test of statistical psychometric knowledge are not relevant. In this instance, therefore, the true–false item is indubitably superior to the free-response format.

Could this item be tested equally efficiently by a multi-choice item, with all its advantages of reduced effectiveness of guessing and easy marking?

A correlation indicates:
(a) The extent of agreement between two sets of scores.
(b) Differences between the means of sets of scores.
(c) Associations between categories of scores.
(d) Differences in distributions of scores.
(e) The shape of the distribution of scores.

Provided that it could be shown in item trials that these or, if necessary, other distractors worked efficiently, it is evident that, as with the previous example, this true–false item can equally well be framed as a multi-choice item.

These two items illustrate our claim that the true–false item format is not particularly useful. Usually multi-choice items can be written that are equally good. However, such a claim cannot be adequately supported by two items, especially since it could be argued that these might have been especially chosen to demonstrate this point.

Thorndike and Hagen (1977) cite some examples of adequate true–false items. Let us examine these since it cannot be argued that these are specially chosen because they can be translated into the multi-choice format.

EXAMPLE 3

Tuberculosis is a communicable disease. True or false?

This (taken from Thorndike and Hagen, 1977) would seem to be a suitable item for the true–false format since it requires one single piece of knowledge. As with example 2, a free response would involve too much judgement by markers to be reliable. However, even this can be translated into a multi-choice item. For example, 'Tuberculosis is: (a) contagious, (b) infectious, (c) contagious and infectious, (d) non-communicable, (e) hereditary'.

It seems to us this item taps the requisite item of knowledge just as well as the true–false item suggested by Thorndike and Hagen, but in addition (1) it reduces the probability of correct guessing, and, even more pertinently, (2) it exposes more precisely the subject's knowledge of the spread of tuberculosis.

These examples illustrate clearly that in standard form the true–false item can usually be better replaced by the multi-choice type of item. However, in certain circumstances, the true–false item may be irreplaceable.

The true–false item is seen at its most useful when we present information or data and ask questions about it to test comprehension. This is particularly valuable as a test in scientific subjects where ability to analyse data is essential.

EXAMPLE 4

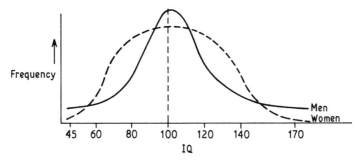

Distribution of intelligence in a large sample of men and women

From the information in the graph above, indicate whether the following statements are true or false.

(a) There are more men than women of very low IQ – < 45. T F
(b) There are more men than women of very high IQ – > 140. T F
(c) The distribution of intelligence among men is approximately bimodal. T F
(d) The distribution of intelligence among women is approximately normal. T F
(e) The mean IQ of women and men is approximately the same. T F
(f) There are more women than men of IQs between 120 and 140. T F
(g) There are more men than women of IQs between 50 and 60. T F

These true–false items are a powerful method of seeing to what extent subjects can understand data. In addition, there has been smuggled neatly in questions concerning the shape of normal and bimodal distributions. To test the understanding of graphs by multi-choice items would certainly be more clumsy.

The kind of questions in example 4 constitute the main value of the true–false format in item writing.

A series of true–false items can be appended to one statement.

EXAMPLE 5

The following statistical techniques may be described as multivariate:
(a) t test, T F; (b) factor analysis, T F; (c) chi square, T F; (d) analysis of variance, T F; (e) analysis of covariance, T F; (f) Kendall's tau, T F.

First, this is obviously more effective than having each of the six techniques as a separate true–false item. Furthermore, in this case, it is more informative than a multi-choice item because each option has to be classified. In a multi-choice item, if a subject knew that factor analysis was multivariate, the others by definition would not be so. Thus, used in this way a series of true–false items can be used to elicit extremely detailed information on topics.

CONCLUSIONS CONCERNING TRUE–FALSE ITEMS
Generally, the true–false item on its own does not appear to be useful. Usually a comparable and more efficient item of the multi-choice type can be written. However, the true–false item is useful (1) in testing comprehension of given material and (2) in examining knowledge in great detail, as in examples 4 and 5. However, its major disadvantage must be noted: guessing can obviously be an important factor in answering these items. The ease with which the format can be applied to

questioning the understanding of material does however make this item form worthy of use.

Matching items

A third category of items, commonly used in objective tests, requires subjects to match items in two lists. For example, if we wanted to explore a candidate's knowledge of the authorship of books, one list would contain authors, another titles and the items would have to be correctly matched. In the field of zoology, for example, a list of mammals and a list of categories could be used, for example, edentates, ungulates and marsupials. As previously, I shall give examples of these items, together with comments, to bring out the strengths and weaknesses of these items and to illustrate the simple guidelines for writing good items.

EXAMPLE 1
Indicate by letter which author wrote which book in the following lists (leave blank a book written by none of these).

AUTHORS	BOOKS	LETTER
A. Dickens	1. *Vanity Fair*	. . .
	2. *Waverley*	. . .
B. Scott	3. *A Tale of Two Cities*	. . .
	4. *Paradise Lost*	. . .
C. Smollett	5. *Humphrey Clinker*	. . .
	6. *Pamela*	. . .
D. Thackeray	7. *The Black Dwarf*	. . .
	8. *The Moonstone*	. . .

As this example makes clear, the matching item is best suited for eliciting factual information. We could as easily have asked 'Who wrote *Vanity Fair*?' However, this matching item is a simple method of asking the question which makes marking easy. Multi-choice items could have been constructed, 'Dickens wrote: (a) *Vanity Fair*, (b) *Waverley*, etc.' However, we should have needed a separate item for each book in our example, other than the blanks, to test the same quantum of knowledge. Thus, for eliciting detailed information of this type, the matching item is superior to multi-choice – it is far neater.

True–false items could also deal with this subject matter: 'Dickens wrote: (a) *Vanity Fair*, T F; (b) *Waverley*, T F, etc.' This example makes it clear that for this particular material the true–false item is not as good as the matching. In the first place four items would be necessary, one for each of the authors. Second, we could not use the same examples in each item because then the answers to the first item would affect the answers to the others. It is obvious, therefore, that for this type of factual information the best item-style is the matching item, followed by the true–false item, and in this case the multi-choice item is the least efficient.

One point to notice is that the list from which the responses are made must be longer than the first list or else guessing becomes progressively easier. Thus, if a subject knows four out of five in equal lists, then the fifth is inevitably correct. The way to counter this fact is to have lists of unequal length or to indicate that some items cannot be matched (or both) as in our example. These measures obviously decrease the probability of correct guessing.

In our first example of matching items, it was clear that the matching item was superior to the true–false item. The obvious question arises, therefore, as to whether this is always the case. Let us look again at examples 4 and 5 given in our examination of true–false items.

TRUE–FALSE EXAMPLE 5 (page 44)

This item certainly could be recast as a matching item.

TYPE OF TECHNIQUE	TECHNIQUES	LETTER
A. Multivariate	*t* test	. . .
	Factor analysis	. . .
B. Non-parametric	Chi squared	. . .
	Analysis of variance	. . .
C. Univariate	Analysis of covariance	. . .
	Kendall's tau	. . .

Indicate by letter which type of technique, if any, describes the statistical techniques in the list above. It is possible that none or more than one descriptor will fit some items in the list.

This matching item certainly fits this material as well as the true–false format, and we can find out the additional information concerning those techniques to which the answer 'false' was appropriate. Examination of the item reveals that this is necessarily the case since the matching format requires, essentially, that subjects decide whether each option is or is not multivariate, non-parametric, and so on.

This example 5 illustrates the point that the choice of item format depends upon the material and the knowledge being tested. In this case of detailed statistical knowledge, the matching item is probably better than the true–false item, and both are superior to the multi-choice variety. This, of course, is not necessarily always so.

TRUE–FALSE EXAMPLE 4 (page 43–4)

However, in the test of understanding data, there is simply no obvious way in which the item could be written as a matching item. This indeed gives us the clue concerning the relative merits of true–false and matching items. The former are definitely superior as tests of material presented in the question. Usually, as in true–false example 4, a matching item could not be written. Multi-choice items could be constructed, but they would be clumsy, and the choice of convincing distractors would be difficult. In addition, such items would inevitably tend to be linked, thus making them inefficient.

For testing detailed information the matching technique may be superior to the true–false one, provided the questions allow sensible lists to be constructed.

One point needs to be stressed concerning the use of true–false and matching items as tests of information – the danger of testing trivia.

Although it is important to realise that chi-squared is non-parametric and t tests univariate, the ability to utter the statement 'the t test is univariate' that would score the necessary mark implies no understanding either of the t test or univariate statistics. A 7-year-old could be taught this information. Similarly, to know that Scott wrote *Waverley* does not seem important compared with the ability to make a critical analysis of the novel.

Conclusions concerning multi-choice, true–false and matching items

In constructing tests of ability, aptitude and attainment we should expect to write items largely of these three types. How do we decide which type to use? A number of issues have to be considered.

SPECIFIC FACTORS

In making our decision of types of item, we must bear in mind the notion of specific factor variance. If test items are of one kind, there is a danger of a specific factor related to the particular item-format. In a battery of tests such a specific might even resemble a genuine group factor, although it would be, of course, nothing other than a bloated specific – the skill at answering items of a particular kind. Thus a variety of types of item is useful.

BOREDOM

A source of error in testing arises from boredom – especially in tests of ability and similar spheres, where effort and concentration are required. A variety of items is likely to make the test less monotonous for subjects (see Cronbach, 1970).

EFFICIENCY OF ITEMS

Clearly we want our items to be as efficient as possible. As we have demonstrated in our examination of the different item types, each is most useful in certain conditions. Perhaps a basic approach to item writing could be formulated thus:

(1) The standard item which suits most kinds of material and question is the multi-choice item.
(2) For detailed factual information where the content of items is related, a good neat test is provided by matching and true–false items.
(3) For testing comprehension of material presented in the question, the true–false items are particularly useful.
(4) For the reasons discussed in points 1 and 2, it is sensible to aim at a test with all types of item, although there is no need to have equal numbers of each type.

Choosing the item type

In my view, the way to choose how a given piece of information should be tested is to attempt to construct items of each type. Sometimes this is simply not possible, thus eliminating automatically at least one category. With all three items written, a decision is usually possible. Below, the information to be tested is the shape of the bimodal distribution.

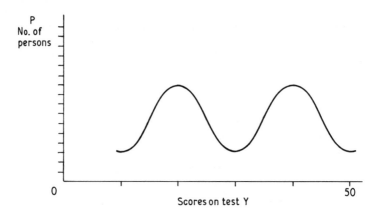

(1) The multi-choice item: *The distribution of scores on test Y is known as the*:
(a) Gaussian curve
(b) Poisson distribution

(c) Bimodal distribution

(d) Normal curve

(e) Two-point curve

(2) The true–false item: *The distribution of scores on test Y a bimodal distribution.* T F

(3) The matching item: To write a matching item to test this point we would have to have a list of possible curves and a larger set of illustrations similar to the one above. This would be extremely wasteful of space, unless we wanted to test the student's knowledge of the shape of a variety of distributions.

Thus, if our sole interest is in one particular piece of information, as here, the multi-choice item is best. The true–false item offers a too-high probability of guessing, and the matching item is only suited to a mass of detailed information. It should be noted how the type of item which best suits the material becomes obvious on attempting to write each type of item.

THE CRITERIA FOR CHOOSING ONE ITEM RATHER THAN ANOTHER

(1) Clarity. Choose the form of item which is likely to be clearest for subjects. In the example above, (1) and (2) are similar.

(2) Guessing. Choose the form which reduces guessing as far as possible.

(3) Neatness or precision. Choose the form which encapsulates the question as briefly as possible.

(4) Relation of items. Check that the form of the item (the options or the matching lists) does not imply or reveal the answer to other items.

(5) Where items seem equally good, choose the item type of which you have the least.

Other item types

Of course there are many other types of item. What I have done, however, is to discuss in some detail the construction of three types which together are capable of putting almost any material into a testable form. Nevertheless, some points are not easily captured by these items, and I shall now briefly discuss some other item forms, pointing out any special advantages which they have.

(1) Limited-response items. These items require subjects to provide their own answers. However, the possibilities are limited or restricted (these items are sometimes known as restricted-response items). This virtually ensures objective marking, for with careful

wording of items there will be only one possible response.
(2) Free-response items. Here there is no limitation of response. Subjects can put anything. However, with correct wording of the question, there is only one possible answer.

I shall give examples of both item types referring to the same material so that the comparative merits of each may be weighed up. In writing both these types of item our general hints about item writing must be borne clearly in mind, especially that warning concerned with testing trivial or worthless information, just because it is easy to test.

EXAMPLE 1
In this example the material to be tested is knowledge of the standard deviation.

(1) Free response: *What does the standard deviation measure?*
(2) Limited response: *The standard deviation measures . . .*

Neither of these items is particularly good because, although 'variance' or 'variation' is the required answer, it is quite possible that candidates will indulge in a lengthy discursive sentence. It would be preferable here to indicate that a one-word answer was required. This, however, would render the free-response item restricted. In this instance the limited-choice item is certainly superior to the free-response, given that we make it clear that a one-word answer is required.

The free-response item could be improved; for example, 'The mean measures the central tendency of a set of scores; what does the standard deviation measure?' This item, although free, should produce answers such as 'variance', 'dispersion' or 'spread of scores'. Nevertheless, as I have argued, the free-response format is not as efficient here as the limited-response format. It is interesting to note that this item can be easily put into our other item forms:

(1) T F: *The standard deviation measures variance.*
(2) Matching:

A	B
1. Mean	Variance
2. Standard deviation	Central tendency
3. Median	Agreement
4. Correlation	Disagreement
	Scatter
	Association
	Clustering

Indicate which items in B are measured by the statistics in list A.
(3) Multiple choice: *The standard deviation measures:*
    (a) The degree of agreement between two variables.

(b) The standard score on a test.
(c) The dispersion of scores on a test.
(d) The average score on a test.
(e) The extreme deviation score on a test.

It seems that given that all types of item can be constructed, the multiple-choice form is by far the most efficient here.

This first example illustrates clearly the major difficulty in writing either free- or restricted-response items – the necessity of so wording the item that subjects who have the requisite skills or knowledge put the correct answer. This means it is necessary to produce items to which only one answer is possible, and such an answer must of course be accurate.

EXAMPLE 2

Here the material to be tested is knowledge of oblique factors in factor analysis.

(1) Free item: *What are oblique factors?*
So much could and has been written about oblique factors that any adequate answer would inevitably be long. The hapless problem of attempting to score the item would then arise. Obviously, for this is a grossly stupid example, we must be more specific in our item writing. We must decide exactly what we want to ask.
(2) Limited item: *Oblique factors are* . . . (one word).
Although this format restricts the length of the response, it is clearly by no means a better item. Thus we could find: 'correlated', 'rotated', 'significant' (for only significant factors are rotated), 'complex' (by Guilford's arguments), 'simple' (by Cattell's), and so on. How then can this item be made more specific?

If we want to test the knowledge that oblique factors are correlated, this is surely most easily done with a true–false item: 'Oblique factors are correlated. T F'. If it is felt that guessing would be too influential, then a multiple-choice item should be constructed: 'Oblique factors are: (a) uncorrelated, (b) unrotated, (c) correlated, (d) orthogonal, (e) Euclidian'. This item tests the information quite neatly, and all the distractors have been chosen because they are terms descriptive of factors or other multi-dimensional vectors, although only the correct answer fits. Thus if we want to test a knowledge of the correlation of oblique factors, it is clear that the multi-choice format or the true–false format are each simple and easy to write. To write the free- and restricted-item equivalents, it is necessary to force the subject, by the wording of the item, to concentrate on the correlational aspect of obliquity. Thus:

Free item: *In what way do oblique factors differ from orthogonal factors?*

This would be scored as correct provided that subjects stated that oblique factors are correlated. However, this item is still poor because subjects could correctly write that oblique factors were oblique to each other, not at right angles. Hence this format, albeit better than the original, is still not good enough.

What information of psychological significance can be obtained from the angles between oblique factors?

At last the question has been nailed; there is now only one possible brief answer. If subjects know about oblique factors, they must mention the correlations; if they do, they score.

There is no doubt that the construction of items such as these (which at least look worthy of testing in item analysis) is far more difficult than the construction of a similar precise multi-choice item. The gain to the test constructor of free items such as the one above is that for subjects they are more interesting, less obviously a test of knowledge and involve some further element of reasoning – this is because the free item actually involves more information than the multi-choice item. Thus our multi-choice item could be solved provided that subjects knew oblique factors were correlated. However, to solve the free-choice item, subjects have to know (1) that oblique factors are correlated, (2) that the correlation is related to the obliquity and (3) that the correlation is of psychological significance. The free item is therefore richer and more difficult. To test (2) of our free item, a further multi-choice item would be needed. It is its relative complexity that makes the free item appear more attractive than the multi-choice item, which is inevitably stark and simple.

Limited item: *From the angles between oblique factors, their . . . can be worked out.*

This limited-item format of the question is attractive in that with only one word to complete, perfect reliability will be assured, the response being either right or wrong, involving no judgement. It is more precise than the free item in forcing subjects to put the desired answer (as is almost always the case with limited- as compared to free-response items), but for this reason may be somewhat easier.

There is an interesting point concerning the wording of this limited-response item, namely the last words 'worked out'. This was deliberately left somewhat general. If the more precise 'calculated' or 'computed' were put in their place, I felt that they would give too much of a clue that some statistical term was required. In trying out this item it would be interesting to compare it, on a small sub-sample, with the item using the word computed to see to what extent the facility value of the item was changed. Alternatively, if the item turned out too hard, on the second trial the new form could be substituted.

In my view the material in this item is well suited to the limited-choice form. It seems far more precise than the free item, while the multi-choice item seems too simple and merely testing rote memory.

EXAMPLE 3
From a poem entitled 'The Illiterate':

> *Him Procrustes close fits to his bed*
> *Stretched inch by inch for every book . . .*

What is the next word?

Given the title of the poem, only one word could fit this limited-response item: 'unread'. Notice that without the title 'The Illiterate' the response becomes exceedingly difficult. To answer the question demands an ability both to scan and rhyme words. It might surprise some readers to see how objective questions can be constructed for such abilities.

A free-response item cannot be constructed from this material but a multiple-choice item could be:

Which of the following words best completes the line?
(a) unread, (b) unsaid, (c) read, (d) said, (e) unknown.

The problem with the multi-choice item lies in writing the options, and there is no doubt that the best options here would be obtained from studying the limited responses to the item.

So far in our examples the limited-response item has always seemed superior to the free-response equivalent because of its added precision. However, this need not always be the case. Where we are seeking purely information of a specific nature, the free-response item can be effective.

EXAMPLE 4
Here the material to be tested is knowledge of variance and sum of squares.

(1) Free response: *What is the sum of squares?*
   For this precise definition, there is only one response, and its various possible forms would be easily recognizable by markers (i.e. be of high reliability).
(2) Free response: *What is the relationship between the variance and the sum of squares?*

Again, there can be no doubt concerning false or accurate answers.

In cases such as these, the limited-choice response would be no improvement; indeed, it is in fact more difficult to write since the extreme specificity of the correct response virtually forces the test constructor to write in part of the correct answer. Thus: (1) 'The sum of squares is the sum of each . . . . from the mean.' The two words required here are not so obvious that the ignorant could fill them in, nor does the item necessarily jog the memory of the half-ignorant. The second item would read: (2) 'Given the sum of squares, the variance is found by . . . .'

The limited- and free-response items are useful, further methods of putting items in testable form. Which is the better depends upon how specific the information to be tested is. When it is highly specific, the free-response item is efficient; where it is not so clearly defined, the limited-choice item is better.

Again, in choosing which item form to use, it is often sensible to write items of all kinds for the same material and then select the best according to the criteria which we have discussed throughout this chapter. It is to be remembered that a section of free- and restricted-choice items in a test (given that they are no less efficient than the other forms) makes a welcome change from purely objective items for a candidate. However, these rule out machine scoring.

Finally, Thorndike and Hagen (1977) list a number of points in writing this type of item which we have covered in this chapter. Some seem so obvious that they hardly merit comment: words should be accurate; required answers should be correct; problems should be specific and should not in completion items leave so many blanks that the item becomes incomprehensible.

Enough of different item types. By attempting to construct items of each type relevant to a given subject matter, it should be relatively easy to produce sufficient items for the first-item trial. If items are selected against the criteria discussed in the previous section, we should aim for both item efficiency and for as wide a choice of item types as possible.

Arrangement of items for a test trial

As has been indicated in the first chapter of this book, clear instructions and easy comprehension of what subjects must do all aid reliability and validity. Hence, in arranging items for a test trial there are a few simple rules which are so obvious as to merit little comment or discussion:

(1) Arrange items of each type together. This means that subjects can

get used to the type of item and need to grasp only one set of instructions per set of items.

(2) Arrange items in order of difficulty. This will prevent the obsessional student from spending all his time or too much time on items which he cannot do and thus not attempting items on which he can score – a result which could render all forms of item analysis inaccurate.

(3) Within the limits of (1) and (2), randomize the material as much as possible. This cuts down on boredom and its associated fatigue.

(4) Do not put together so many items that the average subject takes more than (for adults) 1½ hours to complete them. For younger children, the concentration span in ability tests will be more limited. Take advice on this from teachers who know the subjects.

(5) To ascertain how long the test takes, arrange for subjects to indicate where they are on the test at various points during the testing session.

(6) If these methods of test construction and administration are followed, it is almost inevitable that in the field of aptitude, ability and attainment a good, reliable and valid test will emerge from the statistical test-analytic procedures described later in this book.

Guessing

One further problem remains to be discussed in the construction of ability, aptitude and attainment tests, one indeed which I have already mentioned in this chapter, in passing – that is, guessing. It is obvious that with objective items guessing will distort scores to some extent. If tests are used for some serious purpose such as selection for jobs or promotion, it is evident that subjects will be highly motivated to guess. Guessing, of course, lowers the validity and reliability of tests. What, then, is to be done about guessing?

(1) Requirement to guess. One possible solution is to require subjects to guess, in the test instructions. This is easily done: 'Do not leave blanks. If you do not know or are uncertain of the answer, guess the correct solution.'

(2) Fill in all blanks at random before scoring the test. This is equivalent to guessing.

Given (1) and (2), *all* scores will be distorted by guessing. Hence the validity of the test will not be grossly distorted. Unfortunately, even with instructions not to leave blanks, not all subjects obey so that, unless scorers resort to (2), some kind of guessing corrections must be used (if guessing is deemed to be important).

GUESSING-CORRECTION FORMULA

The common guessing-correction formula is:

$$X \text{ correct} = X - \frac{W}{n-1}$$

where:

  X correct = Score corrected for guessing
  X = No. correct
  W = No. wrong
  n = Number of options in the items.

Four points need to be noted concerning this formula.

(1) It assumes that all wrong answers are due to guessing. This is not necessarily so, since subjects can frequently have misinformation.
(2) It assumes that where guessing has occurred there is an equal chance for each option to be chosen. This is not so since in a multi-choice item a subject may correctly eliminate all but two options. Hence the guessing-correction will be an underestimate for that subject (but see point 4).
(3) Items with different numbers of options require different guessing-corrections.
(4) The guessing-correction applies to the average subject. In individual cases it will be wrong.

From this it is clear that the guessing-correction is at best a rough estimate.

Generally, I agree with Vernon (1950), who argues that in practice, provided that a test has a reasonable number of items, guessing may be ignored. This is particularly true of multiple-choice items. The true–false item is clearly more affected, and this is a reason for not using these items unless it is the only satisfactory item form. If tests are highly speeded, this encourages guessing. However, it is not good testing practice to speed tests to such an extent that candidates cannot finish them. It introduces the extraneous variable of speed into the test, and effectively produces a short test. In brief, guessing is not a major problem with tests, and guessing-corrections are only useful in tests of true–false items, which, however, are not recommended.

Conclusions

I hope that enough has now been written for the rationale of item writing for tests of ability and achievement to become clear. With a large pool of properly constructed items which do not measure trivia, which happen to be easy to measure, it should be possible to develop good tests of human abilities using the statistical procedures which are discussed in later chapters. I also hope that the exposition of the details of item writing (which may have been irritating in its detail) has also revealed why so many objective tests, especially of attainments, are so poor. Many objective tests are produced by inexperienced, enthusiastic amateurs. It is not enough to apply powerful statistics to test items. First the items must be good. Item writing is not easy. With the principles in this handbook, gross deficiencies should be eliminated.

3

Making tests reliable II
Personality inventories. Item writing

Personality inventories are widely used methods of personality measurement, especially in psychological research, because they can be constructed with many of the attributes of good tests – reliability, discriminatory power and well-standardized norms. From the nature of personality variables, test validity is, however, more difficult to establish.

Problems in constructing personality inventories

As was the case with ability tests, the individual items are crucial to inventories, and in this chapter, therefore, I shall deal with the problems of writing items and examine the merits of the various types of item.

When writing items for personality inventories, the test constructor has to take into account the following difficulties, which, if not circumvented, will lead inevitably to tests of low validity.

(1) *Response set of acquiescence.* This is the tendency to agree with items regardless of content, and is more likely to occur, according to Guildford (1959), when items are ambiguous or indefinite.

(2) *Response set of social desirability.* This is the tendency to respond to items in terms of the social desirability of the response: the more socially desirable a response is, the more likely it is that it will be given by subjects, a response mode which Edwards (1957) showed affected the Minnesota Multiphasic Personality Inventory (MMPI).

(3) *Response set of using the uncertain or middle category.* Where there is a middle category of responses, reflecting indecision or uncertainty about the response, many subjects tend to use it – the safe compromise. This tends to lower the validity of test items, since most item-analytic methods depend on extreme scorers.

(4) *Response set of using the extreme response.* This occurs when a

multi-point rating scale is used. Some subjects, regardless of item content, favour the extreme response (Vernon, 1964).

(5) *Face validity of items.* In personality tests it is by no means certain that the response to an item can be taken as true. Cattell and Kline (1977) refer to questionnaire data as Q and Q^1 data. The former are treated as if they reflect subjects' behaviour, the latter as a response to a particular item, a response which either loads a factor or not, regardless of whether it reflects subjects' behaviour.

(6) *Sampling the universe of items.* In tests of ability and aptitude – discussed in the last chapter – it is relatively easy to ensure that items belong or are likely to belong to their intended universe – certainly at a gross level. A language item is not easily mistaken for a science item or a mathematical item. However, in the sphere of personality and temperament, this is not the case.

Sometimes, indeed, even experienced and skilful item writers (e.g. Cattell, 1957) are surprised by items loading on factors other than those which they were designed to tap, and by items failing to load on factors at all. This problem from the viewpoint of classical test theory concerns the difficulty of defining the population of items. From this springs a problem in producing an adequate sample of the population of items for the test, and without this the test cannot be valid. In brief, the true score cannot be clearly defined.

(7) *Sampling the universe of subjects.* As above, in tests of personality, it is more difficult to ensure adequate sampling of the population than it is with tests of ability. With ability tests there is usually a clear target population for whom the test is intended, and thus in principle, at least, sampling can be efficiently carried out. However, with tests of personality other than those designed only for abnormal subjects, we ideally need samples from the general population which cover the whole range of possible scores. Such samples, as we have argued, need to be large and are difficult to obtain.

(8) *Problems in establishing adequate criteria for validity.* Here there is, as we have fully discussed in our section on validity, considerable difficulty in obtaining adequate criteria. For example, if we were trying to measure authoritarianism, we would be forced to rely on ratings, since there are no other external measures (unlike public examinations for the sphere of abilities). Ratings are inadequate (see chapter 1), and in any case, if they were not, a test would be otiose. Similarly, if highly efficient tests of authoritarianism exist, which are thus suitable as criteria of validity, a new test is not likely to be useful.

Thus we are reduced to inferential construct validity studies based upon, usually, multivariate analysis of our test with other variables, and to studies of special groups hypothesized as having particular scores on the variable concerned.

These are the major problems involved in the construction of personality questionnaires, and they must be borne clearly in mind as soon as item writing begins. The last two difficulties, although critical, come more into play after items have been selected.

Writing items for personality inventories

It almost goes without saying that it is essential that personality-test items can be marked objectively and with perfect reliability. The design of item formats must therefore make this possible. The item forms used in the best known inventories – those found the most successful in practice – are set out below.

(1) *The Yes–No item.* This has been used by the present writer in the construction of his personality tests, Ai3Q (Kline, 1971) and OOQ & OPQ (Kline and Storey, 1978). It is easy to write and quick and comprehensible for subjects. This is the form of item in Eysenck's personality tests. A typical Yes–No item reads: 'Do you enjoy sunbathing on the beach?'

(2) *The Yes ? No item.* This is a variant of the Yes–No item above, with the uncertain category inserted because some subjects become annoyed and uncooperative if forced to put either Yes or No to items about which they feel little.

The difficulty with the Yes ? No item is that this middle category is highly attractive and yet rarely informative. Bendig (1959) demonstrated that there was with the MPI (Maudsley Personality Inventory – an early version, in essence, of the EPI, Eysenck Personality Inventory) little difference between the dichotomous and trichotomous item form, and thus concluded that the original dichotomous items were preferable because they forced the unwilling to choose. In my view, there is so little difference between the Yes–No item and the Yes? No item that it becomes a matter of little more than personal preference which form a test constructor uses. Cattell and colleagues use the trichotomous form for some of the items in their factored personality tests.

(3) *The true–false item.* These items consist of statements (often using the first person) which subjects have to indicate as true or false for them. An example of a true-false item is 'I hate being crammed up into a lift.' This is the item form used in the MMPI. Essentially, it is little different from the Yes–No item, although casting the item as true–false rather than Yes–No may affect the English of the item to some extent.

(4) *The like–dislike item* (single word or phrase). This is an extremely ingenious item form which is used at present by Grygier (1961) in the Dynamic Personality Inventory (DPI), a test based upon the Krout Personal Preference Scale (Krout and Tabin, 1954). Wilson and

Patterson use it in addition in their Conservation Scale (Wilson and Patterson, 1970). Examples of items would be: (1) 'lighters', (2) 'fur-beaver collars', (3) 'bass drums'. Subjects indicate like or dislike. Clearly, writing such items demands only the skill of knowing which words to choose. Grygier and Grygier (1976) in their handbook to the DPI argue that these items are essentially projective in nature and that the DPI is effectively a projective questionnaire. However, whether this is so or not, there is no necessity that such items must be projective, and it would appear to us that this is a highly useful, albeit unusual, item form.

(5) *Items with rating scales*. These items consist of sentences to which rating scales are appended. Comrey (1970) is the most prominent user of these items, favouring them because they overcome the difficulties of correlating dichotomous items (see my discussion below, in chapter 6) and because subjects feel they are more sensible than dichotomous items, although the response set of putting the extreme response can be a problem. Comrey uses two 7-point scales: 'always – never' and 'definitely – definitely not' depending upon the wording of the item. A typical example might read: 'I enjoy drinking with friends in a pub: always, very frequently, frequently, occasionally, rarely, very rarely, never'. An obvious problem with these scales is the different interpretations individuals will make of these frequency terms.

(6) *Various trichotomous items*. These are really variants of the trichotomous form of the Yes–No item (type 1 in our list). Cattell, for example, in the 16 PF test uses these because they make more sense in respect to some statement than 'yes', 'uncertain', 'no'. Examples of the trichotomies are: generally, sometimes, never; true, uncertain, false; agree, uncertain, disagree. These variants simply give more flexibility in item writing than the rigid Yes–No or true–false format.

(7) *Trichotomous items with choice*. These are variants of (6) which allow almost any idea to be put into a neat item format. They involve three completing phrases, one of which the subjects have to choose. Here is a typical example: 'If I hadn't much to do I might: (a) phone a friend for a good chat, (b) settle down with a difficult crossword, (c) go to a jazz session.' Some test constructors have utilized these items, (e.g. Briggs and Myers, 1962) with two, three and more choices. Indeed, they can be regarded as a separate category.

(8) *Forced-choice items*. With forced-choice items, as I have described above, subjects are forced to choose which of usually two statements the more accurately applies to or is true for them, although there may be more choices. However, I have included forced-choice items as a separate category not because conceptually they differ from trichotomous items with choice, but because Edwards (1959) made so much of his forced-choice items, which were specifically developed as

pairs, balanced for social desirability, in an effort to eliminate a social-desirability response set.

(9) *Other forms*. The basic types of item described in (1) to (8) above embrace most of the items used in the best-known personality inventories. All, as regards form (as distinct from content), are relatively easy to write, given a few guidelines, which we shall discuss below, and are neat and simple to complete and score.

Obviously other item types are possible and in the Myers–Briggs Type-Indicator, for example, we find a type of item which is more like a projective test, although it is objectively marked. Subjects have to indicate which of a pair of words appeals to them. Perhaps it is best considered as a variant of the like–dislike item (type 3 in our list).

Cattell *et al.* (1970) use similar items in the MAT (Motivational Analysis Test), although they would argue that these are objective-test items rather than personality-test items; the construction of objective tests is described in chapter 4.

All the items which we have considered so far are self-report items. They require subjects to answer them as truthfully as possible, although, as I have pointed out, test construction methods are such that they do not have to be true. Some items, however, although in form the same as those described in our eight categories, differ in instructions. Thus in Edwards' (1967) Personality Inventory, subjects complete items as they believe others see them to be. This, it is hoped, eliminates in part at least social desirability.

Although there are other types of item used in personality inventories, there is no doubt that in our eight categories can be found items that have proven successful in testing personality. Furthermore, there is almost no content which cannot be made effectively into an item of one of these types. Usually, indeed, as was the case with items for ability and aptitude tests, a variety of item types can fit material. In brief, with these forms of item there is no reason why good personality inventories cannot be constructed.

Guidelines for item writing

Given that there is a choice of item types, as I have described above, we must now discuss some of the methods adopted by test constructors to overcome the problems of item writing which I have listed and to ensure further that our items are otherwise adequate.

Much of what I shall say is obvious and little more than common sense. Nevertheless, examination of many published tests and tests used for internal selection by large organizations has convinced this author that these things need to be said. Too often test constructors, blinded by the brilliance of the technology of item analyses, forget the critical fact that a test can be no better (but it can be worse) than its items. Guilford (1959) whose personality questionnaires were amongst the first to be developed through factor analysis (scales, indeed, which have largely stood the tests of forty years' research) makes several useful suggestions for the writer of personality-test items. In our experience these guidelines have shown themselves effective.

(1) *Reduce the insight which subjects may have into the items.* This is done not for the joy of deception but for the reason that if subjects perceive an item to be measuring trait X, then their response will reflect their view of their status in respect of this trait rather than their actual status. Now, some subjects' views of their personalities may be quite wrong. It is clear that too-open items may create this source of bias. As Guilford (1959) argues, the ideal is to score a subject on traits which he does not know, by asking questions about what he does know.

(2) *Write clear, unambiguous items.* This is important to reduce error due to misunderstanding the items. High reliability depends to some extent on this feature of the test.

(3) *The items should refer to specific rather than general behaviour.* Thus an item like 'Do you enjoy sport?' is far too general – the term 'sport' is vague, as is enjoy. It would seem preferable to make the question more specific: 'Do you regularly play any game?' or 'Do you regularly watch a particular sports team?', 'Do you follow horse racing?' With these items, short of falsification or real change, a subject will give the same response whenever he is tested.

(4) *Each item must ask only one question or make one statement.* Take for example 'I think blacks and other races should be forced to emigrate'. If this item were intended to measure racism, it would be poor. Some racists (as the genus is found in South Africa) distinguish sharply between blacks and other races. Others regard all non-Anglo-Saxons as a non-human mass. Thus some racists could endorse the item while others could not (just blacks should be compelled to emigrate). Other more sinister racists might be prepared to see blacks and other races remain but as virtual slaves. Some others again, Germans perhaps in Britain, would respond No depending on their interpretation of 'other races' (see point 2, above). This item is clearly quite hopeless; the wording is vague and two questions are asked at once. A more precise item would read, 'I think negroes should be forced to emigrate'. Not only is clarity improved (blacks and other races are replaced by a more accurate term) but now only one question remains.

(5) *Avoid as far as possible terms of frequency.* These are usually so subjective as to be highly ambiguous. Examples will clarify this point.

Example A: 'Do you dream frequently?' Here all depends upon the meaning of 'frequently'. Some subjects may feel that dreaming once a month is frequent and endorse the Yes response. Others may argue that one dream per sleep is not frequent because research shows that people have three or four dreams per night, and answer No. This item, then, becomes a nonsense. The responses indicate the opposite of what actually occurs. Thus, Example A (improved): 'Do you dream twice a week or more?'

Example B: 'Do you sometimes feel worried for no reason?' This item obviously constitutes a similar problem to that above. However, it is worse because 'sometimes' literally means 'more than once'. Hence almost all subjects are bound, if truthful, to endorse this statement. However, this could well be a useful item since we all know that in fact people do vary in their frequency of causeless anxiety. It is not the content but the form of the item that is under criticism. How can an item essentially concerned with frequency be put more precisely? Thus, Example B (improved): 'Have you felt worried for no particular reason within the last (2 weeks) (4 weeks)?'

(6) *As far as possible, avoid terms reflecting feelings.* Instead, try to put the item into a behavioural context. I have illustrated this point already in (3) above, where in the interests of reliability over time I made an item more specific. In so doing I changed 'enjoy' to 'play'. The point here is that whereas either a subject plays or does not, in the case of 'enjoy' there is a real problem. Meticulous, highly educated, linguistically precise subjects may hesitate long over its meaning: 'Yes they like it, but enjoy is perhaps a little strong; find pleasure in, yes . . .' Of course an item such as in point (5), examining anxiety feelings or worry, also presents this problem. However, to put this item in a behavioural form, such as 'Does your heart beat fast and your mouth go dry for no reason?', seems highly artificial. The point is this. Where an item can realistically be written in which vague words of feeling can be replaced by actual behaviour, this should be done. Where this is not so, it is certainly worth trying out items where feelings are described. The item analyses will reveal their success or failure.

(7) *Ensure through the instructions that subjects give the first answer that comes to mind. Do not allow the subject to mull over the meaning of items.* A good personality-test item that is truly pertinent to the behaviour of subjects should evoke an instant and powerful response. If it does not, it is unlikely to tap behaviour of much relevance to personality measurement. Some examples will clarify this point.

Example A: 'Do you enjoy watching goldfinches?' This item, except perhaps for ornithologists, will evoke nothing but perhaps laughter at its apparent bizarreness. Most people are simply uninterested.

Example B: 'Do you like bread and butter?' This is obviously not a bizarre question. However, most subjects in the west, at least, where this is a staple diet, will not feel at all strongly. Generally, the feeling is that it's all right if there is no alternative.

Example C (taken from trial items for the author's own Ai3Q test; Kline, 1971): 'Do you let your dog lick your face?' This item was intended to tap cleanliness and was keyed No. Obviously those without dogs would endorse No, it was argued, but cleanliness is often a reason for not owning pets. To my surprise, this item provoked an exceedingly powerful response. Some individuals on coming to this item actually abandoned the test trial saying that the whole thing was disgusting; one subject even told me that he had never been so insulted, that he would never allow so filthy an act, and so on in that vein.

There can be no doubt that this item tapped some underlying repressed material – as the subject of animals often does, although whether oral, bestial, or anal, or all, is by no means clear. The relevance to the instructions to tests is clear. It is this first response that is likely to be the indicant of personality. As soon as subjects think carefully over items, not only defensive processes intervene but even more conscious distorting processes – such as the desire to impress, to please the experimenter – may all create bias. Even more important, some items cannot stand critical evaluation, almost by the inherent necessity of having to put so much information into a brief item form. This is why the emphasis in item writing is on clarity and specificity.

Example C above could be mulled over, and there would be no problems. Either one does or does not allow a dog to lick one's face. There are no difficulties in deciding whether (a) the dog is a dog, (b) whether what it does is licking or (c) whether its the face or somewhere else. However, most personality-test items are not so definite. Perhaps, incidentally, it is noteworthy that the item was not successful and had to be rejected.

Example D: 'Do you have vivid dreams?' This clearly illustrates our point. Most subjects probably have an immediate response of either Yes or No. However, careful consideration makes the item impossible. After all, how vivid can dreams be? My dreams appear vivid to me but to another person they might not do so. I do have vivid dreams, but I also occasionally have somewhat flat and dull dreams. Such thoughts render responses difficult.

Example E: 'Have you got plenty of friends?' As in the first example, this item on reflection is exceedingly difficult to answer accurately. Again the problem concerns the meanings of certain words, in this case 'plenty' and 'friends'. It is the careful, thoughtful and conscientious subjects who face these difficulties. They can argue thus: I have plenty of friends, I think, but what is 'plenty'? What in fact is the mean number of friends that people have? Without this information and a knowledge of the variance round the mean, it is impossible to answer whether I have plenty or not.

While all such thoughts are indubitably true, in fact this item does evoke an automatic response in many subjects. 'Friends', too, can cause problems. Subjects can argue: What is a friend, as distinct from an acquaintance, or is there any difference at all? Take x, is he a friend? In some ways, we enjoy going out together, but if I needed him, he'd be pretty useless. Now y . . . and so on.

It is clear from these examples that it is necessary to use instructions that ask subjects to complete items as quickly as possible. Inevitably, of course, such instructions are not always followed, and in a study of obsessionals carried out by the present author, one item, concerned with whether the subject made up his mind quickly and kept to the decision, showed clear evidence of many different responses, although it was endorsed Yes.

This last point introduces an objection to personality questionnaires which must now be discussed.

Objection: the items are really essentially meaningless

This is evidenced by the examples D and E above. To expect intelligent subjects to answer quickly is not only an insult to the subjects (as Alice Heim has argued in connection with some interest tests; Heim and Watts, 1966), but, further, it is argued, how can such items measure anything?

This objection receives an empirical answer: item analysis of whatever kind demonstrates that our set of items measures a homogeneous factor, while validity studies show what that factor is. The fact that items are of dubious meaning becomes irrelevant if responses to those items do in fact discriminate well or correlate with external criteria. This objection, powerful though it may seem, is not, therefore, of great weight.

Such are the guidelines to item writing which Guilford (1959) has described and which help in writing items that turn out to do the job for which they were intended. Certainly, the present writer in the construction of his own personality-test items has always managed to produce reliable and probably valid tests using these methods. Whether without these guidelines he could have done so, is obviously unknown.

Eliminating response sets

In addition to writing items with these guidelines in mind, it is necessary to diminish, as far as possible, the influence certainly of the most important response sets. How this is best done is set out below.

Acquiescence

Response sets were defined by Cronbach (1946) as stylistic consistencies, stimulated by the form of response of personality inventory items. As I have previously pointed out, one of the most important is acquiescence (see Messick, 1962), the tendency to agree with an item regardless of content.

BALANCED SCALES

Messick (1962) argues that a balanced scale is one important precaution in minimizing the influence of acquiescence on test responses, a balanced scale being one where there are equal or almost equal numbers of items keyed Yes or No, true or false.

However, two points deserve note here. First, a balanced scale does not entirely eliminate the tendency: acquiescence still may occur but, as Knowles (1963) points out, such a scale will not confuse the acquiescent subject with the high scoring subject, and this is important. Of course, it could be argued that an acquiescent high scorer will be missed by a balanced scale. If this is true, in more than a few isolated cases, subsequent validity studies of the test would be bound to fail.

Second, spurious inflation of the score through acquiescence will be avoided only if equally meaningful, unambiguous and compelling items can be written, keyed in both directions. If only poor items can be written keyed No, these items will contribute to the low validity of the scale. Some examples will clarify this point.

Example 1. Here is an item to tap the extravert trait of enjoying parties: 'Do you enjoy parties?' The reversal of this would be: 'Do you dislike parties?' In these items the English is satisfactory because it is idiomatic and usual to talk of disliking and enjoying parties. They are also satisfactory because, as it happens, the high scorer enjoys parties and the low scorer dislikes them. The polarity of the items is therefore effective. Often, however, this is a source of error in attempting to reverse items.

Example 2. The following item is designed to tap pleasure in statistics – claimed to be an obsessional trait: 'Are you one of those people who find tables of statistics and figures a complete bore?' This is a reversed item, with the keyed answer No. However, as should have been obvious before the first test trial showed the item to be failing, it is perfectly clear that it is possible not to find statistics a bore and yet not delight in them. In more general terms, reversing an item, where that item refers to some extreme of behaviour, is unlikely to work because of the continua which underlie most responses to items. Reversing items usually implies a dichotomy of response. In other words, where an item response is a dichotomy, reversing the item for a balanced scale is possible; where the extremes of a continuum are used, reversal will not be successful.

Example 3. A similar example concerns the trait of liking to give orders. A reversed item such as, 'Do you dislike having to give orders?' cannot be successful because it is possible not to dislike giving orders without actually enjoying doing so. Thus a continuum not a dichotomy underlies this response. The item cannot be reversed.

Example 4. This item concerns neatness: 'Schools greatly overemphasize neatness.' Here it was argued that the obsessionally neat individual would consider that this trait could not be overemphasized. Here, therefore, the item has been so written that the negative response actually taps the trait involved. Hence from the viewpoint of item writing, this is a viable negative item.

These examples illustrate the two most important points in writing negatively keyed items: they can be written, first, where the negative response is the actual relevant behaviour, and second, where there is a dichotomy rather than a continuum underlying the response, as in our example 1, above.

CLEAR, UNAMBIGUOUS ITEMS

A further point was raised by Guilford (1959) in attempting to eliminate acquiescence from personality inventories. He claimed that acquiescence was least likely to occur when items were clear, unambiguous and referred to specific behaviour. Since these qualities are among those which I have already suggested should be built into items, I shall say no more about them other than to illustrate the claim with a few examples.

Thus the item 'Do you play a musical instrument from music?' is so specific that an individual would have to be remarkably high on acquiescence to endorse it if it were not true. On the other hand, the item 'Do you enjoy music?' is so vague (for what is the criterion of enjoying music?) that acquiescence is likely to be a factor in endorsing this item. Two points are raised by the latter example. Notice first that the item is *not* comparable to 'Do you enjoy parties?'. In this latter item the criterion of enjoying parties is known to everybody: frequent and enthusiastic attendance. Hence the item is almost a shorthand form of 'Do you go to a lot of parties?' It is therefore less likely than 'Do you enjoy music?' to be influenced by acquiescence.

Related to this point is the vague term 'enjoy music'. This phraseology is useless for an item: thus the word 'enjoy' can cover feelings as diverse as those of great performers and composers when listening to, writing or playing music, down to those of the person who enjoys muzak while Saturday shopping. Similarly, the term 'music' covers so large a variety of different things – jazz, pop, folk, rock, baroque, early, classical, romantic, modern, twelve-tone, just for example – and in addition can pertain to listening and performing, that identical item-responses can reflect totally different behaviours. For example, a Yes for subject 1 may reflect an enjoyment of singing counter-tenor in early polyphonic Venetian church music. For subject 2 it may reflect a pleasure in listening to 'Dance with Me' while driving on his job up and down the motoways of England. Any item which causes such different behaviours to be categorized together is almost certainly useless.

TESTING FOR THE INFLUENCE OF ACQUIESCENCE
So far, all our efforts have been aimed – through balancing scales and writing items of great clarity and specificity – at reducing the influence of acquiescence or at rendering it less likely that acquiescence will lead to individuals apparently scoring high on the variable the test purports to measure. However, as we have argued, even with balanced scales, acquiescent responding can occur, and it is not always possible to write items of such clarity that we can feel confident it has been eliminated. For this reason there are techniques designed to check whether acquiescence has been an influential factor in item responses, and these will be described in chapter 6.

Social desirability

Edwards (1957) demonstrated in the case of the MMPI items that there was a high positive correlation between the social desirability of an item as rated by judges and the proportion putting the socially desirable response. Social desirability, therefore, he argued must be an important determinant of response to items, and thus a major source of test invalidity. Although it is probably impossible to eliminate entirely the influence of this response set, there are various techniques which are useful in reducing its effects and these are set out below.

FORCED-CHOICE ITEMS OF MATCHED SOCIAL DESIRABILITY
In the Edwards' Personal Preference Schedule (EPPS) (Edwards, 1959), as we discussed in our study of item types (see p. 61), Edwards' items consisted of two statements matched for social desirability, one of which subjects had to choose. This is the drastic solution to eliminating the influence of social desirability on items. However, this method is not advocated for the following reasons.

(1) To obtain matching items, which are also relevant in terms of content to what we want to measure, is extremely difficult (Edwards, 1957). Indeed, a powerful objection to the EPPS is that it

is little more than an exercise in test construction, and that there is little evidence of its measuring variables of any power (see Kline, 1979).

(2) Any small differences in social desirability within the pairs of items tend to become magnified when they are presented together, as in the forced-choice format, thus rendering most of the effort in matching items valueless (Corah *et al.*, 1958; Edwards, Wright and Lunneborg, 1959).

(3) Judged social desirability is an oversimplification of the phenomenon. What is normally done is to obtain a mean of judges' ratings for each item on social desirability. This assumes that social desirability is unidimensional (which is certainly *a priori* unlikely). Thus, what would truly be required would be a multi-dimensional scaling of social desirability among items and a score on the dimensions isolated – a procedure that could by no means be recommended in the light of point (2) above! In addition to this, as Messick (1960) points out, social desirability itself allows for considerable individual differences: what is socially desirable for a *Guardian* reader is almost certainly not for a London docker.

For these three reasons, to take the drastic and probably somewhat inefficient step of attempting to pair items matched for social desirability is not recommended.

AVOID ITEMS THAT ARE CLEARLY SOCIALLY DESIRABLE OR
UNDESIRABLE
There are a number of characteristics and qualities which few people would be willing to admit, at least in the milieu of the educated Englishman. These are so obvious that when we illustrate them below with example items, they will seem palpably absurd. Here are some examples of items which are clearly socially desirable or undesirable:

(1)	I am a very poor loser.	T F
(2)	I have no sense of humour.	T F
(3)	I am generally a cheat.	T F
(4)	I am not up to much sexually.	T F
(5)	I am sexually psychopathic.	T F
(6)	I cannot control my temper.	T F
(7)	I am an envious and jealous person.	T F
(8)	I am mean.	T F
(9)	When possible I avoid work.	T F
(10)	I lie to get out of trouble.	T F
(11)	I hate negroes.	T F
(12)	I am basically anti-Semitic.	T F

In our experience of test construction, we should be highly surprised if any of these twelve items in our examples proved adequate even for a research test. For a personality test to be used for selection, they would be quite worthless. Imagine item (11) in a test used for social workers or item (12) for a man hoping for work in a firm owned by Jews.

MEASURING SOCIALLY DESIRABLE OR UNDESIRABLE TRAITS

Where socially undesirable or desirable traits are to be measured, item writing must try to avoid the direct approach of the items above. Two examples can clarify this point.

Example 1. Item for measuring parsimony. Since (see item 8, above) a direct approach will not do, I argued in the construction of Ai3Q that a mean person might well think that old-fashioned sayings about thrift were sensible, whereas the less parsimonious would not be impressed. I therefore tried out 'Waste not, want not: every child should have this imprinted on his mind'. There would seem to be little that is socially desirable about either response (Yes or No) to this item. In fact, this item was successful in all item analyses.

Example 2. Item for tapping vindictiveness. Few subjects would endorse the item 'I am vindictive'. It was argued, however, that vindictive individuals might well project their vindictiveness on to others, as a defence against it. Thus I constructed the item: 'Vindictive savagery is the motivation of most revolutionaries'. I considered that few subjects would have actually encountered revolutionaries, so that their opinions would necessarily reflect their own defences and wishes. This item proved successful, and I believe *projection* to be a useful device for writing items that are too socially undesirable to be directly phrased.

Example 3. Item to tap laziness. If we use projection, we might phrase the item thus: 'Industry is poor today because the workers are generally lazy'. It is to be noted that if this item is considered by some readers not to be a projection of laziness but a fact, then the item analysis will truly reveal it: the item will not work.

USE OF A LIE SCALE

Some writers (e.g. Eysenck in the EPI and EPQ) insert a set of special items to check up on those putting the socially desirable answer. They consist of items referring to small peccadillos which most people have at some time alas committed. The high scorer is considered to be putting socially desirable responses, hence his test scores can be ignored. Although Eysenck and Eysenck (1976) argue from a factor analysis of the EPQ items that such a lie scale may, under research conditions, measure an interesting personality variable, for practical testing with a significant outcome for subjects, this method is quite useful.

Here are some typical lie-scale items: I never tell lies; I would never fill in my tax forms less than accurately; I always claim precisely what I spent from my expense account; I always return wrong change in shops.

PROPER ITEM ANALYSIS AND VALIDATION OF THE TEST
Nevertheless, I would still argue that given proper item analysis during test construction, and given good test validation, as was the case with the response set of acquiescence, the effects of social desirability may be ignored.

(1) Item analysis. By definition a socially desirable item must be biased, that is its response split will not be even. Thus by picking only items with a response split that is not uneven, socially desirable items will be eliminated. Furthermore, if most of the items are evenly split and they load on a general factor, then other items loading on this factor cannot be highly influenced by social desirability. A similar argument applies to item analyses using the biserial correlation of each item with the total score. Thus good item analyses should eliminate items influenced by social desirability, unless, by some horrid chance, they select items all of which measure this trait. This possibility can be checked by validating the test.
(2) Test validation. More important than all other tests of contamination by social desirability is our test validation. If we show the test to be valid, then it is irrelevant whether or not it is affected by social desirability. One demonstration of a test's independence of social desirability is to show in a validity study that it is unrelated to the Crowne–Marlowe Social Desirability Scale (Crowne and Marlowe, 1964), a test consisting of items which are clearly socially desirable.

CONCLUSIONS CONCERNING SOCIAL DESIRABILITY
There is no doubt that social desirability can influence the responses to test items and hence scores on personality tests. Nevertheless the influence may be minimized. Here are some conclusions:

(1) Care should be taken to avoid items that appear to be socially desirable.
(2) Item analysis will reject items that are clearly biased towards one response.
(3) The validity of a test should always be demonstrated, thus finally removing all questions concerning the influence of social desirability.
(4) It does not seem necessary to take elaborate precautions against social desirability, as was done by Edwards (1957).

Other response sets

THE TENDENCY TO ENDORSE EXTREMES
This is a tendency which affects rating scales and those tests, such as the Comrey Personality Scales (Comrey, 1970), where the item format includes a rating scale. In my view, the advantages of rating scales (in terms of satisfaction for the test subjects who feel the items can be better answered in this way) is offset by the problem that some subjects tend to endorse the extremes. To avoid confusion with high scorers, a balanced scale is not useful since in this response set either end of the scale is equally attractive. One method of avoiding this problem is not to use this type of item. If we were for some reason keen to use items of this type, careful item analysis and validation of the test variable could probably eliminate those items which particularly attracted this response set.

Indeed, in connection with all response sets, it cannot be stressed too much that, as Guilford (1959) argued, response sets are most operative where items are vague, ambiguous and unspecific. Item writing following our guidelines will *per se* minimize response sets. Furthermore, good test validation will demonstrate that the influence of these distorting factors is trivial. However, it will not be trivial unless precautions are taken. In this case, avoid this item format.

TENDENCY TO ENDORSE THE MIDDLE CATEGORY
Without doubt the best way to overcome this response set is to use dichotomous items, where it is, by definition, ruled out. Although some subjects object to dichotomous items on the grounds that they are unanswerable because (for them) the middle category applies, research (Bendig, 1959) showed such a high correlation between dichotomous and trichotomous items that the risks attendant upon the latter do not justify their use (see p. 60).

In fact, well-worded items can be written such that the middle category is not attractive. Clearly, this category appeals where the extremes are both equally boring. For example: 'Would you prefer (a) to see round a pickle factory, (b) to go round a local museum, (c) uncertain?' How can such poor items be identified if we use dichotomous items in our test trials? One method used by the present author was to insert the special instruction on the trial tests that any items which subjects felt needed a middle category should be marked with a cross. Items frequently so marked, unless the item analysis is particularly good, are best abandoned.

Of course, items that need a middle category generally fail to pass their item analyses and are automatically rejected, and again, test validation can show that the middle-category response set is not an important source of test error.

So much for response sets. If these methods are utilized, it seems to us that the influence of response sets is minimal. Validation of the tests will then show us whether this is in fact the case.

Item content

So far in our discussion of item writing we have concentrated upon item form. We have assumed in our item writing that we knew what traits we were trying to test. Nevertheless, it is fair to ask just how we decide upon the content of the items. General statements on this topic are difficult since much depends upon the individual case as to why we want to develop a personality test. To illustrate how test content is decided upon, I shall give a few illustrative examples.

A theoretical example

Kline (1968) carried out an experimental study of the anal character (Freud, 1908) in which a large number of empirical propositions were put to the test. Is there an anal character? If there is, is it measured by other personality questionnaires? Is it related to toilet training? Does it vary cross-culturally as would be expected from psychoanalytic theory? To answer such questions it was clearly necessary to construct and validate a measure of the anal character. To do this I had to decide what traits had to go into the test.

What follows is a brief summary of how the item content was drawn up prior to changing into items. The resulting test (Ai3Q) does seem to stand scrutiny (see Kline, 1978). Psychoanalytic descriptions of the anal character (e.g. Abraham, 1921; Jones, 1923; Menninger, 1943) were minutely examined, and all traits and specific examples of behaviour were listed. Examples from Jones (1923) are set out below.

(1) Procrastination followed by intense concentration, boring persist-
    ence, self-willed independence – a belief nobody can do anything as
    well as oneself.
(2) Inability to depute work.
(3) Minute attention to detail . . .
(4) 'All collectors are anal erotic.'
(5) Tenderness to children.
(6) Tendency to domineer . . .

A long detailed list of traits and behaviours was collected in this way.

These were then changed into items utilizing all the methods and techniques discussed in the present chapter.

Practical example

It might be useful to have a measure of aggression, perhaps in a centre for deciding on treatment and handling of delinquents or young prisoners. The basic approach here would be to list all the expressions of aggression that we can think of, convert them to items and try them out on a relevant sample. It must be noted that this technique does not assume that there is a dimension of aggression. Rather it would be exploratory. Thus a factor analysis of items would demonstrate whether there was one dimension, several correlated dimensions, several uncorrelated dimensions or no real syndrome of behaviours that could meaningfully be labelled aggressive.

Obtaining item content

By way of example, here is a selection of aggressive behaviours that could be changed into items: constantly fighting (other than play); fights, if crossed in any way; uses broken bottles in fighting; uses heavy objects in fighting; possesses razors, razor blades, knuckle-dusters, bicycle chains, flick knives, studded belts, heavy boots; kicks opponents when down; has rendered someone unconscious; has suffered injuries himself in fighting; shouts if crossed; throws things across the room; lies to get rivals into trouble; invents harmful stories about people. Such a list would then be converted into items using the methods discussed in this chapter.

Conclusions

Given the complexity and the inevitably imprecise guidelines for constructing personality test items, as demonstrated in our discussion, a brief step-by-step summary of personality-test item writing might prove valuable. This I set out below. The full rationale for all these points is contained in this chapter.

  (1) List traits and behaviours from descriptions in the psychological literature.
  (2) Change each trait or behaviour into items (as many as possible). This is best done by the conventional inventory-item formats:

(a) Yes–No items; (b) Yes? No items; (c) true–false items: (d) like–dislike items; (e) forced-choice items; (f) rating-sacle items. The choice depends upon the particular material involved, and the value attached to the particular advantages and disadvantages of each type of item.

(3) Regardless of the item format used, try not to make the purport of each item too obvious.

(4) Make each item clear and unambiguous.

(5) As far as possible, ensure that each item refers to some specific behaviour.

(6) Only one point should be contained within each item.

(7) Avoid terms of frequency and other subjective words.

(8) Where possible, items should refer to behaviours rather than feelings.

(9) Ensure that the items are answered quickly.

(10) Avoid the major response sets, such as acquiescence and social desirability.

(11) Acquiescence is best reduced by writing clear items and using balanced scales.

(12) Check by item-analytic procedures that acquiescence is a trivial factor.

(13) Social desirability is best avoided by careful item writing.

(14) Check by item-analytic techniques that social desirability is a trivial factor.

(15) Avoid by item-format choice the response sets of endorsing the extreme or middle categories.

(16) Check by validation procedures that response sets are not important. If tests are valid, then response sets cannot have affected their scores.

4

Making tests reliable III
Constructing other types of test

In this chapter I shall discuss the development of items and materials for other types of psychological test. Many of the guidelines which have been discussed, especially in the last chapter, will apply here, and these will not be mentioned again. I shall concentrate here on the methods particular and specific to the tests. I shall deal with objective tests of personality or temperament, projective tests, measures of mood and interest and finally attitude scales. First, I shall begin with objective tests.

Objective tests

Definition

The definition used here is that of Cattell and colleagues (e.g. Cattell, 1957): a test of which the purpose is hidden from the subject (and thus cannot be faked) and which can be marked with complete reliability between markers. The great advantage of such tests lies in their practical application. If scores cannot be wilfully manipulated by subjects, the tests can be used in selection procedures. This means that over the years a large body of real-life criterion data in respect of occupational success and objective test variables can be built up. In addition, of course, this absence of deliberate distortion is useful even in less pressurized applications, such as vocational guidance and psychiatry. In these contexts we cannot be certain that subjects will not distort their results.

One point should be noted before we leave the subject of deliberate distortion. With objective tests deliberate sabotage is still possible. Thus, if the test is the 'Slow Line-Drawing Test', subjects can draw lines not as slowly as possible, only fairly slowly. However, they do not know what this will do to their scores nor even indeed what the scores are. Such deliberate disobedience of instructions is in itself symptomatic of certain personality traits and, indeed, can be utilized as an objective-test variable.

This last sentence gives us a clue to a major and profound difficulty in objective-test construction. Given our definition, almost anything that can be objectively scored and which is not a direct response to a question (as in personality inventories), and thus obvious to subjects, could be an objective test. For example, this page of the manuscript could be used to yield the following objective-test variables:

(1) Length of time completing the manuscript.
(2) Number of words on page.
(3) Number of nouns.
(4) Number of verbs.
(5) Number of crossings-out.
(6) Pressure of nib in writing.
(7) Number of proper nouns.

Of course the psychological significance of such variables is not known – a second major problem with objective tests. Thus in our study of the construction or, more accurately, the creation of objective tests this difficulty has to be overcome. How do we choose an objective test (since, by definition, so many are possible) with any hope of validity? For, if it is apparently valid (i.e. face-valid), it is not any longer objective, for its purpose can be guessed. What are needed, therefore, are some principles for objective test construction – a taxonomy of objective tests.

Advantages of objective tests

Given this problem of developing objective tests, it is reasonable to ask whether it is worth trying to develop such methods, especially if their only advantage is that they cannot be easily faked. After all, better a valid test that may perhaps be subject to distortion than a non-valid one that resists all efforts at faking.

In fact, as Cattell and Kline (1977) have argued, there is a theoretical advantage in objective tests so considerable when they are compared with inventories that the efforts to develop valid objective tests are indeed worthwhile. This is the simple but inescapable point that the meaning of words and the purport of items changes over time, thus making longitudinal studies of personality of dubious merit. This meaning is, of course, different among cultures, thus rendering cross-cultural studies of personality using inventories extremely difficult, if not impossible, and it is an arguable case that it is different among social classes within the same culture. Kelly (1955) indeed would claim that the meaning of words is so different among individuals that any form of standardized testing is necessarily of little value. Hence the emphasis by Kelly and his followers on repertory grids, where each grid is personal to the subject whose constructs are being investigated. A few examples will make this point beyond doubt.

(1) 'Do you enjoy gay parties?' Before about 1960 this item had no homosexual connotations. A gay party was a party characterized by cheerful, lively good-humour. At present, a gay party is a party for homosexuals.
(2) 'Do you enjoy "Drop the handkerchief"?' This item is culture-bound to America: this is not a game played in Great Britain and the concomitants of the game are thus unknown. Hence the item is not usable in cross-cultural studies.
(3) 'Do you regularly go to the cinema?' Today this item would indicate a genuine interest in films, if answered Yes. Twenty years ago, before the total spread of television, the cinema was simply the most common form of entertainment. The response No would probably have been the one of interest.

Objective tests, on the other hand, should be able to yield data that are unaffected by changes in the meaning of items, and hence such data should be useful in the study of changes over time and between disparate groups – all vital necessities if the study of personality is to be placed on a sound basis.

Principles of objective-test construction

As I have argued, the huge range of possible objective tests (any non-face-valid variables that can be objectively scored) necessitates that objective-test constructors have some principles to guide their test construction. Cattell and Warburton (1967) in their compendium of objective tests of personality and motivation, in which 688 tests leading to more than 2300 variables are listed, regard these as but a small proportion of what could be devised. However, these authors realize that objective-test construction requires a taxonomy before it is abandoned, overwhelmed by the potential (for even in their compendium many of the variables remain untried and of unknown validity), and a useful taxonomy of test materials is included. A summary of this follows.

Psychological tests have three sources of variation:

(1) Instructions. Clearly these are important in determining how a subject perceives the test (although subjects may not always believe them).
(2) The test material. This can be social or physical for example.
(3) Scoring the response.

Since it is clear that these three categories are not independent – for the instructions *must* refer to some stimulus material – Cattell and Warburton prefer to collapse the first two categories, which become: *stimulus-instruction situation*.

STIMULUS-INSTRUCTION SITUATION
In fact, this varies along a number of parameters:

(1) To react or not react. Generally, reaction to the stimulus is required. This is not always so, as for example in tests of pain sensitivity.
(2) Restricted versus unrestricted variety of response. Completely unrestricted response is unknown in testing. It is assumed that subjects (as Cattell and Warburton argue) will not eat the test materials or destroy them. However, responses can be relatively free, as in the Rorschach, or restricted, as in reaction-time measures.
(3) Inventive versus selective responses. The meaning is obvious here. The true–false response mode typifies the latter, the description of a Thematic Apperception Test (TAT) picture the former.
(4) Single versus repetitive responses.
(5) Sequence of responses: ordered versus unordered. This is concerned with the extent to which subjects are required to give responses in a given order.
(6) Homogeneous versus patterned responses. Some tests require responses of the same kind; others necessitate a variety of different responses.
(7) Natural versus limited responses. This refers to the instructions, such as 'Work at your own speed', compared with 'Do not spend long over each question' and 'Work as fast as you can'.
(8) Concluding reaction versus reaction to reaction. Either the subject reacts to the test material or he reacts to his own reaction, for example he may have to evaluate it or associate to it or remember it.

Cattell and Warburton (1967) consider these to be the main parameters of variation in the construction of test materials, concerning which there is little cause for argument. However, three further, more subjective dimensions are presented which, for the construction of objective tests, would appear to be particularly important.

(9) Immediate meaning versus referent meaning. In some tests there is no meaning beyond the test, as in reaction times. However, in certain tests (e.g. where opinions are asked) there is considerable symbolic reference. This is a critical parameter since most forms of distortion and problems in the subjective meanings of words and concepts occur with tests which have referent meaning.

(10) Itemized versus global presentation. This parameter is concerned with the distinction between tests consisting of items and those which consist of a single task.

(11) Nature of the psychological decision required in the task. This concerns the question of whether the response demands (a) cognition (e.g. correct judgement), (b) judgement of feeling or (c) judgement of familiarity or recognition.

Two other possibilities might be, Cattell and Warburton (1967) argue:

(12) Variation in the motives for accepting the test situation.

(13) Variation in freedom to leave the test situation.

This gives us the possibility of 2^{13} types of stimulus-instruction situations.

The value of these classificatory principles is considerable: if we construct objective-test materials that in total include them all, then we should have utilized every possible type of material. This is particularly important since with these tests there is always the risk that more variance will be specific (to the test) than is desirable.

As we have discussed, another important distinction among tests resides in the way in which they are scored. Cattell and Warburton (1967) in their study of test responses invoke the following *parameters of scores from test responses*. Although these parameters are not entirely independent of the stimulus parameters above, as shall be seen, they are sufficiently independent for the total number of test categories to be the product of the test and response parameters.

Before these parameters are set out, it must be emphasized that responses to tests can yield a very large number of test variables. For example, if we were to consider a personality inventory as an objective test, in addition to the standard-scale score or scores, further variables could be scored: time to complete test, time to complete half the test, number of Yes responses endorsed, number of No responses endorsed, number of alterations, number of blanks, number of uncertain responses. All these scores, it will be noted, other than the standard-scale score, are objective because no subject could know what they measured, and they can be measured with perfect inter-maker reliability.

Response-scoring parameters

(1) Objective versus self-evaluative. The point here concerns mainly those tests using self-report items. Is the subject scored as he would expect from the instructions or on something unknown to him? This does not involve deception of subjects. For example, an objective test is the *Critical Evaluations Test* (T8, Cattell and Warburton, 1967). Here subjects are asked to state whether a given performance – for example, a waitress taking ten minutes to bring six meals to a table – is very good, good, poor or very poor. What *inter alia* is scored here is the number of critical evaluations. The subject matter of the items is irrelevant to the scorers. Thus this inventory-like test is, in fact, entirely objective, as defined at the beginning of this chapter. Of course, all the tests to be discussed in this chapter are objective in terms of this first parameter.

(2) Overt behaviour (total organism) versus physiological response (part organism). Typical physiological responses might be blushing or tremor.

(3) Dimension of one possible response versus classification among a variety of responses (parametric versus non-parametric). The parametric measures a dimension of the response: time, errors, repetitions. The non-parametric reveals the number and variety of classes of response. In this sense many creativity tests are scored non-parametrically.

(4) Total quantity or number of responses versus fraction meeting a criterion. This cuts across the third category above, since, as Cattell and Warburton point out, a variety score could be of either category here.

(5) Single homogeneous score verses patterned relational score. The single score is possible only if the test is scored as a whole, as is the case with personality inventories. A patterned relational score can take many forms: difference in time for completion of first and second parts; memory for material under standard and under distracting conditions.

Finally, Cattell and Warburton actually add a sixth category:

(6) Normative versus ipsative scoring. However, this seems to be a classification of a radically different type from those above, since it affects all tests and is more properly relegated to the sphere of standardization than test construction. If we were to include this category, there would be a possible 2^6 types of response score.

Thus this operational analysis of tests should allow us, in our test construction if we aim to utilize each viable type, to construct tests of every variety. Such an approach, however, although useful, still does not help us as regards the content of objective tests. Furthermore, it shows that the potential number of types of objective test is huge indeed: $2^{13} \times 2^6$ – which is well in excess of 50,000. Many, however, are unviable, but even so the number of varieties is still prodigious. The scheme, however, does indicate to what extent each possible type of objective-test item has been tried. We should never be short of items!

If this classification system is to be used in practice for objective-test construction, it must be shortened. Cattell and Warburton in fact claim that sixty-four varieties are of particular importance, drawn from the three most important situations and scoring parameters each generating eight possibilities. The huge number of tests in their compendium does not fill all the sixty-four cells, so this brief version of the taxonomy still leaves ample room for the creative test constructor. This taxonomy, based upon the characteristic of tests, may enable the test constructor to produce a variety of tests, but there is a major difficulty: how do we know that the resulting measures will measure temperamental (as distinct from other) variables. In brief, how can we be likely to produce tests of temperament if we want them rather than dynamics or abilities? As it stands, this taxonomy is not helpful, and for this reason the test constructor requires further information.

The distinction between objective tests of ability, temperament and dynamics

One method of determining what objective tests measure is to factor them with clear marker variables from the three modalities. The factor analysis will then reveal what modality the objective test is measuring. This, however, although effective and a necessary procedure before any objective test is actually used, does not indicate how we may construct the type of test we need. It is an adequate check but not a guide to test construction.

Cattell and Warburton (1967) devote considerable space to this problem, and we shall summarize their arguments briefly here, for they provide some rational basis (in addition to the taxonomy for helping the form of the tests) for item content.

(1) Two kinds of situation are distinguished (situationalism is not in fact the antithesis of trait psychology): incentives and complexities.
(2) As incentives change, so do the scores of dynamic tests. As complexities change, so too do the scores on ability tests. Temperamental tests include all others.
(3) Definition of incentive: an incentive provokes a striving for a goal

and is a symbol of the goal or the goal satisfaction, which itself can be discovered only by process analysis. This is the statistical pattern analysis of a behaviour sequence over time. This sequence is the path of activities leading to goal satisfaction. An incentive situation is thus recognized by its relationship to the goal (i.e. by common fluctuations in strength and constant precedence). Kline and Grindley (1974) did indeed show just such fluctuations between dynamic measures and situations.

(4) Definition of complexity. When the incentive in the environment has been recognized the complexity can be defined: all that which is not incentive.

(5) This means in practice of course that the measurement of dynamics and abilities is intertwined. However, relatively pure measures of each can be obtained. For example, if we have measures of ability that are very easy, differences in score are not reflections of ability but dynamics (how hard people are trying, for example). Thus levels of complexity and incentive can be so manipulated that objective tests can become almost pure measures of each modality.

(6) Needless to say, all tests constructed thus have to be checked in factor analyses to ensure that their pattern of loadings is in accord with expectations – all putative ability tests loading together and similarly for motivational, dynamic measures.

With this rationale, the distinction between incentive and complexity, the objective-test constructor has some guide at least as to what his tests are likely to measure, although all still has to be checked in subsequent factor analyses.

However, as must now be obvious to the reader, these principles and taxonomies are interesting and possibly stimulating, but perhaps too abstract to be of practical use in constructing actual tests. Cattell and Warburton (1967), aware of this, also present what they candidly admit to be no more than intuitive hunches concerning the construction of objective tests based upon their considerable experience in this field. These I shall now briefly discuss.

Practical hints for objective-test construction in personality and motivation

The following five things to be avoided are regarded by Cattell and Warburton as the popular predilections of the amateur, best abandoned before beginning the real task of constructing objective tests.

(1) Avoid ending up with face-valid questionnaire items.

(2) Avoid problem or puzzle items. These are more likely to measure ability factors.

(3) Do not place too much reliance on the 'stress situation'. As Cattell and Warburton (1967) argue, this may be fine for tapping aggression or fear, but there is a wide variety of other emotions.

(4) Aesthetic and stylistic preferences may well show up some aspects of personality. It is absurd, however, to expect such tests to reveal all aspects apart from the obvious fact that responses to these tests must be influenced by level of education and culture.

(5) Avoid the simple use of projective tests. Wenig (1952) has shown that such tests measure a complex of dimensions which demand factor-analytic unravelling.

Finally,

(6) Use questionnaire items to specify accurately the relevant behaviours. From this a good objective test may be devised.

Overcoming some common problems associated with objective tests

There are a number of problems which can make the interpretation of any test score (not only objective tests) dubious, and these have to be accommodated in the construction of objective tests. A detailed discussion of these, to which readers must be referred, is contained in Cattell and Warburton (1967). However, the main points can be briefly summarized.

DIFFERENTIAL MOTIVATION OF DIFFERENT SUBJECTS

The differential motivation of different subjects to do the tests is particularly important in research studies, although presumably in selection and guidance this source of individual differences is minimized. After all, if an objective test demands considerable concentration, for example, why should a subject make the effort to do it as well as he can? On the other hand, some subjects have to do their best at everything. Cattell and Warburton (1967) discuss five objective-test designs which to some extent can minimize this difficulty.

(1) Divide the test into two parts. The score obtained is a ratio or difference score, and two parts being compared, with the reasonable assumption that for each subject the motivation for each part is the same and thus its effect is cancelled out. An example of this technique is the test for ego strength – memory under distraction, where the score is the difference between memory for digits and memory for digits interspersed amongst jokes. This is clearly a useful design for objective tests.

(2) Utilize as motivations basic ergic drives rather than sentiments. In the terminology of Cattell (see Cattell and Child, 1975; Cattell and Kline, 1977) ergs are basic drives, such as hunger, sex or fear, while sentiments are the culturally learned drives, such as religious feelings or sentiments towards the family. Since, as Cattell and Child (1975) have discussed, there is less variance in ergs than sentiments, it reduces differences due to motivation if ergs are deliberately involved as motivations of test performance. Fear (electric shocks) and sexual desires (pictures of nudes) are relatively easy to manipulate in this way, although it must be realized that these drives cannot be fully excited, within accepted ethical codes of testing.

(3) Restrict scoring to stylistic or formal aspects of the performance. These variables are held to vary less with motivation than most others. Cattell and Warburton select handwriting as an example, which tends to remain recognizable for each individual across a wide variety of situations.

With these first three methods of overcoming motivational distortions, one point, which is obvious but important, needs to be noted: they apply mainly to tests of temperament rather than dynamics.

(4) It is likely that a subject's motivational level over the whole battery can be factored out – possibly into one or more factors – from other substantive factors. If this is so, variables which tend to load substantially on such factors can be dropped.

(5) Finally, the objective-test constructor can deliberately seek to engage the motivation of his subjects in such a way that each becomes highly involved in the test procedures, although care must be taken that this is done through value systems which subjects share. This, unfortunately, is a principle which it is easier to understand than to put into practice.

PERSONALITY AND THE TEST SITUATION

Personality is concerned with social behaviour, but tests involve social behaviour only in the test situation. This, of course, is another major testing problem, and one which situationalists (e.g. Mischel, 1968) have used *inter alia* to cast doubts on the effectiveness of personality tests. Indeed, Mischel has argued that the factors obtained from traditional personality inventories are essentially test situational factors.

To overcome this difficulty Cattell and Warburton (1967) have invented individual test situations which indubitably involve social interactions. Unfortunately, however, these authors also argue that such miniature situations are difficult to devise, and difficult to use in practical psychology, thus considerably lessening their value for anything other than theoretical purposes. Indeed, they hope that future research will allow the factors defined by the miniature-situation tests to be measured by other objective measures of a more simple kind. If this happens, the situation tests can then be dropped. Without them, however, the objective-test constructor cannot feel certain that he has measured social behaviour. A few group tests loading on social interaction factors have been developed (and are listed in Cattell and Warburton, 1967) but much remains to be done in this area.

THE INFLUENCE OF ABILITY AND ACHIEVEMENT ON OBJECTIVE-TEST SCORES

This is a major difficulty which must be removed in the construction of objective tests of personality (temperament and dynamics). For example, it is known (Cattell and Child, 1975) that as a measure of interest, information on relevant matters is powerful. A moment's reflection, however, illustrates clearly how this problem can distort such a measure. A scholar's minor interest in horse-racing (Cambridge is near Newmarket) might result in a fund of knowledge not to be equalled by a lesser intelligence whose sole relaxation it was. The information test, therefore, would be false.

Thus techniques of test design must be developed which minimize ability and achievement. In fact, the following methods are suggested by Cattell and Warburton (1967).

(1) Reduce the demands as far as possible in objective tests on ability variables – eduction of relations, vocabulary, general knowledge, for example.
(2) As our example previously showed in the case of motivation, divide the test into two parts and use a ratio or difference score. This cancels out the ability level of the subject, as it does the motivational level.
(3) Submit tests to factor analysis and eliminate those that load on ability factors.
(4) Use as wide a sample of content, skill and interest in the objective test battery as possible.

The behavioural variables should include a diversity of role situations since personality factors are likely to be expressed through a variety of roles. Content, too, should be chosen such as to engage the interest of the whole range of the population. This is also important because it is *a priori* unlikely that one particular test format, however good, could tap the whole personality sphere, that is the whole gamut of factors.

GROUP OR INDIVIDUAL TESTS

Aim to produce simple, group-administrable tests rather than individual tests. This is important both for research, where large samples are necessary, and in practical psychology, where group administration is virtually a necessity. It must be pointed out, however, that to produce a group version of an individual test requires considerable ingenuity and research effort to demonstrate that in fact both forms do measure the same variable. Certain objective tests, however, such as physiological indices, may be impossible to translate into group form.

In addition to these semi-formal guidelines, Cattell and Warburton (1967) discuss the intuitive bases of some of their tests, because in objective-test construction a certain flair is still necessary since no algorithm has yet been devised. It will be sufficient to list these, since test constructors can either utilize these sources or not, that is some constructors will have the imagination to invent tests on this basis, while others will fail to do so because no rules for so doing can be laid down. The most important are (1) clinical intuition, (2) observation in everyday life of incidents critical for personality, (3) everyday folklore – proverbs and saws, (4) emotional situations in games, for example card games, (5) observed conversational behaviour and (6) literary sources.

Cattell and Warburton (1967) also claim that a number of what they refer to as vague psychological principles were helpful in constructing tests. However, the present writer has found these far too diffuse to be useful (e.g. 'the selective action of perception and memory with respect to general orientations') in practical test construction, although they are helpful in understanding the bases of some of Cattell's objective tests.

Finally, Cattell and Warburton argue that some of the experimental psychological findings (such as those concerned with conditioning and learning, and EEG and personality, for example; see Eysenck, 1967) can be useful in the design of objective tests.

Such then are the hints with respect to form and content for objective-test constructors attempting to produce tests that will correlate with some external criterion. This is likely to be the approach favoured by those attempting to construct new objective tests for a particular purpose – selection for a post or guidance. It is hoped that all these hints will be found valuable in stimulating test construction. Nevertheless, it must be emphasized that no tests should be used unless they have been demonstrated to measure their intended variables.

Objective test dimensions

Cattell and Warburton also discuss how objective tests can be designed with reference to explicit concepts, by which they essentially mean personality factors. Of course, the principles to be discussed below could be used to design tests measuring non-factor-analytic dimensions. However, factor-analytic concepts are by definition supported by evidence (their factor loading), hence they form a sensible target for measurement (in contradistinction to many clinical concepts which may have no reality beyond the imaginations of their creators).

The essence of this method is to utilize marker variables for well-established factors (of which various lists are available, e.g. Howarth, 1976, for personality questionnaire factors), and then to design tests that are intuitively likely to load on these factors. Subsequent factor analyses reveal the tests that load on the factors. This method is ideally suited to the development of objective-test measures equivalent to known factors in other tests – a useful procedure since from the viewpoint of selection, at least, objective tests cannot be faked. However, as Cattell and Warburton exemplify, this method can lead to the discovery of new factors not found in any other type of testing. This can easily be imagined if a set of objective tests forms a factor located between two marker factors.

In developing objective tests against the empirical criteria of established factors, a number of points merit note, if accurate results are to be obtained:

(1) Replication of all factor structures on different samples is essential. Ideally, as Nunnally (1978) shows, such studies demand ten times the number of subjects to variables. However, if a finding is replicated, so strict a criterion is perhaps unnecessary.

(2) A study of the tests loading on a factor helps one to sharpen the concept of the factor concerned. Thus sometimes the objective test loadings help to clarify further what had previously seemed to be a well-known factor.

(3) Much more interesting than this is that the factor loadings can help to clarify what the objective tests measure (an omnipresent problem with objective tests).

(4) From the factor loadings of tests it is often possible to devise new tests. In other words, actually seeing how variables load (i.e. hindsight) is highly useful in helping to construct tests. Thus one most important guide to creating objective tests are the actual factors emerging from them. These may be difficult to identify without further study both of the factor-analytic and the experimental variety, but at least in attempting to measure such factors the objective test constructor is aiming at a statistically important concept.

CONCLUSIONS

So much for the two approaches to devising objective tests of temperament. It can be seen that there are some useful guidelines available to workers in this the most difficult areas of testing, guidelines both for item form and content. Nevertheless, although I have shown how some obvious problems may be circumnavigated, it is clear that much depends on (a) intuitions based upon general psychology and previously known temperamental factors, and on (b) the actual factors emerging from studies.

I have not given more detail concerning the construction of objective tests because in my view there is so huge a number of such tests already devised, but of unknown validity, that the test constructor in search of new tests would be best advised to examine empirically what has already been done before embarking on the arduous task himself. Many of the best-known and well-validated objective tests have been constructed by Eysenck and his colleagues at the Maudsley Hospital, and most of their measures relate to their three super-factors, extraversion, neuroticism and psychoticism. Details of these tests may be found scattered throughout Eysenck's voluminous publications, but a useful source for many of them is Eysenck (1971).

The most extensive effort at objective-test construction, however, has been made at Illinois by Cattell and his colleagues. Indeed, their work has formed the basis of our discussion, and as was indicated earlier in this chapter. Cattell and Warburton (1967) offer a list of objective tests so huge that its psychological significance has not yet been elucidated to the full. The would-be objective-test constructor should certainly search this list and try out all likely tests before attempting to devise tests himself.

Objective tests of motivation or dynamics

So far what has been said concerning the construction of objective tests is relevant to the measurement of human temperament. Obviously, the taxonomy of types of tests is equally applicable to objective tests of motivation. So, too, is the second approach, based upon study of the factor-analytic results. However, certain principles for the development of objective motivational tests, which are not applicable to tests of temperament, have been suggested by Cattell and his colleagues, and these I must now discuss.

The principles for the construction of objective tests of motivation have been described in detail in Cattell (1957), Cattell and Warburton (1967), Cattell and Child (1975), and by the present author (Cattell and Kline, 1977). Thus here will be found a summary sufficient for the demands of this book, that is one suited to the needs of the practical test-constructor.

THEORETICAL BACKGROUND

In the Cattellian approach to motivation it is assumed that motivations are revealed in attitudes. Thus, for example, the fact that an individual is highly interested in money is held to reflect his drive strengths.

Cattell and Child (1976) utilize a dynamic lattice to demonstrate how such attitudes might relate to drives. In this example the money is desired to build up self-esteem (the self-sentiment), to provide a good home (sentiment to spouse) and to ensure that children are successful (protective erg). Notice that it is assumed here that human beings are motivated by a finite number of drives, thus following the notions of McDougall (1932). These drives are considered to be of two kinds: (1) ergs, basic to all human beings, (e.g. the sex drive) and (2) sentiments, the culturally moulded drives (e.g. feelings for home). Whether we are interested in something, the attitudes we have, depend essentially on how, through these activities, we may express our drives and sentiments. An interest in psychoanalysis, for example, could be a method of expressing a sex drive. All this means that the objective-test devices aimed at tapping motivational factors are concerned with attitudes and interests.

One further facet of the theoretical approach adopted by Cattell and his colleagues deserves mention. This concerns strength of interest. Two people can both be interested in the same things but their interests can differ markedly in strength. The work reported by Cattell and Child (1975) shows clearly that from the objective-test analysis of attitudes, factors of strength and interest emerge as well as factors reflecting the structure of interests, that is the basic human drives, ergs and sentiments.

It is against this background of theoretical assumptions that the principles of objective motivational test construction have to be understood. This is the rationale for attempting motivational measurement via tests of attitude and interest. Cattell and Kline (1977) set out sixty-eight psychological principles upon which motivational measurement can be based, principles also to be found in Cattell and Child (1975) and which are given in Table 4.1.

Table 4.1　Some principles of motivation measurement applied to constructing test devices

---

With increase in interest in a course of action expect increase in:

(1) Preferences. Readiness to admit preference for course of action.
(2) Autism: misperception, distorted perception of objects, noises, and so on, in accordance with interest (e.g. Bruner coin perception study).
(3) Autism: misbelief. Distorted belief that facts favour course of action.
(4) Reasoning distortion: means-ends. Readiness to argue that doubtfully effective means to goal are really effective.
(5) Reasoning distortion: ends-means. Readiness to argue that ends will be easily reached by inapt means.
(6) Reasoning distortion: inductive.
(7) Reasoning distortion: deductive.
(8) Reasoning distortion: eduction of relations in perception (e.g. analogies).
(9) Utilities choice. Readiness to use land, labour and capital for interest.
(10) Machiavellianism. Willingness to use reprehensible means to achieve ends favouring interest.
(11) Fantasy choice. Readiness to choose interest-related topic to read about, write about or explain.
(12) Fantasy ruminations. Time spent ruminating on interest-related material.
(13) Fantasy identification. Prefer to be like individuals who favour course of action.
(14) Defensive reticence. Low fluency in listing bad consequences of course of action.
(15) Defensive fluency. Fluency in listing good consequences of course of action.
(16) Defensive fluency. Fluency in listing justifications for action.
(17) Rationalization. Readiness to interpret information in a way to make interest appear more respectable, and so on, than it is.
(18) Naive projection. Misperception of others as having one's own interests.
(19) True projection. Misperception of others as exhibiting one's own reprehensible behaviour in connection with pursuit of interest.
(20) Id projection. Misperception of others as having one's own primitive desire relating to interest.
(21) Superego projection. Misperception of others as having one's own righteous beliefs relating to interest.
(22) Guilt sensitivity. Expression of guilt feelings for non-participation in interest-related activities.
(23) Conflict involvement. Time spent making decision under approach–approach conflict (both alternatives favour interest).
(24) Conflict involvement. Time spent making decision under avoidance–avoidance conflict (both alternatives oppose interest).
(25) Threat reactivity. Psychogalvanic resistance drops when interest threatened.
(26) Threat reactivity. Increase cardiovascular output when interest threatened.
(27) Physiological involvement. Increase cardiovascular output when interest aroused (threatened or not).
(28) Physiological involvement. Finger temperature rise when interest aroused.
(29) Physiological involvement. Increase muscle tension when interest aroused.
(30) Perceptual integration. Organize unstructured material in accordance with interest.

(31) Perceptual closure. Ability to see incomplete drawings as complete when material is related to interest.

(32) Selective perception. Ease of finding interest-related material embedded in complex field.

(33) Sensory acuity. Tendency to sense lights as brighter, sounds as louder, and so on, when interest is aroused.

(34) Attentivity. Resistance to distraction (lights, sounds, etc.) when attending to interest-related material.

(35) Spontaneous attention. Involuntary movements with respect to interest-related stimuli (e.g. eye movements).

(36) Involvement. Apparent speed with which time passes when occupied with interest.

(37) Persistence. Continuation in work for interest, in face of difficulty.

(38) Perseveration. Maladaptive continuation with behaviour related to interest.

(39) Distractibility. Inability to maintain attention when interest-related stimuli interfere.

(40) Retroactive inhibition when interest-related task intervenes.

(41) Proactive inhibition by interest-related task.

(42) Eagerness: effort. Anticipation of expending much effort for course of action.

(43) Activity: time. Time spent on course of action.

(44) Eagerness: money. Anticipation of spending much money for course of action.

(45) Activity: money. Money spent on course of action.

(46) Eagerness: exploration. Readiness to undertake exploration to achieve interest-related ends.

(47) Impulsiveness: decisions. Speed of decisions in favour of interest (low conflict).

(48) Impulsiveness: agreements. Speed of agreeing with opinions favourable to interest.

(49) Decision strength. Extremeness of certainty for position favouring course of action.

(50) Warm-up speed: learning. Speed warming-up to learning task related to interest.

(51) Learning. Speed-learning interest-related material.

(52) Motor skills. Apt performance to affect interest.

(53) Information. Knowledge affecting and related to course of action.

(54) Resistance to extinction of responses related to interest.

(55) Control. Ability to co-ordinate activities in pursuit of interest.

(56) Availability: fluency. Fluency in writing on cues related to course of action.

(57) Availability: free association. Readiness to associate to interest-related material when not orientated by cue.

(58) Availability: speed of free association. Number of associations when interest aroused.

(59) Availability: orientated association. Readiness to associate interest-related material with given cue.

(60) Availability: memory. Free recall of interest-related material.

(61) Memory for rewards. Immediate recall of reward associated with interest.

(62) Reminiscence. Ward–Hovland effect. Increased recall over short interval of interest-related material.

(63) Reminiscence. Ballard–Williams effect. Increased recall over long intervals of interest-related material.

(64) Zeigarnik recall. Tendency to recall incompleted tasks associated with interest.
(65) Zeigarnik perseveration. Readiness to return to incompleted task associated with interest.
(66) Defensive forgetfulness. Inability to recall interest-related material if goal not achievable.
(67) Reflex facilitation. Ease with which certain reflexes are evoked when interest aroused.
(68) Reflex inhibition. Difficulty in evoking certain reflexes when interest aroused.

Source: R.B. Cattell and D. Child, *Motivation and Dynamic Structure*, London: Holt, Rinehart and Winston, 1975.

As fully described by Cattell and Child (1975) many of these principles have been realized into tests and replicated factors of strength of interest, and some clear ergs and sentiments have emerged. Indeed, a group test, the MAT (Cattell *et al.*, 1970), and an adolescents' version, the SMAT, have been published.

However, as was the case with objective tests of temperament, the objective-test constructor would be well advised to try out the tests in the Compendium of Objective Tests (Cattell and Warburton, 1967) before attempting to develop any of his own measures. Indeed, the construction of objective tests is a specialist's art, and for psychologists who want some tests for practical use, either for research or selection, to attempt to construct such tests is unlikely to be successful, unless considerable resources of time and research assistance for trying out versions and validation are available. I have ignored here the special methods for the measurement of dynamic conflict because at this time the research evidence for the validity of the techniques is too speculative for it to be sensible to use them other than to explore further this indubitably important area of motivational research. (For further details, readers should refer to Cattell and Child, 1975.)

Further points concerning the construction of objective motivation tests

Although our table 4.1 gives us the basic principles in the light of which objective motivation tests can be constructed, some further points deserve note.

IPSATIZATION OF SCORES
If we consider principles 42, 43, 44, 45 and 60 in table 4.1, it should be obvious that time and money voluntarily spent on some activity and

relevant information about it are measures of a subject's motivation towards it. However, as I have previously pointed out, such measurement is bedevilled by individual differences such as ability and amount of free time and money. To avoid this obvious source of error, scores are ipsatized, that is a subject's score on a test is the deviation on that test from his mean score. Thus if a millionaire spends £400 on a flute, this clearly indicates less interest than a music student's doing the same thing. Ipsatization removes these irrelevant sources of variance.

SENTIMENTS AND ERGS

As was indicated in our necessarily brief outline of the theoretical context of these objective tests of motivation, there are two aspects to motivational measurement: strength of interest and basic motivational goals, drives; in this approach, ergs and sentiments. The principles of test construction contained in table 4.1 are aimed at the first problem: motivational strength.

It is therefore pertinent to consider the construction of tests directed to the measurement of ergs and sentiments. In fact, as Cattell and Warburton (1967) point out, these principles are applicable to tests of drives because, to quote their example, an autism test (principles 2 and 3 in table 4.1) can be used to measure wishful thinking towards a large variety of objects: food (hunger erg), women (sex erg) or problem solutions (curiosity erg). Thus all depends, as ever in test construction, on the ingenuity of the test constructor. However, the specific properties of the particular test employed must influence what aspects of drive-motivated behaviour are measured. From this it follows that to measure in tests the full richness of an individual's motivation, a wide selection of tests is necessary (incorporating as many of the principles in table 4.1 as possible), measuring an adequate sample of his attitudes, thus ensuring full coverage of the variety of his sentiments and ergs.

SAMPLING ATTITUDES

In the previous paragraph it was noticed (I hope) that the phrase an 'adequate sample of attitudes' was used. This was because the ideal of incorporating all a subject's attitudes is clearly impossible. This being so, it is important in the construction of objective tests to determine which attitudes should be sampled. Cattell and Warburton (1967) argue that this can be done first *a priori* by deliberately selecting attitudes which it is thought likely will be related to what are considered to be the most important drives (e.g. hunger and sex), and then later empirically by inserting attitudes (where the drives are only intuitively guessable or even unknown) into studies with marker variables of replicated drives. This problem again indicates the considerable difficulties the objective test constructor faces in the study of motivation.

In most of their studies (as described in Cattell and Warburton, 1967; Cattell and Child, 1975) about sixty attitudes are examined, each likely to load up on both an erg and sentiment. A few examples will clarify this point. (Nevertheless, before I set them out, it must be realized that this approach is limited: our hypotheses may be wrong, and we may omit what turn out to be highly important variables.) Thus, (1) I want to be the kind of person everyone likes to have around. This taps the gregariousness erg and the self-sentiment. (2) I want to go home and rest after a busy day. Rest-seeking erg and home sentiment are measured by this attitude. (3) I want to see deaths from accident and disease reduced. This taps the fear erg.

Examples of objective tests

Enough has now been said about the construction of objective tests. All the principles and guidelines have been set out and all that remains is to give a few examples. I select ours from the Compendium by Cattell and Warburton (1967). They have been selected to indicate the ingenuity that has gone into the construction of these measures and the diversity of tests so far constructed. In addition, our choice indicates clearly the difficulties of objective test construction. Here is a sample of test titles from the 400 objective-test devices so far designed:

Willingness to play practical jokes.
Readiness to make an early decision while dark adaptation is proceeding.
Amplitude of voice under normal relative to delayed feedback conditions.
Awareness of social etiquette.
Basal metabolic rate.
Eidetic imagery.
Cancellation of letters (a vigilance task) compared under two conditions.
Readiness to imitate animal sounds.
Critical flicker fusion frequency.
Speed of arousal of negative after-images.
Preference for crayoning own rather than provided drawings.
Frequency of hand tremor in a decision situation.
Amount of laughter at jokes.
Pupil dilation after startle.
More fidgeting while waiting as measured by the fidgetometer (see p.98).
Speed of design copying.

Height of tower block construction (6-year-olds).
Care in following detailed instructions.
Accuracy of gestalt completion.
Distance covered in a brass finger maze, with and without shock.

These titles give a clear indication of the rich variety of tests which have been devised. I shall now describe some of them in more detail. This will clearly illuminate the problems and make clear why I do not advise such test construction to be lightly undertaken.

WILLINGNESS TO PLAY PRACTICAL JOKES

This is an objective test of the questionnaire variety. The subject expresses his willingness to play practical jokes. The rationale of the test is that timid subjects should welcome formal opportunities to get their own back and thus enjoy such jokes. Factorial studies show that this assumption was supported, and that, in addition, stable subjects enjoy these activities, an unexpected finding.

This test illustrates the problems of designing objective tests, because we would have expected this test to load on the exvia factor, since extraverts like such jokes and introverts dislike them.

WILLINGNESS TO MAKE AN EARLY DECISION WHILE DARK ADAPTATION IS PROCEEDING

In this test the subject sits in a dark room. A bright light is then turned on, and the subject is told to stare at a white screen. He is further told that when the light is switched off, he will see a letter. As soon as he does so, he is to call out its name. Three letters are used. The variable is the time taken before calling out the letter. It is argued as the rationale for the test that subjects of good inhibitory capacity should show faster dark adaptation.

This test needs few facilities but is obviously suitable only for individual use, although a group form might be possible utilizing the equipment of a language laboratory. Kline and Gale (1969) showed that such methods allowed a projective test, the Blacky Pictures (Blum, 1949), to be used successfully in a group administration without losing the element of privacy associated with individual testing, and essential in this objective test.

BASAL METABOLIC RATE

In this test the subject's smallest oxygen consumption for six minutes is converted to calories per hour per square metre of body area. It was originally thought that this test would be related to exuberance, responsiveness and to powers of good mobilization, and to extraversion. In fact, it does load on the first three factors but also on timidity and impracticalness. As Cattell and Warburton (1967) wryly argue, it is clearly not easy to theorize with any precision about the psychological aspects of physiological functions.

FIDGETING AS MEASURED BY THE FIDEGETOMETER
The fidgetometer is a swivel chair with electrical contacts at various points which are closed by movements. The score is the amount of movement recorded over a fixed period of time. The design of this chair is such that subjects notice nothing unusual about it. The rationale of this test is that anxious people should fidget more, as should those high on the factor of cortical alertness. In fact, research has never demonstrated a relationship between scores on this test and the anxiety factor, although cortical alertness is involved.

The fidgetometer is a good example of an objective test in that it is hard to fake and easy and accurate to score. It also illustrates clearly the problems with objective tests since it is suitable only for individual use and despite its ingenuity (although it really is an electrical version of a device invented by Galton), it loads only low on one factor. Such a test should be better!

These examples are sufficient to indicate the hazards and difficulties of objective testing. Enough has been said to enable the test constructor to go ahead but I must again repeat my warning: this is not a way for the faint-hearted. Certainly, the finest personality tests – culture-fair, objective, hard to distort – will turn out to be objective. However, a massive research effort is necessary to achieve this end.

Projective tests

As I have previously argued, projective tests are really within the category of objective tests as they have been defined here. However, since some of the most famous (or perhaps notorious) psychological tests are projective tests – for example the Rorschach and the Thematic Apperception Test (TAT) – and since the term projective tests is still meaningfully used in psychology, I have considered it appropriate to deal with the construction of projective tests separately.

In chapter 2 I fully discussed the nature of projective tests and the objections which have been raised against them by academic psychologists on the grounds of their weak reliability and validity. I do not intend to repeat those points here. Suffice it to say that essentially, as Semeonoff (1977) argues, a projective test is a stimulus, usually somewhat ambiguous, designed to elicit the inner needs, tensions, anxieties and conflicts of subjects – their 'idiodynamics', to use the phrase of Rosenzweig (1951). The rationale of the projective test is that when subjects are asked to describe an ambiguous stimulus, their description cannot reflect the stimulus (it is too vague), it therefore must reflect something within themselves. This same argument applies to all forms of projective testing, such as drawings, sentence completion or doll play. The art, therefore, of projective testing traditionally has two aspects: (a) designing stimulus material so that it will in fact elicit interesting and personal responses, and (b) interpreting the responses.

It will be immediately noticed that the objections to projective testing as succinctly put by Eysenck (1959) are mainly aimed at the second aspect, the interpretation, and that this is where the objective-test concept of Cattell scores heavily because Cattell and colleagues use the Rorschach, but objectively scored. Thus the objection does not concern the stimulus material itself, although it must be questionable if one set of Rorschach ink blots or TAT pictures were capable of comprehending the whole personality sphere. After all, if we recollect our psychometric model of test variance in chapter 1, it must be that there is some specific variance in these tests, and this alone would distort the results. Nevertheless, there is nothing *per se* in the objections raised by Eysenck to suggest that projective testing is useless if it could be objectively scored and if the wild interpretations, favoured by many projective testers, were abandoned.

Justification for the construction of new projective tests

Several thousands of studies have been carried out with the Rorschach test alone. The TAT had more than 2000 researches up to 1978 (see Buros, 1978) and much sophisticated clinical research has been carried out with these tests as with a number of other projective tests. With so much research and relatively meagre positive findings, surely projective testing is best abandoned. Furthermore, even if it is not abandoned, surely there can be little call to construct yet more projective tests. How could, the argument runs, a single investigator or even a small team hope to discover anything useful by inventing new projective tests when fifty years of Rorschach testing has proved negative?

These objections to projective testing as it is traditionally carried out seem well made. Nevertheless, there are a number of arguments that support the development of new projective tests, and these are set out below.

ARGUMENT 1

First, Holley, in a series of studies of the Rorschach test and other projective devices, has shown (e.g. 1973) that the Rorschach, when subjected to objective scoring and a powerful multivariate statistical analysis, is an impressive instrument discriminating clearly between various psychiatric groups. From this he argues that perhaps the Rorschach is indeed as useful a test as its clinical adherents would have us believe, and that the failure of many academic researches to support its validity was due not so much to the weakness of the test itself but to the poverty of their generally univariate methods. If this argument is sound, of course, it may well be equally applicable to studies of other projective tests.

It should be pointed out that Holley's findings have been replicated by many of his students, notably Vegelius (1976), who has greatly developed his statistical approach. Hampson and Kline (1977) also used his methods in a study of criminal personality using various projective tests such as the House Tree Person Test (Buck, 1948) and the TAT, and again these methods were found most promising.

The basic approach to scoring in Holley's method is simple in the extreme. The protocols of the projective tests are subjected to a minute content analysis and scored for the presence or absence of features, 1 or 0. Thus if subject A has described ink-blot 5 as a skull, he receives a score of 1 for skull. All other subjects are scored on this variable – 1 if they have mentioned skull, 0 if not. In this way it is possible to score objectively almost any objective-test response. Interview data are equally amenable to this method. Studies of the reliability of scoring between markers indicate a very high degree of reliability. Well above 90 per cent agreement was found on almost all variables by Hampson and Kline (1977).

One point about this scoring system deserves note (other than its extreme tedium!). When completed there are invariably a large number of variables which have been scored 1 by only one person. These distort any subsequent correlations because all the 0's make subjects appear more similar than they actually are in terms of their responses. It is therefore convenient to abandon any variable which has been scored by less than around five or six subjects.

The statistical analysis used by Holley is Q factor analysis, that is correlations between subjects, not variables, are computed and subjected to rotated factor analysis. The resulting factors therefore identify groups of subjects. This method is highly suited to the study of special groups, such as is demanded by the study of psychiatric categories or criminals.

The special feature of this analysis is the use of the G index of correlation (Holley and Guilford, 1964) for correlating the subjects. This coefficient has the advantage compared with ϕ and the tetrachoric correlation coefficient that its size is not affected by the size of the item split, that its standard error is not unduly large and, perhaps most important of all, it does not vary according to the polarity of the item, an essential feature if the correlation matrix is to be further subjected to statistical analysis. Finally, as Vegelius (1976) has shown, like ø but unlike the tetrachoric correlation (Nunnally, 1978), the G index is mathematically suitable for factor analysis.

Once the Q factors (subjects) have been isolated, a simple coefficient, D, is used to see which variables best distinguish the groups, a useful aid in identifying the factors and in determining the best variables to extract from the projective tests.

There are a few points worthy of mention concerning this analysis. First, as it stands, it is clearly suited to the study of groups – either when we wish to discriminate among groups previously categorized or when we are seeking to discover whether any meaningful classifications can be made. In the first instance, for example, G analysis might be useful in cross-cultural studies or the study of successful and failing subjects in a training course. In the second case, G analysis is valuable if sub-groups are expected: a study of dyslexics or depressives would be clear examples. Clearly, however, it is only in classificatory studies that G analysis can be employed. It is not a panacea for the analysis of projective tests.

That being said, it is arguable that discriminant function analysis would provide as good a solution, although the use of 1's and 0's might provide difficulties. A comparison of the two methods in a number of studies would be valuable. From this it is clear that the most generally useful feature of Holley's studies is the objective scoring system, although if we are interested in group differences, G analysis is undoubtedly a neat and simple procedure.

Thus I would argue that the approach to the Rorschach adopted by Holley is a strong argument for not abandoning the projective test as a useful psychological test. Hence its support for the value of developing some new varieties. Indeed, we can go further. It would appear useful to attempt to develop projective tests having the objective scoring system in mind, that is ones likely to produce responses amenable to such scoring. In the study by Hampson and Kline (1977) it was found that some tests, notably the HTP (House Tree Person Test), were easier to score in this way than others. The TAT was scorable objectively, but it was felt that some of the richness of the protocols was lost in the process.

In conclusion, therefore, the work of Holley supports the value of designing new projective tests that are likely to be easy to score by this objective method.

ARGUMENT 2

A second, more general argument for the retention of projective tests and the development of new varieties lies in the nature of projective-test data. The responses to projective tests are unlike a subject's responses in any other situation in which the tester can see the subject. If the test is stimulating, we see aspects of the subjects we should otherwise know nothing about. Thus to waste such data must be a poor strategy. This leads us to our third point.

ARGUMENT 3

New projective tests should be specific rather than general. One of the objections to the Rorschach raised by Eysenck (1959) is the inherent unlikelihood of one test being able to measure the whole personality. In physics, for example, a thermometer measures heat, a voltameter, electrical charge. More formally, as we have seen, it would involve the Rorschach's loading on a wide variety of common factors and having little specific variance. This same argument applies to many other projective tests. For example, the TAT is now used to assess a large variety of variables (as a glance through Semeonoff, 1976, demonstrates), even if originally it was designed to measure the needs and presses (and there are many of these) of Murray's (1938) Personology.

More recent projective tests, however, have been aimed at narrower, more specific targets. Thus Blum's (1949) Blacky Pictures test seeks to measure Freudian psychosexual variables, and each card has a specific purpose, for example one card for the castration complex. Corman's (1969) PN test has a similar definite target for each card. Neither of these tests, however, has convincing evidence for their validity. Thus I would argue that since projective-test data is irreplaceable, it is worth developing new projective tests but ones deliberately aimed at specific aspects of personality. Since few projective tests have been shown to be valid, this leaves open a huge field.

ARGUMENT 4

The fourth argument for the development of new projective tests relates to percept-genetic methods (Kragh and Smith, 1970), developed in the Universities of Lund and Oslo, which suggest that new projective tests could prove valuable. Percept-genetics is the study of the development of percepts, hence the name. One experimental method used by Smith and Kragh in their studies over the years involves the tachistoscopic projection of a stimulus at gradually decreasing speed until the subject can give a veridical description. Kragh (1955) has argued that the development of the percept of this stimulus (for at the beginning of the sequence nothing is reported) reflects the basic development of the personality of the individual, even allowing glimpses of actual life-events, and thus the technique is held to allow important insights into subjects' habitual defensive processes. It should be pointed out that part of percept-genetic theory states that normal everyday perception involves just the same percept development which takes place instantaneously. The tachistoscopic presentation enables the experimenter to observe this normally instantaneous process.

Although the ramifications of percept-genetic theory are irrelevant to the subject of our book, sufficient clinical evidence has been collected by Kragh and Smith (1970) and by later workers at Lund (e.g. Westerlund, 1976) to suggest that powerful tests could be constructed using these percept-genetic methods. Indeed, the Defence Mechanism Test has been developed in just this way by Kragh (1969), and it has been found useful in a variety of applied settings. I have experimented with these methods, and in one study with special stimuli (Kline and Cooper, 1977) defence mechanisms were seen. However, a further investigation with different (and hypothesized to be better) stimuli was not successful (Kline, 1980). Nevertheless, the percept-genetic technique of presenting stimuli does seem likely to be a useful way of presenting projective tests.

CONCLUSIONS

I would therefore conclude this section on the justification for producing new projective tests with the following summary of our argument.

It is worthwhile producing new projective tests provided that they are (a) objectively scorable and (b) aimed at specific psychological targets. Tachistoscopic presentation of the stimuli may well prove valuable, and at the present time it is unwise to abandon data that are not obtainable by other means.

Constructing a projective test: the Vampire Test (measure of orality)

As I hope must now be clear, the art of constructing projective tests lies in the selection of the stimuli. The task is simple: find stimuli that will be relevant to the aspect of personality that we wish to test. As with objective tests, the guide for stimuli must be psychological theory, research findings and clinical intuition. These are only guides, and all ultimately must depend on the validation studies of the results.

The best way to explicate the construction of projective tests is to give an illustrative example. Over the past two years the present author has been attempting to develop a projective test of orality, the Vampire Test, and a brief description of the rationale for the test materials will now be given. It must be pointed out, however, that as yet this test is incomplete, and the evidence for its validity is so far negative. However, this should not reduce its utility as an example of projective-test construction.

PURPOSE

Previously we had developed two questionnaire measures of oral personality traits, OPQ and OOQ (Kline and Storey, 1978). The purpose of the projective test was to investigate whether such traits were in any way related to orality (mouth activities, feeding, sucking, biting, weaning) as postulated in psychoanalytic theory (Freud, 1905).

RELEVANT THEORY AND RATIONALE

As indicated, the psychoanalytic theory of oral character traits claims that they are defences against oral eroticism – the infantile pleasure in biting and sucking. It was decided, therefore, that stimuli would be selected such as were likely to elicit such defensive processes, on the rationale that responses to them would differ between subjects fixated at the oral level (i.e. with many such defences) and those not fixated.

CHOICE OF STIMULI

Two projective tests with similar aims and rationale but without much evidence of validity already exist: the Blacky Pictures (Blum, 1949) and a French version with certain adaptations, the PN test (Corman, 1966). The Blacky Pictures test has two oral cards: one shows Blacky, a dog, being suckled, the other shows Blacky tearing his mother's collar. This test, which has been extensively reviewed by Kline (1973a), suffers from the defect that its crude cartoon drawings impinge too much on subjects' conscious experience, thus detracting from any psychological impact that the drawings might contain. This was certainly the case when the present writer used this test (Kline, 1968; Kline and Gale, 1969).

The PN test is better drawn, and the main character is not a dog but a pig. Nevertheless, both tests, for adults, are unsatisfactory because it is expected that subjects will identify with these animals and give less-defensive responses than they would with human characters. In fact, the childlike nature of the stimuli for British adults seems to constitute a barrier.

For these reasons it was decided that stimuli not requiring identification would be used. Three stimuli were chosen which, it was hoped, would touch on the essence of orality as it is described in the psychoanalytic literature (see Fenichel, 1945, for a summary). Ambiguous stimuli were not used since definite hypotheses concerning stimuli could be made. Ambiguity can be helpful, since if a stimulus is too well defined, it literally leaves nothing to the imagination. Where a more general stimulus is appropriate, a degree of ambiguity is useful.

(1) *A woman suckling her baby.* Here was portrayed the basic oral situation. A young woman gives suck to her baby. Her full breasts can be clearly seen. Her head is bent slightly to suggest tenderness. See figure 4.1.

(2) *A wolf like creature buries its fangs in its victim's neck.* This was intended to portray the savagery of oral sadism: biting to kill, as it is supposed to be in the unconscious. A wolf was selected because this portrays the basic oral ferocity. See figure 4.2.

(3) *A vampire-like creature sweeps down.* This vampire motif was chosen because it was hypothesized that the attraction of the vampire stories and legends which on a literary level seem banal and tedious lies in their vicarious expression of oral sadism. See figure 4.3.

PRESENTATION

These stimuli were presented tachistoscopically according to the percept-genetic methods, which we have previously described. These methods were chosen because defences were claimed to be tapped by them, making them ideal for our purposes.

RESULTS

So far the results with these tests have been disappointing. Although some defensive responses were elicited, there was no evidence that subjects thus responding were different from other subjects on other measures of orality. This does not, of course, mean that the Vampire Test is useless. The other tests may be inadequate, or the link between oral traits and orality may be non-existent (see Kline and Storey, 1980, for a full discussion of these findings). It must be pointed out that some problems were found with the experimental method of presenting these stimuli, which might account for the failure of the test. All scoring was objective, as described above.

FUTURE WORK

It is intended to use these stimuli as an ordinary projective test and obtain descriptions of them. Further percept-genetic research will also be conducted.

CONCLUSIONS

Our description of the development of the Vampire Test was chosen, obviously, not because the test was successful but because it illustrates how the selection of stimuli takes place. If further studies indicate the test is not successful, other stimuli will be developed in case (in terms of the factorial model) the results are being distorted by specific variance. Possible other stimuli might be, for example, plates of delicious food, a

Figure 4.1

Figure 4.2

Figure 4.3

starving man, portrayal of famine, a close-up of dental treatment, a man luxuriously swallowing beer or champagne

Thus it should be clear that the same technique of stimulus selection can be applied to any variable which has been fully described in either the clinical or research literature. However, as our example demonstrates, it is not necessarily a simple matter to hit upon adequate stimuli.

The construction of other motivational tests

The main motivational tests, tests of dynamics, are of the objective or projective variety. Other kinds of motivational tests do exist, but I shall devote little time to these since in principle their construction entails nothing different from what has been previously discussed.

Questionnaires relevant to dynamics

Some dynamic questionnaires have been constructed measuring not temperamental traits, as do most personality questionnaires, but motivational goals, Edwards' Personal Preference Schedule (EPPS) (Edwards, 1959) is an example of this. Other than trying to write items relevant to drives rather than traits, methods of test construction for such questionnaires are identical to those for constructing tests of temperament. Indeed, it will be remembered that in our discussion of item types for personality questionnaires, we used the EPPS as an example. Thus nothing further needs to be said about the construction of this type of test.

Interest inventories

Some interest tests have been constructed which list interests and have subjects rank or rate them; scores on various interests are then computed. The Rothwell–Miller test exemplifies this approach to the measurement of interest (Miller, 1968). As with the previous category, these tests are constructed in the same way as personality questionnaires. Criterion-keying is often employed, although factor-analytic methods can be used provided that the test scores are independent of each other.

The Brook-Reaction Test

A test of interest that has been developed in Great Britain is the Brook-Reaction Test (Heim *et al.*, 1969) which entails subjects free-associating to ambiguous words delivered orally, one per twelve seconds. Responses are classified in terms of interests and omissions, and bizarre associations are noted. This description should enable readers to see that the Brook-Reaction Test is, in fact, by our definition an objective test. It makes use of certain of the principles set out in table 4.1, such as free association and fantasy interest.

Mood and state scales

Mood and state measures are tests of transient states such as anger or grief rather than the more enduring, relatively stable traits of temperament. I shall now examine the constructional methods suited to them. However, treatment will be brief because those methods that we advocated for the construction of personality questionnaires as tests of temperament are all useful. Thus the steps can be set out as follows below. Our example, for ease of exposition, will be the mood *fatigue*.

Item writing

CONTENT
List all behaviours and feelings that seem relevant to the state of fatigue.

FORM
Convert these into items, as described in our section, on questionnaire items in chapter 3 (p.60). All our remarks concerning the advantages and disadvantages of different item types are relevant here, as is our whole discussion concerning hints on item writing and the avoidance of the major response-sets.

Indeed, in respect of writing items, the construction of mood scales and personality trait scales are not separable. In fact, the difference will be discernible in terms of content: the mood-scale items will clearly refer to transient and unstable feelings and behaviours. Mood and state scales can sometimes be most clearly distinguished from temperamental trait scales in terms of *instructions*.

INSTRUCTIONS
For mood and state scales it is essential that subjects understand that they complete each item according to their *present* feelings not their

usual feelings. To ensure this occurs, it is obviously helpful to write this into the items as well. For example:

STATE: I am really tired now
         My legs are aching with fatigue
         At the moment I can barely keep my eyes open
         Just now I keep dropping off to sleep

TRAIT: I am usually tired with no energy
         My legs are often aching with fatigue
         Very often I just can't keep my eyes open
         Very often I find myself just nodding off to sleep

Thus it is advisable to have instructions such as 'Answer these questions about moods and feelings', or 'Complete the statements about them, as you feel *now, at this moment,* even if this is not how you usually feel'.

Item analysis

Again, all the points made about item analysis of temperamental scales apply here. I shall not repeat them except to delineate the bare essentials.

ITEM TRIALS
Numbers should be sufficient to ensure reasonable freedom from statistical error.

FACTOR ANALYSIS OF ITEMS
If this method is used, the same difficulties as with temperamental tests have to be overcome.

BISERIAL CORRELATION OF ITEM AND TOTAL SCORE
This is clearly appropriate here and as one fitting the model of measurement error and being easy to use, it is highly useful.

CRITERION-KEYING
In the case of mood and state scales, this is also a viable method since it is possible to obtain experimentally defined criterion groups. If these are matched in other ways, or if they can be rationally assumed to be matched, the usual disadvantage of criterion-keyed test construction, that it does not ensure unidimensionality of the test variable, is no longer relevant. An example will clarify this point. We could fatigue our criterion group by giving them a battery of difficult tests and other tasks and perhaps having them complete a difficult assault course. Their final

task would be to complete our fatigue inventory. Items would be selected which discriminated this group from controls, or which discriminated the post-experiment scores from scores obtained from the same group either before or some time after the experiment when experimental fatigue had dissipated. It is to be noted that this latter method of constructing a criterion-keyed test by administering it to the same sample in two conditions is also a demonstration of the validity of the test since a valid test should be able to discriminate in this experimental design. This procedure demands, of course, replication on a further group.

VALIDATION OF THE TEST

If we were to construct our test of fatigue by the methods of biserial correlation and criterion-keying, then test validation requires that we demonstrate, other than by the face validity of the items and the fact that they measure a definite variable, that the mood or state of fatigue is measured. The best test of this would be the experimental design advocated for the selection of items in criterion-keying. Thus we would hypothesize increases in scores after the experimental procedures. Similarly, we could obtain the scores of individuals when we considered them fatigued after examinations or expeditions, and contrast them with the scores of non-fatigued controls and with their own scores taken at a later time.

Finally, we should note carefully the argument adduced by Cattell (1973) and Cattell and Kline (1977). There it was pointed out that even if a factor analysis of a mood test, however constructed, demonstrates that a factor runs through the test, this does not mean inevitably that it measures a mood or state. Such an R analysis can reveal traits as well as states. What is needed from the logical viewpoint is either a P analysis, where a factor within one person and fluctuating over time is revealed, or a dR analysis, where the changes in scores of individuals on retesting are factored. An argument against this view is that if a test shows itself valid in the experimental validation described in the discussion of criterion-keying, above, then to subject it to P or dR analysis is irrelevant. This is true; however, it does not dispose of the argument for P or dR analysis in the study of moods.

For many states (e.g. depression or anger), experimental manipulations are not as easy as is the case with fatigue, for practical and sometimes ethical reasons. Here the dR analysis of large samples, tested on two occasions without experimental manipulation, should allow test validity to be demonstrated.

Summary

State scales can be constructed exactly as temperament scales except that in item writing, and by careful test instructions, the emphasis of subjects' responses is on present feeling. Validation is best obtained by experimental arousal of the mood or state where possible, otherwise P or dR factor analysis is required. R analysis on its own without further evidence of validity is not sufficient.

Attitude measurement

There are three commonly used types of attitude scale: Thurstone scales, Guttman scales and Likert scales. However, I intend to discuss only the construction of Likert scales fully because there are severe problems with the other two methods which render their use dubious. These difficulties will now be briefly mentioned.

Thurstone Scales

The basic method in the construction of a Thurstone attitude scale involves three steps: (1) a large number of statements relevant to the attitude (newspapers are a useful source) is collected together; (2) these statements are rated by judges on an eleven-point scale, from 'strongly favourable' to 'strongly disfavourable'; (3) items are then selected where there is good agreement among judges. In addition, the items should cover the whole range of the eleven-point scale. A subject's score can be the mean rating of the items with which he agrees or the highest scale score of the items endorsed by him.

Since, as Edwards (1957) argues, around 100 judges are necessary if a reliable scaling is to be achieved, there are obvious difficulties of sampling. Again, if the judges do not accurately reflect the population which we are trying to measure, the whole procedure is thrown off course.

Nunnally (1978) has summarized a series of objections to Thurstone scales with great skill. He argues that the major difficulty with the model is that items so rarely fit it. The essence of the model is that each item should tend to receive the keyed response only at one zone of the attribute dimension. Thus if we have an item 'war is hateful', this should be endorsed only by those, say, at the middle point of the attitude to war scale. However, those who are highly anti-war would probably also endorse it. Thus the model does not properly fit the structure of attitudes. In other words, the item is monotonic, and this is essentially true of most attitudinal items. However, the scaling model is not monotonic. It assumes a continuous attribute and item curves of normal distribution. The practical problems associated with judges, together with the fact that the dimensions of the model cannot be met by items, strongly contraindicates the use of Thurstone scales in the measurement of attitude.

Guttman scales

I have previously mentioned Guttman scales when it was pointed out that the Rasch model (where the items were not distinct in difficulty) gave rise to a probablistic version of the Guttman scale. This, however, is an unusual view of Guttman scales which merits, here, a little more detailed description.

Guttman scales fall into the category of models known as deterministic models, where it is assumed that the item-characteristic curves are without error. In a Guttman scale, if the items are ordered in difficulty, say 1 to 20, if a subject endorses item 8, he is bound to endorse items 1 to 7. If he fails to endorse 9, he will also not endorse items 10 to 20.

In terms of item-curve characteristics, the model assumes that up to a point on the attribute, the probability of response alpha is 0 and beyond that point it is +1. This means that each item has a perfect biserial correlation with the total score and has perfect discrimination at some point on the attribute continuum.

In the construction of Guttman scales (computer programs are now available to handle the necessary massive sorting tasks), the basic aim is to produce items so chosen in order of difficulty that to endorse any item means that all items lower than it will be endorsed, and to fail any item means that all items higher than it will be failed. This is clearly easier in tasks where an order is relatively easily established, such as mathematics or musical theory, than in less-structured subjects.

There are many objections to Guttman scaling. The first and most important in our view is one stressed by Levy (1973), although not with reference to Guttman scales. Levy emphasized the importance of the basic model of a psychological test being appropriate for the object of measurement. Now, it seems to us unlikely that the item-characteristic curves of a Guttman scale fit any data in the real world of psychology. Items are unlikely to correlate perfectly with total scores on the attribute; thus a model which assumes such a correlation is unfitted for handling the data.

A further objection is that items can be selected to conform to the Guttman-scale pattern simply by choosing items widely spaced out in terms of difficulty or endorsement rate. However, the item-characteristic curves are not as they should be to suit the model. This wide dispersion of items in terms of difficulty means that scales are short and hence not highly discriminating.

A similar objection is raised by Nunnally (1978) who points out that the achievement of a Guttman scale in terms of item endorsements by no means guarantees unidimensionality. Thus an easy, a medium, a fairly difficult and a very severe item, each measuring different things, would be likely to form a Guttman scale. However, on what attribute or latent trait would the item-characteristic curves be set out?

A final objection cited by Nunnally (1978) is that at best the Guttman scale is only an ordinal scale.

These objections in our view cannot be refuted and there seems little value in attempting to construct such scales.

Likert scales

Likert scales consist essentially of statements, followed by five- or seven-point rating scales indicating the extent of subjects' agreement with them. Since this type of scaling assumes only that individual items are monotonically related to the attitude being measured, and that the sum of the item scores is linearly related to the attitude, it is clear that in Likert scaling there are no unwarrantable assumptions.

However, I do not intend to devote much space to the construction of Likert scales since this type of attitude scale is fundamentally no different from the standard personality questionnaire that is produced by the method of correlating each item with the total score. In other words, the model underlying Likert scales is the classical model of error variance, and these tests are best constructed by the item-analytic techniques previously described. Their distinctive nature springs from the items – statements relevant to attitudes – and the item form, the scale indicating extent of agreement.

CONSTRUCTIONAL STEPS

Here I shall discuss only those points where there are any substantial differences from the procedures previously set out.

Items. In attitude scaling it is essential to state explicitly the object of the attitudes. In our example we shall take Jews (the author hopes that his being Jewish will avoid any slurs of anti-Semitism: no anti-Semitism is intended). First collect together all statements that refer to Jews. Extreme statements, both positive and negative, should be avoided, since in a normal population many items will show little variance, and will in this instance be affected by social desirability. Similarly, neutral items will show little variance. Hence the aim is to find statements that are mildly positive or mildly negative. The test should contain, to make it seem more realistic and not too obvious in purpose, roughly half positive and half negative statements. This balance will be useful in combating acquiescence. A few example items will clarify this point:

(1) Jews have made a considerable contribution to modern science.
    (mildly positive)
(2) Without Jews modern science would be years behind.
    (positive, too extreme)
(3) Jews tend to keep together as a clan.
    (negative, mild)
(4) Jews have infiltrated into almost all important organizations.
    (negative, too extreme)
(5) Jews are in fact superior, the chosen race.
    (positive, too extreme)
(6) Jews are concerned mainly with money and materialism.
    (negative, too extreme)

Item form. As described, Likert scales demand five- or seven-point rating scales indicating extent of agreement with each item. Nunnally (1978) has a full discussion of the proper use of rating scales. In summary it can be shown that:

(a) Graphic scales are easier to complete and are less liable to error than numerical scales. A graphic scale is:

Completely *agree*	.	.	.	.	.	*Completely* *disagree*

| 1 | 2 | 3 | 4 | 5 | 6 | 7 |

   In the numerical case, descriptive words are set out beside the numbers.
(b) Reliability increases with the number of scale steps, and this increase decreases sharply at 7. Hence the advocacy of a seven-point scale.
(c) Odd numbers of steps give results little different from even numbers. However, the odd number allows a neutral response which in attitude scales (although it may encourage response sets) seems useful.

Thus with items based on statements about Jews and seven-point rating scales of agreement, we are now in a position to try out the items and subject them to item analysis.

Item analysis. A large and representative sample reflecting the population for whom the test is designed should be used for item analysis. Ten times as many subjects as items is the ideal, but two smaller samples (N's each greater than 100) could be used.

As with item analysis of personality inventories, each question has to be correlated with the total score. To do this, scoring has to be reversed for the negative statements. An example will clarify the point.

(1) Jews are clannish. (negative attitude)
(2) Jews are a highly cultured group in European society. (positive attitude)

To item 1, the score is 8 (scale steps +1) minus the actual scale number put by a subject; to item 2, the score is the actual scale number. Each subject's *total* score, reflecting his standing on the variable 'positive attitude to Jews', consists of the sum of scores obtained from the items. The steps are:

(1) Score each item taking into account reversal of negatives, as described for items 1 and 2, above.
(2) Total up each subject's scores based upon item scores.
(3) Calculate the alpha coefficient (see p.125)
(4) Correlate each item with the total score, using Pearson product-moment correlation.
(5) Select items passing the criterion correlation (in both samples, if two are used).
(6) Arrange for equal numbers, if possible, of negative and positive items.
(7) Compute the alpha coefficient of the new test of selected items.
(8) Twenty-item scales, as discussed in our chapter on item analysis with alpha coefficients of 0.60 or larger, are to be aimed at.
(9) If necessary, rewrite any items and subject to new item analyses.
(10) Try out and subject to item analysis the final selected scale.
(11) Items could be weighted according to their correlation with the total score. However, as Nunnally points out, the correlation of weighted and unweighted scales is so high that it does not appear worthwhile to go to the trouble of computing such weights.
(12) Validate the test variable by the appropriate experimental tests.

There seems little doubt that these procedures should produce a homogeneous and face-valid measure of attitude to Jews, which the procedures of step 12 should demonstrate to be valid or not.

One further point deserves note. When multi-point scales are used there is greater item variance than is the case with dichotomous items. Hence a factor analysis of Likert-scale items could lead to a clear factor structure, far more so than with personality inventories using dichotomous scores. Hence it might be viable to factor analyse the item correlations and select those loading on the factors. The procedures and rationale for the factor analysis of test items in test construction have been fully discussed, so that I shall do no more here than briefly indicate the necessary steps.

(1) As for item analysis.
(2) As for item analysis.
(3) As for item analysis.
(4) Compute correlation matrix for all items (Pearson product-moment).
(5) Subject correlation matrix to rotated factor analysis.
(6) Select items loading on general factor or other factors (see 'Notes', below).
(7) Administer selected items again and check results.
(8) Validate test as in step 12 of item analysis, above.

NOTES
For the factor analysis as large a sample as possible is desirable. If the sample is not three times larger than the number of items, replication is essential.

In attitude scales a general factor may be present – in our example, attitudes to Jews. However, it is arguable that this attitude is itself dependent on factors such as dogmatism (Rokeach, 1960), or authoritarian personality traits (Adorno *et al.*, 1950), or on personality factors such as Cattell's *L*, distrust. If this is the case, then the factor structure of the attitude scale would not be clear and any general factor might only appear at the second-order or even higher. For this reason, factor analysis as a method of test construction should only be used in cases where there are good *a priori* reasons to hypothesize a clear general factor or some other pattern.

Summary and conclusions

(1) Objective tests were defined and their advantages pointed out.
(2) A taxonomy of tests was suggested based upon two parameters: stimulus instructions and response scoring. This will enable a test constructor to construct every variety of item form.
(3) Objective tests of ability, temperament and dynamics were distinguished.
(4) Some practical hints on objective-test construction were set out, with reference to personality and motivation.

(5) Methods to overcome problems in test construction were discussed.

(6) Specific problems of objective tests of dynamics were discussed.

(7) A list of basic principles based on the psychological literature for testing motivation was set out.

(8) Differences between testing for motivational strength and goals were discussed.

(9) The construction of projective tests was described, after the value of constructing such tests was demonstrated.

(10) The construction of other tests of motivation was briefly discussed.

(11) The construction of mood scales was described.

(12) The construction of Likert tests was discussed.

5
Computing test-reliability

In the first chapter I briefly discussed the two concepts of reliability and validity, central to psychometric tests. In this chapter I shall set out the methods and procedures for establishing the reliability of a test. As was pointed out, reliability, in the practical sense, has two meanings, one referring to internal consistency and one to the replicability of the scores. Each is important, although in practice the second is essential for good tests, while the first, referring to internal consistency, is the reliability accounted for by the classical model of test error.

However, from the viewpoint of the psychological test constructor, there are various practical issues which must be discussed – concerning the reliability of tests, the advantages and disadvantages of various ways of assessing reliability, the importance of internal-consistency reliability in practice as distinct from theory, together with sources of unreliability. It is with these that I shall open this chapter.

Importance of internal-consistency reliability in test construction

Internal-consistency reliability is central to the theory of measurement error – the higher the reliability, the smaller the error and the greater the relation of the test score to the true score (see chapter 1). From this the obvious inference is that high internal consistency should be a major aim of test constructors, and this is certainly the view of many psychometrists (e.g. Cronbach, 1970) or of the test reviews in the many editions of *Buros' Mental Measurement Yearbook*.

However, Cattell and his colleagues, who have produced some of the best-known tests in many fields of psychological measurement – for example, the Culture-Fair Intelligence Test (Cattell and Cattell, 1960), the 16 PF Personality Test (Cattell *et al.*, 1970) and the Motivation Analysis Test (Cattell *et al.*, 1970), have consistently argued that high internal consistency can be (and often is, in the complex fields of human temperament and dynamics) antithetical to high validity. Since validity is defined as the extent to which a test measures what it purports to measure, this must be the principal aim of test construction. Reliability is important only in as much as it is held to ensure high validity. How then can it be that Cattell should hold a view not only opposed to the majority in the field but one which seems to run against the statistical basis of test construction?

The meaning of true scores

In chapter 1 great care was taken to define the meaning of true scores – the scores on the infinite universe of items – for effectively this is the critical point at issue.

Since I shall argue here that the importance of internal-consistency reliability has been exaggerated in psychometry (i.e. I agree with Cattell), and that it *can* be antithetical to validity, it is essential to state that I fully accept the statistical arguments previously advanced. However, what is not brought out in the mathematical treatment (and this is why true scores are the critical issue) is the psychological significance of true scores as theoretically defined. Examples will best clarify the viewpoint.

Suppose that we are trying to measure a variable such as verbal ability. It is highly likely that the items which appear to tap verbal ability do in fact do so; for example, vocabulary, definitions, synonyms, antonyms, construction of artificial languages with grammars, précis, comprehension and summarization. This is to say that verbal ability is a relatively homogeneous set of skills clearly defined and bounded. It would be highly surprising if subjects good at précis were not good at comprehension and had poor vocabularies. This means that there is good psychological reason to expect that a proper sample of items would be internally consistent, homogeneous and reliable, and that any items that could not be thus defined were, in all probability, measuring a variable other than verbal ability. In this case, therefore, the fallible test would be expected to be highly reliable because the universe of true items was itself homogeneous. Indeed, most good tests of ability do have high alpha coefficients because in the sphere of abilities each factor is generally distinct and discreet. If a test is valid – that is if its items are from the universe of items which we intend – in the ability sphere high reliability is probably a *sine qua non*.

However, this example also gives a clue to the argument against too high reliability, that high reliability is antithetical to high validity. Les us suppose that our test of verbal ability consists of antonyms, synonyms, comprehension, vocabulary and précis questions. Such measures when well constructed have high reliabilities around 0.90. However, if in the quest for high reliability we were to use only one item type, say antonyms, this reliability could indubitably be raised. However, it is clear, hopefully, to most readers that this latter test is highly unlikely to be a more valid test of verbal ability.

In terms of the classical-error model, we can clearly see why this test of higher reliability is less valid. The high reliability of the antonyms test reflects the fact that our sample of test items (antonyms) closely correlates with the hypothetical universe of items, that is all possible antonyms. However, this true score reflects not verbal ability but ability at antonyms. Thus, by limiting our items and constructing the universe of items, reliable tests can be made but only at the expense of validity. Thus we can see from this example how to argue that high reliability is antithetical to validity is not contrary to the classical model of error measurement. As we argued, all depends on the psychological meaning of the true scores (verbal ability rather than ability at antonyms).

In our example from the sphere of ability, most test constructors would not make the mistake of producing a highly reliable test by restricting themselves to one type of item, because the concept of verbal ability is well understood and antonyms are not enough. However, in other areas of psychological measurement, especially those of personality and motivation, this is not so. Indeed, many workers, for example Cattell, Guilford and Eysenck, use factor-analytic tests to map out the field and define the concepts.

In this instance, therefore, where the variable cannot be defined *a priori*, there is a real danger of producing tests of such high reliability that essentially the universe of items is too limited to be of great psychological interest, or to put it more statistically, the true score would be specific and correlate with almost nothing else. This is particularly true where we are concerned with attempting to measure a variable, such as extraversion, which is a cluster or syndrome of characteristics. Typically extraversion (e.g. Eysenck and Eysenck, 1975) is held to embrace sociability, talkativeness, cheerfulness, confidence and interest in the outer rather than the inner world, *inter alia*. An extraversion scale which includes all these variables will be homogeneous because they do in fact cluster together. However, inevitably, it will be less homogeneous and therefore of lower reliability than a scale concentrating on the sociability component of the factor. However, the latter would indubitably be less valid as a test of extraversion.

From this discussion it must be clear that high internal-consistency reliability can be antithetical to high validity where the variable we are measuring is broad. This claim, as we have seen, in no way invalidates the statistical theory of error measurement which implies that high reliability is essential for error-free measurement. All turns on the meaning of true scores and the constitution of the universe of items. However, it does follow that a test should be made as internally consistent as possible, but not at the expense of limiting the item content. It is therefore essential in test construction to have a clear idea of the items we are going to put into the final test (as regards content) and not merely select from the item pool those items which yield the highest reliability. This leads to the creation of tests of bloated specifics (Cattell, 1973). Thus we can conclude that, as our model of test error suggests, reliability is highly important but not all-important.

Sources of unreliability

We must now turn to an important question which the theory of error measurement impinges upon but is not directed at – sources of unreliability. This is of great concern to the practice of test construction, perhaps even more than the theory, for if the sources are known, it may be possible at least in some instances to eliminate them by virtue of our test-construction procedures.

(1) *Subjective marking.* A common source of error is subjective marking. This allows for differences between markers and between the same marker on different occasions. Clearly, this would lower the inter-item correlations and hence coefficient alpha would drop. The obvious solution to this problem is to utilize only types of items which can be objectively scored. With such items only clerical error can contribute to unreliability. All useful item types for various tests have been discussed in chapters 2 to 4.

(2) *Guessing.* This has been discussed in chapter 2 (p. 55), on writing items for ability tests. Guessing does lower the reliability of tests. However, as was argued, it mainly affects true–false items, which are not advisable in any case. With a large number of items, guessing can be ignored.

(3) *Clear items.* As was pointed out in chapter 3, clear, unambiguous items improve the reliability of personality test items (p. 63).

(4) *Test length.* As was shown in chapter 1 (p. 13), the longer the test, the more reliable it is. Twenty items is usually sufficient for reliability.

(5) *Test instructions.* Instructions for tests should be unambiguous and clear. Ambiguous instructions induce unreliability. Instructions can easily change the difficulty level of items. For example, 'make this pattern with four blocks' is easier than 'make this pattern with the blocks' when subjects are presented with six blocks. If instructions

have to be changed, then statistics need to be reworked.

(6) *Test–retest unreliability.* Nunnally (1978) draws a distinction between errors that occur within a test and errors that occur between tests, these latter being test–retest unreliability. Clearly, important factors are changes in test conditions and changes in how people feel on test occasions. Subjective scoring can play a part as can real item differences if parallel forms of a test are used. Real changes in status on the tested variable are not to be confused with unreliability or measurement error.

(7) *Other sources of error.* Other sources of measurement error reside in the subjects rather than in the items. Little needs to be said about these other than to mention them. A subject may feel unwell as the test progresses so that his performance deteriorates, or *vice versa*. For some the room may be uncomfortably hot or cold. Subjects may mistake the format and thus continuously indicate wrong responses, or they may turn over two pages at once and thus miss a set of items. Fatigue and boredom can set in and influence the later items. Clearly, there is a large number of such possible causes of error.

Such, then, are the main sources of error in tests which all reduce reliability.

Sampling subjects in the study of reliability

All the inferences that can be made from test reliability about the relation of test scores to true scores assume, of course, that the correlations or variances in the equations are accurate. Whether this is true or not depends upon adequate sampling of subjects in our studies of reliability.

In sampling there are two variables that are of critical importance.

Size of sample

Since, as with any other statistic, the standard error of the correlation coefficient is related to the size of the sample from which it was derived, it is essential that large samples be used to minimize this kind of sampling error. The decision regarding the minimum size of the sample that will allow this source of error to be ignored is to some extent arbitrary. Guilford (1956) discussing this point in relation to factor analysis suggests a minimum of 200 subjects. Nunnally (1978), a little more rigorous, argues for 300. The present writer has looked at the standard errors of correlations with given *N*s, and it seems to me that with 200 subjects this source of error is negligible. Thus I recommend that reliability studies of tests should be carried out on samples of not less than 200, although larger samples are desirable. The K–R20 formula, which demands percentages of subjects putting the keyed response, requires large samples for accuracy, and 200 here is certainly the minimum desirable.

Constitution of sample

However, even more important than the size of the sample is its constitution. A large sample of the wrong kind can give us totally misleading reliabilities.

First, it is essential that the sample reflect the population for whom the test is designed. If we are constructing a test for use with high-level executives, the reliabilities must be obtained from such a specialized sample. If it is a test for the general population, then our sample must reflect the general population. Similarly, a test designed for psychiatric use must be shown to be reliable among psychiatric patients. It is no good showing that a test for abnormals is reliable among undergraduates, for example.

In a test designed to be used among a variety of groups it is often useful to show that it is reliable for each group separately. Here it could be argued that the sample sizes be allowed to fall below 200. For example, if a test showed consistent, high reliability on a sample of 100 students, 100 outpatients at a psychiatric hospital and 100 school teachers, then we could feel confident that it was adequately reliable in these groups. Notice that the one 300-subject sample would not be representative of any population.

From the viewpoint of testing reliability, the samples do not need to be selected with the same care as they must be for standardization (see chapter 8). Thus the general population sample need not exactly reflect the varied parameters of the population. However, it must not be all students or postmen or some particular group who, as it happens, can be tested.

The reason that the samples must reflect the population for whom the test is designed is that among special groups the inter-item correlations can change, as can the item variances. Thus if we consider again K–R20 (1.8) – the special case of the alpha coefficient for dichotomous items:

$$r_{kk} = \frac{k}{k-1}\left[1 - \frac{\Sigma PQ}{\sigma_y^2}\right] \tag{1.8}$$

we can see that as the variance (σ_y^2) changes, so will the reliability. Thus, if in the case of an ability test we give it to subjects for whom it is too easy or too hard, there will be little variance (the tests will be largely correct or incorrect respectively). Similarly dependent on the sample, P (correct response) and hence Q $(P-1)$ will vary. Thus, if we give a test designed to discriminate severity of symptomatology among neurotics to normals, P will be small, Q large and the variance small – as happens with the MMPI in normal samples.

Conclusions

It is therefore essential that test reliability be computed on relevant samples of adequate size.

Computing reliability

In this section I shall set out the steps necessary for computing the various coefficients of reliability which I have so far discussed.

Coefficient alpha

There can be no doubt that coefficient alpha is the most efficient measure of reliability in terms of the classical model of error measurement, and in ideal circumstances (given adequate time and facilities) it should always be calculated. The formula (1.7) was:

$$\frac{k}{k-1}\left[1 - \frac{\Sigma\sigma_i^2}{\sigma_y^2}\right] \tag{1.7}$$

where k is the number of items, σ_y^2 is the standard deviation of the test squared, and $\Sigma\sigma_i^2$ is the sum of the standard deviations squared of the items.

For dichotomous items *the K–R20 formula* can be used, where

$$r_{kk} = \frac{k}{k-1}\left[1 - \frac{\Sigma PQ}{\sigma_y^2}\right]$$

where $\Sigma PQ = \Sigma\sigma_i^2$ and P = proportion putting keyed response and Q = $1-P$.

COMPUTATIONAL PROCEDURES FOR KR 20 FOR TEST Y (COMPUTATION 5.1)

(1) Calculate the variance of the test scores. This gives us σ_y^2.
(2) Calculate the proportion of subjects putting the keyed response to

each item. This gives us *P* for each item.
(3) For each item subtract *P* from 1. This gives us *Q*.
(4) For each item multiply *P* and *Q*. This gives us *PQ*.
(5) Sum PQ for all items: ΣPQ.
(6) The K–R20 formula can then be simply applied, *k* being the number of items.

COMPUTATIONAL PROCEDURES FOR COEFFICIENT ALPHA
(COMPUTATION 5.2)

(1) Calculate the variance of the test scores. This gives us σ_y^2.
(2) Calculate the variance of each item.
(3) Sum the item variances. This gives us $\Sigma \sigma_i^2$.

The formula for the variance is:

$$\sigma^2 = \frac{\Sigma x^2}{N}$$

where x = the deviation of each score from the mean score.
   In practice it is easier to work directly from raw scores and the formula can be written

$$\Sigma X^2 - \frac{(\Sigma X)^2}{N}$$

where *X* is the raw score.
   A computer program for coefficient alpha may be found in the appendices.

Split-half reliability

Split-half reliability varies according to the particular split of items that we happen to use. Nunnally (1978) argues that it should be regarded as an estimate of coefficient alpha and that in the dichotomous case we should always therefore use K–R20. However, this misses one important point. The split-half reliability is far more simple and quicker to calculate than the K–R20. Furthermore, in this writer's experience of test construction the difference between K–R20 and the split-half reliability has been trivial, of no significance whatever for the practical test constructor. I advocate its use only when no computer programs are available for calculating the alpha coefficient and a quick estimate of test reliability is required in the course of test construction to ensure that all is going well. With the advent of cheap, efficient computing there is no real excuse to use split-half reliability other than for a quick estimate. For this reason I provide no computer program for it.

COMPUTATIONAL PROCEDURES FOR THE SPLIT-HALF RELIABILITY:
FIRST HALF VERSUS SECOND HALF (COMPUTATION 5.3)

(1) For each subject, compute his test score on the first half of the test: X.
(2) For each subject, compute his test score on the second half of the test: Y.
(3) Compute the correlation between X and Y.*
(4) Correct the resulting correlation, the reliability, for length using the Spearman–Brown Prophecy formula (1.6):

$$r_{kk} = \frac{2r_{xy}}{1+r_{xy}}$$

This gives us the split-half reliability (corrected for length) of the test.

COMPUTATIONAL PROCEDURES FOR THE SPLIT-HALF RELIABILITY:
ODD-EVEN RELIABILITY (COMPUTATION 5.4)

(1) For each subject, compute his test score on the even-numbered items of the test: X.
(2) For each subject, compute his test score on the odd-numbered items of the test: Y.
(3) Compute the correlation between X and Y.
(4) Correct the resulting correlation, the reliability, for length using the Spearman–Brown Prophecy formula (1.6):

$$r_{kk} = \frac{2r_{xy}}{1+r_{xy}}$$

This gives us the split-half reliability of the test (corrected for length).

Hoyt's analysis of variance method

Hoyt (1941) has utilized analysis of variance in his method of estimating reliability. As Guilford (1956) points out, Hoyt considers the responses to the items as a two-way factorial analysis of variance without replication. Algebraically, Guilford claims that it is identical to K–R20. Since this means that it is also identical to coefficient alpha (of which

*The formula for calculating a correlation between X and Y is:

$$r = \frac{N \Sigma XY - (\Sigma X)(\Sigma Y)}{\sqrt{N \Sigma X^2 - (\Sigma X)^2} \ \sqrt{N \Sigma Y^2 - (\Sigma Y)^2}}$$

where N = the number of subjects, X = scores on test 1, Y = scores on test 2.

K–R20 is a special case), Hoyt's analysis of variance method is worth consideration as an alternative to alpha when ease of computation is important.

THE HOYT FORMULA

$$r_{tt} = 1 - \frac{V_r}{V_e}$$

$$= \frac{V_e - V_r}{V_e}$$

where V_r is the variance of the remainder sum of squares and V_e is the variance for examinees.

FORMULAE FOR THE SUMS OF SQUARES
(1) $\Sigma\ d_e^2$ (sum of squares for examinees) =

$$\frac{\Sigma\ X_t^2}{n} - \frac{(\Sigma\ X_t)^2}{nN}$$

where X_t = the total score for each subject, n = the number of test items, N = the number of subjects.
(2) $\Sigma\ d_i^2$ (sum of squares for items) =

$$\frac{\Sigma\ R_i^2}{N} - \frac{(\Sigma\ X_t)^2}{nN}$$

where R_i = the number of correct responses for item i.
(3) $\Sigma\ X_t^2$ (total sum of squares) =

$$\frac{(\Sigma\ R_i)\ (\Sigma\ W_i)}{(\Sigma\ R_i)+(\Sigma\ W_i)}$$

where W_i = the number of wrong responses to item i.
(4) $\Sigma\ X_r^2$ (remainder sum of squares) = (3) − (1) − (2).

DEGREES OF FREEDOM
Examinees $N-1$, items $n-1$, remainder $Nn-N-n+1$
Variances = Sums of squares divided by degrees of freedom

COMPUTATIONAL PROCEDURES FOR HOYT FORMULAE
(COMPUTATION 5.5)
Variance for examinees:

(1) Square and add the score for each subject: $\Sigma\ X_t^2$.
(2) Divide this by the number of items:

$$\frac{\Sigma\ X_t^2}{n}$$

(3) Add the score for each subject and square the total:

$$(\Sigma\ X_t)^2$$

(4) Multiply the number of subjects and number of items and divide result into:

$$(\Sigma\ X_t)^2\ :\ \frac{(\Sigma\ X_t)^2}{nN}$$

(5) Subtract (4) from (2):

$$\frac{\Sigma\ X^2}{n}\ -\ \frac{(\Sigma\ X_t)^2}{nN}$$

(6) Divide (5) by $N-1$ (degrees of freedom for examinees), that is number of subjects minus 1. This gives us the variance for examinees: V_e

Variance for items:

(7) Compute the number of correct responses to each item, square it and add together: $\Sigma\ R_i^2$

(8) Divide this by number of subjects:

$$\frac{\Sigma\ R_i^2}{N}$$

(9) Subtract (4) above from this:

$$\frac{\Sigma\ R_i^2}{N}\ -\ \frac{(\Sigma\ X_t)^2}{nN}$$

(10) Divide (9) by $(n-1)$, that is the number of items minus one. This gives us the variance for items: V_i

Total sum of squares:

(11) Add the number of correct responses to each item: $(\Sigma\ R_i)$.
(12) Add the number of wrong responses to each item: $(\Sigma\ W_i)$.
       $W_i = N - R_i$
(13) Multiply (11) and (12).
(14) Add (11) and (12).
(15) Divide (13) by (14) = total sum of squares.

Sum of squares for the remainder:

(16) Take (5) plus (9) from (15).

Variance remainder:

(17) Divide (16) by $Nn - N - n + 1$ (degrees of freedom):

$$rtt = \frac{(6) - (17)}{(6)}$$

Test–retest reliability

As I have discussed, if we are to have confidence in a score, it must remain the same if we measure the variable on two occasions, assuming that there are no changes in the variable over time.

There are two methods of measuring the test–retest reliability. The first is to give alternative forms of the test on the two occasions. Here the problem is that it is exceedingly difficult to select two sets of items that are genuinely equivalent. Ideally, each item in one form would have an equivalent in the other form with identical item characteristics – that is the same proportion of the population should put the keyed response, the correlation with the total score should be the same and the item content similar. This is hard to achieve and the correlation between parallel forms given at the same time is rarely above 0.9 and is often much less, so that the use of the term parallel is dubious. Nevertheless, the more one knows what one is measuring, the easier it is to design parallel forms of a test.

The second approach is to give the same test on the two occasions. Nunnally (1978) argues that a defect of the method is that subjects remember their responses, and in the case of ability tests this can considerably affect their second attempt at the test. However, if the time gap is large, this effect is trivial, and if a year is left between testing, it can be ignored. Nunnally also argues that the test–retest correlation on a single form does not fit the classical model of measurement error, because even if there was zero correlation between items, test–retest reliability could be high. This is of course true, but it does not mean that the test–retest reliability is not worth computing. On the contrary, it answers a different question. Coefficient alpha and its like assess the consistency of a test. Test–retest reliability is concerned with a different feature: reliability over time. This is equally, indeed in some ways more, important. A wonderfully coherent but inexplicably fluctuating measure would not be useful. In our view it is essential for any test that the test–retest reliability be high. If it is not, it cannot be valid.

COMPUTATIONAL PROCEDURES FOR TEST–RETEST RELIABILITY
(COMPUTATION 5.6)
Parallel forms of the test, A and B:

(1) Compute the correlation between scores on A and scores on B, the tests having been taken on separate occasions.

Test–retest:

(2) Compute the correlation between the scores on occasion A and scores on occasion B. There should be a time gap of at least six months to avoid a spuriously high result.

The factorial approach to reliability

The classical model of measurement error assumes, as we saw in the first chapter, that the reliability of a test is the ratio of true variance to actual obtained variance, and that test variance consists of true variance plus error variance. The factor-analytic approach to reliability assumes this model but, as Guilford (1956) indicates, breaks down the true-score variance.

FACTOR-ANALYTIC MODEL OF TRUE-SCORE VARIANCE

True-score variance consists of common-factor variance plus specific-factor variance. For example, the true-score variance of a group verbal intelligence test might consist of g_f, g_c and V (three common factors) plus a factor specific to this particular set of items. This means that the total variance of a test equals common-factor variances plus specific-factor variance plus error variance. Following Guilford (1956) this can be written:

$$\sigma^2 t = \sigma^2 a + \sigma^2 b + \ldots \sigma^2 n + \sigma^2 s + \sigma^2 e$$

where $\sigma^2 t$ = test variance, $\sigma^2 a$ to $\sigma^2 n$ are common-factor variances, $\sigma^2 s$ is specific variance and $\sigma^2 e$ is error variance. It is possible to divide this equation through by $\sigma^2 t$. Thus we get:

$$\frac{\sigma^2 t}{\sigma^2 t} = \frac{\sigma^2 a}{\sigma^2 t} + \frac{\sigma^2 b}{\sigma^2 t} + \ldots \frac{\sigma^2 n}{\sigma^2 t} + \frac{\sigma^2 s}{\sigma^2 t} + \frac{\sigma^2 e}{\sigma^2 t} = 1.00$$

This can be rewritten:

$$1 = a^2 x + b^2 x + \ldots n^2 x + s^2 x + e^2 x$$

where $a^2 x$ = the proportion of test variance contributed to total by factor a, and so on. Thus the reliability of a test $rtt = 1 - e^2 n = a^2 x + b^2 x + \ldots n^2 x + \sigma^2 x$ Thus, if we factor analyse a test and square and sum its factor loadings, we obtain the reliability, since the factor loadings represent the correlation of the test with a common or specific factor. From this it is clear that the factorial approach to understanding test variance is simply an extension of the classical model of error measurement, and that it follows from it that reliability (of the internal-consistency kind) can be estimated from the communality of the test, although strictly speaking the communality is defined as common-factor variance and should not include the specific-factor variance as does the reliability.

COMPUTING RELIABILITY THROUGH FACTOR ANALYSIS
(COMPUTATION 5.7)

(1) Factor-analyse the test with as wide a variety of tests as possible.
(2) Square and add the factor loadings of the test.

This method of establishing reliability is highly dependent on the other variables with which the test is factored. Thus, if we had a mathematics ability test and factored it together with personality and motivation variables, there would be almost no factors on which the test could load. An estimate of its reliability based upon this sample of variables would be inadequate. On the other hand, if the test were factored together with two or three tests of all the main ability factors so that each test had a chance to load on its appropriate factors, then this method would be likely to be reasonably accurate. Clearly, it is more suited to assessing the reliability of a factored test, which should load up on one or two common factors only and a specific, than it is to criterion-keyed tests, which may measure a variety of factors some of which might not be included in the factor battery.

Conclusions

The conclusions from this discussion and guide to computing reliability coefficients are clear-cut and can well stand as a summary of this chapter on reliability.

(1) All reliability studies must be carried out on large (200 or more) and representative samples.
(2) Internal-consistency reliability should be established, although for reasons which I have fully discussed, this need not be as high as is often indicated in some textbooks.
(3) Obviously, there is no one figure for reliability. All results should indicate the sample, size and type and the method used.
(4) The alpha coefficient or its simplified form, the KR 20, should be computed where this is possible.
(5) The split-half reliability should be regarded only as a quick guide to the true reliability.
(6) Factored reliability estimates should be used only with factored tests and where a wide variety of other variables has been sampled.

(7) Where tests are speeded and in tests which have been found difficult for subjects, the internal-consistency coefficients can be spuriously inflated.

(8) Parallel-form reliability (where such forms exist) should be quoted.

(9) Test–retest reliability should be computed. The time gap should not be less than six months.

(10) Reliability is important, but it must be remembered that reliability *per se* is not valuable. Its value is that usually it is necessary for validity. A test, however, can be almost perfectly reliable and almost totally invalid.

6
Item trials

In this chapter I shall describe the procedures used to select items for tests, having regard to the aim of reliable, valid and discriminating tests. Our studies of items so far in this book have concerned the art of psychometrics, the writing of good items. In this chapter our concern is the science.

The aim of item analysis is to select items that form a homogeneous, discriminating scale. The most commonly used method is to correlate each item with the total score and to calculate the proportion of the complete sample who put the keyed response. By selecting items with high correlations with the total score which furthermore have endorsement rates of between 80 per cent and 20 per cent, a homogeneous and discriminating test can be produced.

Having been written, test items must be tried out and subjected to item analysis. How this is done is set out below.

Problems with the item-analytic method

The first objection concerns circularity of the procedure. If all our items in the item pool were wide of the mark and did not measure what we hoped, they would be selecting items by the criterion of their correlation with the total score, which can never work. It is to be noted that the same argument applies to the factoring of the item pool. A general factor of poor items is still possible. This objection is sound and has to be refuted empirically. Having found by item analysis a set of homogeneous items, we must still present evidence concerning their validity. Thus to construct a homogeneous test is not sufficient, validity studies must be carried out. This objection, therefore, is easily met.

A second objection can be made to the fact that item analysis, although it ensures test homogeneity, does not ensure factoral purity. It is possible for a test, thus constructed, to load on a number of correlated factors. Thus, if in our ability test, for example, items measuring crystallized ability (g_c) and verbal ability were included in the same item pool, it is likely that item analysis would pick both kinds of item – for these factors are highly correlated. In this respect, therefore, item analysis is inferior to factor analysis as a method of test construction.

This latter objection can only be met by further study of the test. Factor analysis of the test with other factor-measures would show whether the test was unifactorial or not. If not, then a factor analysis of items is necessary (a technique described in chapter 9).

However, if item analysis can produce a test that is factorially impure, the obvious question arises: why use the method? Why not use factor analysis immediately? The answer to this is that, as is pointed out in chapter 9, there are severe technical problems when factoring items that have not been entirely overcome. Furthermore very large samples are required; Nunnally (1978) claims that ten times more subjects than items are necessary. This makes *initial* item factoring of dubious worth, especially since item-analytic and factor-analytic tests are highly correlated (Nunnally, 1978). Hence as a first step, item analysis is a highly valuable method of test construction.

Items

Construct about twice as many items as are needed for the final test. The length of the final test will depend upon its purpose and nature. An ability test for primary school children must not take more than around thirty minutes or else fatigue and boredom will affect the results. A personality test for adults should take no longer than this or subjects will fail to complete it. Ideally, tests should be as brief as possible, consonant with reliability and validity. This means there must be at least fifty items in the item pool (reliability). Items must sample the item universe (validity).

Similarly, in a test assessing neurotic or psychotic symptoms, the proportion putting the keyed responses will be markedly different among psychiatric and non-psychiatric groups.

Important sampling variables

To say that a sample must reflect the population says little unless the critical variables defining the population are stated. Clearly, the critical variables are different for different tests. Thus in tests of ability, age and, in the case of adults, educational level, are essential variables, since an ability test to assess a variable at all levels of ability would have to be exceedingly long. Nevertheless, for most tests, a few sampling variables are particularly important. These are set out below. When trying out items, sampling should take them into account.

Sex of subject

In constructing items for almost any type of test, it is necessary to note that there are likely to be differences in responses due to sex. A few examples will illustrate this point. In tests of ability it is generally the case that up to the age of 16 years, girls are superior in verbal and boys in numerical attainments. Items in these fields are likely to produce different item statistics. Many personality-test items are also likely to show sex differences; for example, those concerned with interest in clothes, interest in sport, interest in appearance, driving cars, drawing, horse-riding. Similarly, tests concerned with hobbies and interests will probably show similar trends. The point here is that it is reasonable to expect differences between males and females in response to such items. I am not claiming that such differences do in fact occur.

One solution to the problem is to sample males and females separately and then select items meeting the criterion of the item analysis in both groups. This is the solution that the present writer has adopted in his own tests, although there are some difficulties involved, partly theoretical in nature, which must be fully realized before adopting this procedure.

The first problem is that although items can almost always be written that pass the item-analytic criterion (item/total correlation > 0.2 and the proportion, P, putting the keyed response between the values 0.20 and 0.80) in both groups, even among the successful items these indices may not be identical. Particularly important here is the P coefficient, for if this is always greater among, say, the males than the females for a large number of the items, this could lead to a sex difference on the test. In practice, however, despite these variations the present writer, using this method, has always been able to find items successful in both groups and yielding tests with no significant sex difference in score.

The second problem is far more fundamental. If we select items that yield similar item-analytic indices among males and females, we *ipso facto* produce a test with no sex differences in scores. On the other hand, we could select items with indices such that females scored more highly on the test. However, what is the meaning of this identity or difference in scores? To put the problem differently, it is clear that means and variances on tests are a function of the particular set of items. Thus it is not meaningful to argue *from test scores* that girls are better than or worse than or the same as boys. This must be a function of the set of items.

In practice this means, in our view, that unless we have some powerful *a priori* reason for expecting a sex difference on a test, items should be selected which do not yield a sex difference. In the case of most personality and motivational variables this is the safest approach. It is to be noted that if there is a *real* difference in the variable between the sexes, no matter how many items are tried, this will appear in the item statistics. Thus, if repeatedly with every item, no matter how phrased or changed, we find a consistent trend, then it is best to use such items even though the test now gives us a sex difference.

We can either accept the difference as true, (i.e. is not just an artifact of the items), or we can provide norms for the scores (see chapter 8) which correct the imbalance. Which of these choices we make must depend on the variable being measured. In brief, then, items should be tried out separately for each sex, and those chosen should not behave differently in the groups. If they do, norms can be provided to right the balance, unless we want the sex difference to remain on theoretical grounds.

This procedure seems by far the most sensible in test construction, and it accepts the artifactual nature of any obtained distribution of scores. One other possibility, however, is to give the test to a sample of subjects (which, if properly chosen, will be half male) and simply pick out the best items. This assumes that there will be no sex differences affecting responses. This is reasonably efficient since, if half the sample perform differently, item statistics will be adversely affected, and hence items with sex differences will tend to be rejected. This is a quicker, less-elegant solution and one which denies the test constructor information on how sex differences affect item responses. Although it may yield good tests, this method is not recommended except where there is extreme pressure on time and resources.

In summary, then, separate item-analyses for the sexes are recommended. Unless there is a clear *a priori* hypothesis to the contrary, items should be selected with no sex difference. If sex differences emerge on the final test, the scores may be standardized later to eliminate this.

Age of subjects

This is a variable which to some extent has to be taken into account for all tests but is especially important with respect to tests of ability and aptitude. With tests of ability it is usual to construct tests for a relatively narrow age band, simply because if each age group is to have sufficient items for reliable discriminations to be made, the test would be exceedingly long.

When trying out items it is essential that the whole sample is similar to that for whom the test is intended. However, it is useful also to item-analyse the test separately for the different age groups within the sample. Thus items can be selected which are effective for all age levels within the sample, although obviously most suited to one particular age level. Here the aim is to obtain items with a difficulty level decreasing smoothly with age. In tests of ability this may be difficult, and it is often better to develop tests for specific year groups, for example separate maths tests for 13-year-olds, 14-year-olds and so on.

As regards personality and motivation tests, it is usual, as we shall see, to construct tests for adults (16 and over), adolescents (12 to 15) and for younger children down to the age of 8, although special versions for even younger groups can be developed.

Here obviously we try out the test items on a sample that matches the target population in age. However, it is useful to examine the item statistics in a sub-sample of the extremes of the age group for whom the test is intended. Thus an adult version should be item-analysed among the 16-year-olds to ensure that the items work with this group. Similarly, in the adolescent version it is important to see how the items work at the extremes (the areas where it is likely that the items will be inappropriate). For example, items about parties may be different for 15-year-olds who arrange their own and for the younger children who do not. With personality tests for the youngest groups of children it is advisable to item-analyse items separately by year groups, since lack of comprehension or insight can grossly affect items.

Other variables

Other variables such as *social class, cultural differences* and the related *educational level* can clearly affect responses to tests of ability. However, proper sampling techniques should randomize the effects of these such that items affected by them will simply not work efficiently and be rejected from any final test. Furthermore, if the test is aimed at the general population, this is right and proper. If the test is high level aimed at highly educated subjects, then our sample will be correspondingly high level. In general, no special attention needs to be paid to these variables given that our samples reflect the population for whom the test is intended.

Item analysis: two useful indices

We shall assume from this point on that our samples are adequate in constitution and sufficiently large. We now come to the actual item analysis. Since the aim is to produce a homogeneous discriminating test, it follows that there are two indices that are useful: (1) the proportion putting the keyed response and (2) the correlation of the item with the total score.

Correlations of items and the total score

There are several indices available for calculating the item-total correlation. These are listed below with comments on their use in item analysis.

(1) *Pearson product-moment correlation.* This is advised by Nunnally (1978) with multi-point items. However, with five-point scales (or below) the PM correlation is dubious.
(2) *Point-biserial correlation.* This is the correlation to use where dichotomous items are used. Other items can be reduced to right/wrong or keyed/not keyed response and this index can be used.
(3) *Phi coefficient.* This can be used if we dichotomize the total score into pass/fail, or above/below the mean. Strictly, it assumes that these are non-continuous categories.
(4) *Tetrachoric correlation.* This can be used as the phi coefficient. However, the assumption is made that the categories pass/fail or right/wrong are continuous. The problem with the tetrachoric correlation is that its standard error is large – twice that of the product-moment correlation. Both r_{tet} and ø, by dichotomizing the total, jettison a certain amount of data.

Anstey (1966) lists twenty-one further indices. However, many of these indices were developed to save time. They are ingenious short cuts which give efficient estimates of the correlation with the total score. However, with access to micro-computing now so easy, the need for these methods has gone. Instead, we can choose what are, for our needs as test constructors, the best methods.

THE CHOICE OF ITEM-ANALYTIC STATISTICS
To dichotomize the scores into high and low, as many of the item statistics require, is to lose much valuable information. There seems no advantage in this approach, and I do not intend to recommend its use. Now, with computers, it is not even time-saving.

Using a continuous criterion, the total score, what then is the best statistic? The best index is undoubtedly the point-biserial correlation, or r_{pbis}. Anstey in his comparison of the biserial and the point-biserial correlation makes two important distinctions between these indices. The biserial correlation assumes that the distribution of criterion scores is normal and that there is a quantitative distinction between the right and wrong answer. The point-biserial correlation makes no such assumption about distributions and assumes a quantitative distinction between right and wrong responses. Furthermore, the biserial correlation can, when the distribution is not normal, exceed 1; it also assumes linearity of regression between item and criterion.

If also we remember that, according to the classical model of error measurement, the item-total correlation is equal to the average correlation of an item with all other items, the r_{pbis} is exceedingly meaningful. In brief, this correlation gives us the best measure of the item-total correlation which is essential in constructing a homogeneous test.

THE DIFFICULTY OF UNCOMPLETED SCORES

A practical problem, especially in tests of ability where some subjects have run out of time, is that some items at the end are left uncompleted. This tends to inflate their correlation with the total test score. As can be seen from Anstey's indices, attempts have been made to take this into account in computing the correlation. However, as Anstey (1966) indicates, this is hardly worthwhile. In our view, it is best to administer items in such numbers that all can be completed. After all, if 10 per cent of the sample have not done an item, this is just 10 per cent lost information, and no statistical juggling can affect this. If this is impracticable, it is probably better to administer items randomized so that the numbers not completing any one item are negligible.

Proportions putting the keyed response

Little needs to be said about this statistic. The only difficulty is the one mentioned above – items that are unattempted. Generally, all that has to be done is to count the number of responses to each item.

The procedures of item analysis

I shall now set out the practical steps necessary for item analysis. The method I shall illustrate is the one recommended by Nunnally (1978) and used by the present writer in the construction of his own tests, i.e. the r_{pbis}. Before describing the computations and procedures, one small point remains to be noted. In the item-total correlation the contribution made by the item to that total is included – hence this is higher than its correlation with all other items. Where a large number of items is tried out (say around 100) the effect is negligible. However, Nunnally (1978) contains a correcting formula:

$$r_{it} \text{ (corrected)} = \frac{r_{it}\, \sigma_t - \sigma_i}{\sqrt{\sigma_i^2 + \sigma_t^2 - 2\sigma_i\, \sigma_t\, r_{it}}}$$

where r_{it} = correlation of item and total score, σ_i = standard deviation of item, σ_t = standard deviation of test. This should be applied if the items are much fewer than this.

I shall assume that the trial set of items has been given to a large sample of suitable subjects as discussed above and has been scored. I also assume that items are dichotomous. The formula for the r_{pbis} is:

$$\frac{M_H - M_L}{\sigma}\, \sqrt{Pq}$$

where M_H is the mean score of the high group on the item, M_L is the mean score of the low group on the item, σ is the standard deviation of the test, P is the proportion of persons putting the keyed response to the item and q is $1 - P$.

Computational steps in item analysis

(1) Compute the mean and standard deviation of the whole group on the test.
(2) For each item, compute the mean score on the test for subjects putting the keyed response to that item (M_H) and note the number of subjects doing this (N_H).
(3) For each item, divide M_H by N. This gives P.
(4) For each item, $1 - P = q$. This gives q.
(5) Given the total mean for each item, the M_L mean can be worked out:

$$(M_H \times N_H) + (M_L \times N_L) = M_T \times N_T.$$

This gives M_L.
(6) For each item, multiply Pq and take the square root.
(7) rpb for each item can now be worked:

$$\frac{M_H \text{ (from step 2)} - M_L \text{ (from step 4)} \times \sqrt{Pq} \text{ (from step 6)}}{\sigma \text{ (from step 1)}}$$

This item analysis now gives us for each item the proportion putting the keyed response (P step 3) and the r_{pbis} with the total.

This procedure is lengthy if we have a large sample and a good collection of items, so that in practice the test constructor may not actually carry this out. This is particularly true if the correcting factor for the correlation (due to the fact that each item contributes to the total score) is applied. Generally, most test constructors have access to computing facilities, in which case all this work can be done by the computer.

Computer calculation

If there is a computer available, the procedure will be as follows:

(1) For each subject, the score on each item (1 or 0) plus the total score is punched in.
(2) The program is required to print out correlations (corrected by the formula already noted) between items and the total score.
(3) The program is requested to print out the proportions putting the keyed response (1) to each item.
(4) NOTE The r_{pbis} is numerically equivalent to the Pearson Product-Moment correlation, hence the computer is asked to compute these.

Short-cut calculation without computer

If no item-analysis program is available, a short-cut hand method can be used which has sufficient accuracy for the practical selection of items, although it would be unwise to use the resulting correlation coefficients for further statistical analysis or to take them too literally. This method involves using the top and bottom 27 per cent of the distribution to estimate P and r_{pbis}. To do this item-analysis tables have been developed by various authors. We shall set out here the short-cut method with Fan's tables (Fan, 1952), which are easy to use and freely available in Great Britain.

ITEM ANALYSIS USING FAN'S TABLES

(1) Select the top 27 per cent on the test (H group) and the bottom 27 per cent (L group).
(2) For each item, work out the proportion putting the keyed response in the H group: P_H.
(3) Do the same for the L group: P_L.
(4) For each item, look up Fan's tables, which for every possible combination of P_H and P_L give the estimated P and r_{pbis} set in matrices, each row being a value of P_H and column being a value of P_L.

Obviously, if a computer is available, it is sensible to use it. Nevertheless, all test constructors are urged to analyse a test by hand at least once because actually seeing how items are scored in the various groups and constantly reshuffling the tests gives a great insight into what is happening to the test items – intuitions which cannot be obtained from computer print-outs.

Selection of items after item analysis

This method of item analysis has given us the two essential statistics required: the P, the proportion putting the keyed response and the r, the correlation of the item with the total score.

As was indicated, it is necessary to do separate item-analyses for the sexes, and in some cases we might want to use more than one sample to ensure item stability. Let us suppose we have conducted item analyses for all our samples. Table 6.1 shows a helpful way of setting out the results.

Table 6.1   Setting out the results

	N=200 M Item Analysis 1		N=200 F Item Analysis 2		N=200 M (Army) Item Analysis 3	
	P	r	P	r	P	r
Item 1: Do you enjoy talking?	0.41	0.52	0.73	0.35	0.40	0.47
Item 2: Do you sometimes feel jealous?	0.25	0.35	0.41	0.28	0.31	0.20
Item 3: Have you ever eaten so ↓ much you were sick?	0.95	0.06	0.90	0.12	0.92	0.03
Item N . . .						

Note: These are not items from a real test, and the item statistics are invented for illustration.

Criteria

In selecting the test items there are various points that have to be kept in mind, and in our final choice we have to achieve a balance between them. The importance of each of these criteria varies to some extent with the kind of test being constructed and its purpose.

The criteria are:

(1) Length. For reliability about twenty or thirty items are needed.

(2) Content. In most tests we want as wide a variety of items as possible. This is equally important, for example, in mathematics tests, where items tapping knowledge of all the curricular demands are necessary, as it is in personality tests, where as wide a range of relevant behaviours – the sociability, cheerfulness and talkativeness of extraversion, for example – should all be measured.

(3) Item-total correlations. This is *the* criterion. The higher the correlation, the better the item. Obviously, it is possible to accept items that are significantly correlated with the total score, but in a large sample this figure may be low. Ideally, all items should correlate beyond 0.2 with the total score.

(4) Difficulty level. This is also critically important. For most tests it is accepted that items with P values between 80 and 20 are satisfactory. Clearly, a good item in other respects with a P value of 0.19 would not be rejected. However, for certain ability tests we may want maximum discrimination at some level of the variable. For example, in secondary-school selection, tests in some areas were required with maximum discrimination at the 115–20 IQ level; in other places, where there were fewer secondary-school places, maximum discrimination was at the 125 IQ level. To achieve this, items of a different difficulty level were needed.

Selecting test items

The simplest procedure to select items for a test that will fit our measurement model (and with no specific difficulty level) is set out below:

(1) Pick out all items which on all item analyses meet the statistical criteria of r_{pbis} and P.

(2) Examine those items which fail one item-analysis, to see whether any particular characteristics of the sample could account for it. For example, among a sample of teachers, the present writer found that an item concerned with discipline had item statistics quite different from those in non-teacher samples. This discovery enabled the decision to be made to use this item. On the other hand, an item concerned with looking after children which showed a strong sex difference was rejected because it was felt that such a difference would always occur. If in comparing the items in the male and female samples we find a good set of items for males and a good set for females, with relatively little overlap, then this is a clear indication that separate tests with these sets

of items are desirable (although this is now probably illegal under the Sex Discrimination Act).

(3) Inspect the content of the items so far selected. Do they cover all the characteristics that we hoped to measure with the test? If not, inspect the unselected items to see whether there are any which measure these traits and which almost reach the statistical criteria. If there are a few, these can be put into the test. If there are not, two possibilities remain: (a) that these items do not constitute a homogeneous test together with the selected items, or (b) our item writing has failed. If we decide on (b), then items must be rewritten and tried out again (see p. 145).

(4) Count the number of items so far selected. If they are in the region of our target number (20–30) and cover the test content, compute K–R20 reliability. This should always be > 0.7, unless for some reason, as discussed in our selection on internal consistency, a lower homogeneity can be expected. If the reliability is satisfactory, then our first item trial can be terminated. A homogeneous, reliable, test, apparently relevant in content, has been constructed.

(5) If reliability is not high, items can be added, the next best in terms of our other criteria, and the K–R20 reliability can be recalculated each time until the additions cease to increase the reliability. This, however, does capitalize on chance. If these new items have poor correlations with the total score, they will not greatly increase the reliability, and consequently it will remain low. New items must be tried out (see p. 145).

(6) If our test trial has resulted in a test that is reliable and satisfactory as regards content, it is worth examining the distribution of scores. Usually a symmetrical distribution is required. In practice, since the highest correlations, using r_{pbis}, tend to be with items around the median difficulty level, a symmetrical distribution is almost inevitable. If it is markedly skewed, then we may need new items to correct this, or we can arrange for a different distribution in our standardization.

The variance should be examined. This should be as large as possible since this means the test is discriminating well. A test with little variance clearly needs new items. If large numbers of subjects are obtaining the maximum and minimum scores, new items at these difficulty levels may be required since clearly the test is not discriminating at these levels, and in larger samples of our population more such subjects would be expected.

(7) If the test seems satisfactory as regards its variance and discriminatory power, compute Ferguson's delta. If this is beyond 0.9, the test is certainly discriminating.

(8) If all is well, and a satisfactory set of items appears to have been constructed, cross-validate the item analysis on a new sample. If more than one or two items fail to reach the statistical criteria of r_{pbis} and P,

which are the only criteria of interest in the cross-validation, then these will have to be rewritten and tried out again. However, this is highly unlikely if good trial samples have been previously used. With the cross-validation sample, compare the male and female means; there should, of course, be no significant difference.

(9) This procedure is concerned only with item analysis. We have not dealt here with problems of multiple-choice distractors or guessing, which we discuss in our chapter on ability tests, or with the elimination of response sets dealt with in our chapter on personality tests.

The issue of reliability, raised under point 5, needs some elaboration. Some authors advocate a systematic approach to reliability, namely that the best items (by the criterion of item-total correlation) be added together until the reliability is as high as is desired, and at this point the test construction is complete. In our view this ignores other important aspects of the test (as discussed above) and places too much emphasis on internal consistency.

So far our description of item analysis and test construction has assumed that enough items have been found to construct a scale that is worthy of validity studies. However, at various points during the selection of items, it can become clear that items need rewriting.

Rewriting items

If certain aspects of the variable have no satisfactory items, if there are insufficient items to produce a reliable test or if on retrial some items fail, the items may have to be rewritten. In rewriting items the hindsight of knowing an item has failed together with the item statistics can be helpful in item rewriting. Some examples will clarify this point.

EXAMPLE 1
This is item 3 in table 6.1 showing how to set out the results of item analyses: 'Have you ever eaten so much you were sick?' The item statistics indicated that too many subjects endorsed the item for it to be successful. Thus, although it was intended to tap gluttony, it utilized a behaviour that almost everyone admits to. A piece of gluttony is required which is of greater rarity. Perhaps 'Have you ever eaten six ice creams in a row?' might do the trick. This is a hypothetical example. The other examples are taken from my own work on personality testing.

EXAMPLE 2
'Would you use someone else's toothbrush?' This received the No response from the majority of the trial sample. This was obviously too

severe a test of tolerance of germs. In its place a milder item was used: 'Would you use a friend's toothbrush?'

EXAMPLE 3

'Are your hobbies and interests similar to those of most people?' This item was not endorsed by many subjects, who showed themselves uncertain by putting a question-mark by the item (as they were allowed to do in the item trial). It was held that the problem here was 'most people'. Who really knows what most people do? In its place I substituted 'many people', and the item was successful on retrial.

EXAMPLE 4

Is smoking a dirty habit? This item worked well in Great Britain, but failed in Amritsar, Punjab, where most of the sample gave a Yes response. However, the stupidity of using this item in Amritsar is attested by the fact this city is the centre of the Sikh religion, which forbids smoking!

These examples are sufficient to show that the item analysis can give us clues as to how items should be rewritten. Once rewritten the new items, together with the selected items, should be administered again to proper samples and subjected to item analysis as described. This should yield a sufficient number of representative items to form a reasonable test.

Failure to form a test

Sometimes, however, even after item rewriting, there are still insufficient items to form a test of even moderate reliability. There are a number of reasons why this might be the case and I shall discuss the remedies that may be adopted in each case.

There is no such variable

It is possible, especially in the field of personality and motivation, where there is little agreement as to what the variables are, even among psychometrists, and almost no agreement between psychometry and clinical theory, that we are trying to measure a variable or syndrome that simply does not exist.

Thus, if we try, for example, to measure the phallic character (Freud, 1905), a hypothesized syndrome of personality traits derived from fixation at the phallic level in Freudian theory, such failure could well occur. No investigator has been able to construct a valid measure of this variable (see Kline, 1972; Fisher and Greenberg, 1977). It seems in this case that there is no correlation among the component traits. Hence a test cannot be constructed. As I have argued in the discussion of internal consistency, when measuring broad syndromes it is permissible to allow reliability to sink lower than with other more homogeneous variables, yet if there is no correlation, even this becomes impossible. If this is the case, the test is best abandoned.

DEMONSTRATION THAT THERE IS NO VARIABLE

The only sound method of testing this hypothesis, other than by deduction from the nature of the variable we are attempting to measure, is to correlate the items and possibly to submit these to factor analysis, although this is not usually necessary.

This procedure will not be given in detail since it is identical to that described under the construction of factored tests. However, in brief, ø coefficients are computed between the items. If most of these are low, less than 0.2 or insignificant, then clearly the test does not form a syndrome. If certain items do cluster together, these can be examined for content. If they are all similar – paraphrases or concerned with obviously similar behaviours – then this is sufficient explanation of the correlation. If they cover part at least of the syndrome, it may be that these do form a genuine variable, that is the syndrome is narrower than that described in clinical theory. In this case it may be worth writing new items of this kind; such new items would then be subjected, together with the originals, to item analysis as described.

There is a danger here that by this procedure we may construct a specific factor – a bloated specific (Cattell and Kline, 1977). However, this would be revealed when we have carried out validity studies – it would correlate with nothing. This correlational analysis is certainly worthwhile if our test has failed and if we are trying to measure a variable which may be conceptually dubious. If we were attempting to measure a well-defined variable such as verbal ability, such correlational analysis would be senseless since failure could not be attributed to the fact that there is no variable.

Items are unsatisfactory

Logically, of course, in every case of failure to construct a test, the reason could be that our items just do not measure what they were intended to measure. Again, this is more likely in the case of personality and motivational tests than it is with tests of ability. However, even here, confusing terms or poorly worded instructions can spoil their efficiency.

However, if we have followed the rules of item writing (which we set out in chapters 2 to 4, devoted to the construction of different types of test) and, more importantly, if we have corrected the poor items in the light of the item analyses for a second trial, as suggested above, then this is not likely (except for the usual few items which are simply abandoned).

Nevertheless, this explanation should only be adopted if we are convinced that no other fits the facts. Indeed, the only way to demonstrate it is to write successful items in further trials.

Items are factorially complex

One of the objections to item analysis is that it is possible to get items loading on two correlated factors which would still show good item total correlations. However, if the factors are not correlated there will be only low correlations with the total score, and a test cannot be constructed.

This cause of failure is essentially only a variant of our first – there is no variable underlying the test, only in this case the failure is due to the fact that there are several variables which the items are measuring. If this is suspected from the nature of the test, then the following procedure should be adopted.

First, phi coefficients between the test items should be computed. These correlations should then be factor-analysed. This will reveal whether the items are in fact loading on several factors. If they are, it indicates that we have several tests compounded together. The items loading on each factor should be examined and other similar ones written if we want to develop separate tests of these factors. However, by this procedure we are in fact constructing factorial tests. The methodology of these instruments is discussed in chapter 9, and I shall say no more about it here. It is to be noted that if the items load on no factor at all, then we are in the position of our first cause, that the test measures no variable at all.

Insufficient good items

Nunnally (1978) mentions one cause of test failure that is easily remedied. This occurs where there is a nucleus of good items with high item-total correlations and hence intercorrelations but insufficient in number to form a reliable test. The addition of the other poor items will not improve the reliability, since they do not correlate with each other.

The fault can be quickly diagnosed. There should be a few good items in terms of r_{pbis} and all the rest would be low. By way of remedy, the content of the few good items should be examined and other items should be written that are similar. This, however, should be done only if the nucleus of good items does seem to cover the content of the test. If the good items are themselves highly similar, we may again be constructing a test of a bloated-specific factor.

It must be noted that this case is identical to a possible outcome of our first cause of failure to form a test – that there is no variable. Correlational analysis of the items might identify a small cluster of items. However, if these had not shown up in the item analysis, there would be few such items.

I have indicated in this chapter the step-by-step procedures involved in item analysing a pool of items and selecting them for a final test. I have also suggested how item analysis can be helpful in item rewriting.

It must be stressed here that our methods guarantee to supply a test of satisfactory internal consistency and discriminatory power which clearly measures some variable. What this variable is, it is up to our validity studies to demonstrate.

7
Computing the discriminatory power and the validity of tests

In the opening chapter, on measurement devices, I pointed out that psychometric tests had three characteristics in which they were superior to other forms of measurement: reliability, validity and discriminatory power. Before going on to discuss the assessment of validity, I shall discuss first the measurement of discriminatory power, for like reliability, this can be assessed with some certainty. Validity, on the other hand, although there are definite techniques to be mastered, always involves some element of judgement.

Discriminatory power

As was indicated in chapter 1, potentially tests can discriminate far better than, say, interviews or ratings, where nine categories are about the most that can reliably be used.

Indices of discrimination, as Guilford (1956) points out, are concerned essentially with ranking subjects. The basis of the coefficient of discrimination, Ferguson's delta (Ferguson, 1949), which was advocated for assessing the discriminatory power of tests, is simple and is set out below. The relationship between the scores of any two subjects is one of either difference or equality. The total number of possible relations among pairs of subjects in a sample of N is $N(N-1)/2$. The total number of equality relationships among the pairs is:

$$\frac{\Sigma f_i^2 - \Sigma F_i}{2} \tag{7.1}$$

where f_i is the frequency of cases at each score, therefore $\Sigma f_i = N$. The total number of difference relationships among the pairs is:

$$\frac{(\Sigma f_i)^2 - \Sigma f_i^2}{2} \tag{7.2}$$

and (7.1) + (7.2) = $(N^2 + N)/2$, since these are the only relationships among the pairs. It is obvious that the number of differences – maximum discrimination – is highest when each score has the same frequency. This occurs when each frequency is $N/(n+1)$, n being the number of test items.

These are the basic statistical facts behind the formula for Ferguson's delta. This coefficient is the ratio between the discriminations made by a test and the maximum number such a test could provide. The formula reads:

$$\delta = \frac{Nu22 - \Sigma f_i^2}{N^2 - [N^2 / (n+1)]}$$

This simplifies to:

$$\frac{(n + 1)(N^2 - \Sigma f_i^2)}{nN^2}$$

where N = number of subjects, n = number of items, f_i = the frequency at each score. δ is 0 when all individuals score the same (i.e. there is no discrimination) and is 1 when there is a rectangular distribution.

COMPUTATIONAL STEPS FOR FERGUSON'S DELTA (COMPUTATION 7.1)

(1) Draw up a frequency distribution of the test scores.
(2) Square and add each frequency: Σf_i^2.
(3) Add 1 to the number of items: $n+1$.
(4) Square the number of subjects: N^2.
(5) Multiply the number of items by (4): nN^2.
(6) This gives us all the terms in the equation. We can then insert them:

$$\delta = \frac{(3) \times (4) - (2)}{(5)}$$

Certain characteristics of δ which Ferguson (1949) has discussed need to be borne in mind by the test constructor. Since a rectangular distribution (the most discriminating) necessitates items with the full range of facility values, this means that the discriminatory power is to some extent antithetical to reliability, for a wide range of facility values reduces item intercorrelations. Of course, as Ferguson argues, the distribution of scores which a test yields is a function of the item difficulty and their intercorrelations, and this affects not only the reliability but also the discriminatory power: = 0.86 for a leptokurtic (with too few easy and too few difficult items), 0.90 for a binomial and

0.93 for a bimodal distribution. All this implies that when a test is to be constructed the extent to which our aim is maximum reliability or maximum discriminatory power depends upon the purposes for which we need it.

Validity

When indices of reliability and discriminatory power are properly executed, there can be no disagreement over the results. In the case of validity, no such neat statistical exercises are possible. Instead, evidence has to be presented which bears on the validity of the test. This evidence is interpreted to demonstrate the validity of the test, but such interpretations are highly subjective. In this section of the chapter I shall examine the best methods of presenting this evidence.

In the first chapter I fully discussed the various kinds of test validity, and here we shall set out the procedures relevant to these different categories.

Face validity

This is a trivial aspect of the test concerned only with its appearance. If for any reason a test has to be face-valid, it is a simple matter to ask subjects taking the trial sessions of the test whether it seems a good measure of the variable or not. Face validity is important for the motivation of subjects.

Concurrent validity

This is assessed from the correlations or factor loadings with tests that purport to measure the same variable. There are a few obvious rules for carrying out good concurrent validity studies, which are set out below, although these are not different from those to be observed in any branch of scientific psychology.

(1) Ensure that the subject sample reflects the population for whom the test is designed, especially with regard to sex, age, educational status and social class. Tests designed for psychiatric use should be administered to the appropriate psychiatric groups.
(2) Ensure that the samples are large enough to produce statistically reliable correlations which can bear factorial analysis. A minimum number for this is 200.

(3) Use as wide a variety of other tests of the variable as possible – to ensure that the correlation is not due to a similarity of specific factors rather than group factors. For example, if our test attempts to measure g, use verbal and non-verbal g measures by different test constructors.
(4) If factor analysis is used, ensure that simple structure is obtained.
(5) In discussing the results, give clear reasons as to what correlations or factor loadings would be expected. This allows the reader to judge the psychological significance of the results.

Concurrent validity studies which meet these criteria should yield relatively unequivocal evidence that cannot be technically impugned.

Predictive validity

Here the main problem is obtaining a criterion to predict. Although this is always difficult, the difficulty varies with the type of test. Ability and interest tests are usually more amenable to demonstrations of predictive validity than are personality tests. In general, the rules to be followed are similar to those given for concurrent validity.

(1) As regards sampling subjects, all our previous comments apply.
(2) Size of sample is vital. If multiple correlations are used with an emphasis on beta weights (the index of how important the test is in predicting the criterion), the sample should be split or cross-validated since beta weights tend to vary from study to study.
(3) Simple structure must be obtained if factor analysis is used.
(4) The reliability of the criterion should be shown.

This last point is particularly important because correlations are lowered by the unreliability of measures.

ATTENUATION OF CORRELATIONS DUE TO UNRELIABILITY
From the classical model of measurement error it can be shown that it is possible to estimate what the correlation between two tests would be, were they perfectly reliable. The formula is (for the derivation, see Nunnally, 1978):

$$\bar{r}_{i2} = \frac{r_{i2}}{\sqrt{r_{ii}\, r_{22}}}$$

where $\bar{r}_{i2}$ is the corrected correlation, r_{i2} is the obtained correlation, r_{ii} is the reliability of variable 1, r_{22} is the reliability of variable 2. This formula corrects for the unreliability of both variables. If we want to correct only for unreliability of the criterion, only the criterion reliability is inserted into the denominator.

COMPUTATIONAL STEPS FOR CORRECTION DUE TO UNRELIABILITY
This formula is so simple that to set the steps out is probably unnecessary. In brief:

(1) Multiply the reliability of the two tests together
(2) Take the square root: $\sqrt{r_{ii}\, r_{22}}$
(3) Divide the obtained correlation of test and criterion by (2)

USE OF THE CORRECTION
In my view this correction formula must be used with great caution, for a number of reasons. First, in the practical application of tests, our test and its criterion are only of a given reliability: to correct for this does not alter this fact, however unpleasant it may be. It is far better to get a reliable test and criterion than correct for unreliability.

In theoretical research, however, where our focus of interest is the relationship between two variables, the corrected estimate may be a better indication than a figure lowered by unreliability. However, here there is always the probability that we delude ourselves with corrected estimates. For this reason corrected estimates of correlations are to be avoided on their own. To quote them alongside obtained coefficients is, however, sometimes meaningful, depending on the purpose and nature of the research. To use them without indication of correction and without giving the original figures is misleading.

Content validity

Content validity, as was indicated in chapter 1, is of interest mainly in the construction of tests where the material to be tested can be clearly defined; mathematics, music, vocabulary or grammar are obvious examples. In terms of our measurement model, the problem of content validity becomes one of sampling the universe of items. In practice, a random sampling of a dictionary would not be likely to yield a sound vocabulary test, since not all dictionary words are of equal importance for an adult to know. Even a random sampling of the commonest words would not be adequate since there are constraints on the words we want to test (depending on the purpose of the test). Thus for overseas doctors our vocabulary test would be far different from that for say overseas teachers.

In practice, content validity can only be assured by getting experts in the field to state what they regard as the vital material, converting this into test items and then sending it out to consultant experts again to see if they can see any glaring omissions or items that are concerned with the same problems.

In the case of personality tests, content validity has little relevance, although the present writer in constructing tests of the oral personality, OPQ and OOQ (Kline, 1979), attempted to demonstrate a form of content validity by listing all the psychoanalytic descriptions of the oral personality in a reduced form – for example 'dependent', 'clings like a leech' – and then converting these into test items.

Cattell (e.g. 1946), in the construction of the 16 PF test, also attempted to ensure content validity by (1) searching the dictionary for all terms descriptive of behaviour, (2) getting rid of those regarded by experts as synonyms, (3) rating subjects on the remaining descriptions and finding clusters of ratings, and (4) writing items aimed at tapping these clusters. This was an elaborate method of sampling the whole universe of variables and attempting to ensure content validity – a bounding of the personality domain. The success of this venture is a matter of dispute (e.g. Cattell and Kline, 1977; Howarth, 1976). Needless to say, a procedure such as that could only be carried out with enormous resources and is not to be recommended to the normal test constructor. Usually, unless clear descriptions exist in the literature, in the construction of personality and motivation tests content validity is not a relevant consideration.

PRACTICAL PROCEDURES FOR CONTENT VALIDITY
Attainment tests:

(1) Specify precisely the population for whom the test is designed.
(2) Specify the skills to be tested, perhaps after job analysis.
(3) Send the list to experts in the field (teachers etc.) to check on omissions.
(4) Convert list to items, using where possible the same number of items per skill.
(5) Resubmit items to experts for checking.
(6) Apply normal test-construction procedures to items. This should result in a test with content validity.

Other tests:

(1) Where descriptive literature exists, search through and convert to description of behaviour.
(2) For each behaviour mentioned, write a number of items.
(3) Where there is no descriptive literature, obtain descriptions of behaviour from informed workers; for example, in a study of the dependency of kidney patients, ask doctors and nurses in charge to describe the dependent behaviour of their patients.
(4) As (2), above, convert descriptions to items.
(5) Apply normal test-construction procedures to test items.

Criterion-referenced tests

In the field of attainment and educational testing, both of children and adults, for example after specific courses of training, considerable emphasis is often placed on what is sometimes thought to be a very different type of test – the criterion referenced test. Berk (1980) has a full discussion of this topic, as does Glaser (1963).

Advocates of the criterion-referenced test contrast it with the norm-referenced test on the following grounds. Normative tests sample the skills and abilities of the subjects, whereas the criterion-referenced tests define and specify the objectives of a course of training and put these to the test, by writing items that measure the attainment of these objectives.

There are two points worthy of note here. Criterion-referenced tests are only applicable in those instances where the objectives of learning can be clearly and unequivocally specified. Second, and this is why the topic has been included here, criterion-referenced tests are tests designed with the aim of maximizing content validity, which we discussed in the previous section. In principle, criterion-referenced tests are not different from norm-referenced tests, although it is true that there is no need for norms. In these tests what is important is simply how much of the test the subject gets right. Norm-referenced test constructors are uninterested in comparative performance; all they want to know is whether particular subjects have or have not mastered the materials.

This distinction is obviously not one of intrinsic difference. Thus a content-valid test is effectively a criterion-referenced test with norms. Similarly, if a criterion-referenced test were standardized, it would become a content-valid normative test.

As has been argued in the case of content validity, the essential feature in the construction of criterion-referenced tests lies in the specification of the objectives of the training course so that items can be written which include those objectives. In many adult training courses the objectives are quite specific, and criterion-referenced testing is the obvious method. The form of the items depends upon what needs to be tested, as has been fully discussed in our chapter on item writing.

Incremental and differential validity

As was indicated in chapter 1, these forms of validity are mainly used in selection procedures in which a battery of tests is used to predict some criterion.

INCREMENTAL VALIDITY: PROCEDURAL STEPS

(1) Correlate test with criterion and other tests in battery.
(2) If it correlates positively with the criterion but insignificantly with the other tests, incremental validity has been demonstrated. Such a test would add to the multiple correlation of the battery with the criterion.
(3) In a factor analysis the test should load on a factor with the criterion but not on a factor with the other tests.

DIFFERENTIAL VALIDITY

There are no general procedures to illustrate differential validity, but if we were to take our earlier example of academic performance, differential validity would be shown by a test if its correlations with different academic subjects were significantly different. In general, therefore, we expect different correlations with different aspects of the criterion to demonstrate differential validity.

Construct validity

As I have argued, construct validity involves demonstrating the psychological characteristics of the variable measured by the test. In so doing, other kinds of validity, already discussed, may be invoked. A general description is set out below.

PROCEDURES

(1) Set out precisely hypotheses concerning the variables with which the test should correlate (concurrent validity).
(2) Set out precisely hypotheses concerning the variables with which the test should not correlate.
(3) Specify groups which should score high and groups which should score low on the test.
(4) Hypothesize the place of the test in factor space. This is a similar hypothesis to those of (1) and (2) above.

These four sets of hypotheses should then be tested on large samples, properly chosen, as set out in our procedures for establishing concurrent validity. The specific groups should be large enough, not only for statistically significant differences to emerge, but also so that confident generalizations can be made. In terms of our psychometric model, construct validity involves demonstrating that the universe of items, of which the test items are a sample, is in fact what we intend it to be.

Conclusions

It is obvious that the validity of a test cannot simply be stated as a coefficient, unlike the reliability and discriminatory power. Instead, the validity of a test is evidenced by a series of results, of the kind discussed above in our various procedures. If the procedures set out in the previous sections are followed, the studies could not be impugned on technical grounds. However, in validity studies all depends on the psychological knowledge and acumen of the test constructor. Thus a concurrent validity study, if technically sound, stands or falls by the tests that are included in it. Similarly, location in factor space demands that the proper parameters of this space are included in the study. If they are not, however well executed, construct validity will not be demonstrated.

Subjective, then, though the assessment of validity is, there are rarely serious disagreements. This is because if a variable is properly understood, then in most cases there is no doubt which other variables it should or should not correlate with, what place it should take in factor space and which groups should perform well or not on it. Where the variable is not understood, the question of validity does not arise. Rather, the validity studies become exploratory descriptive studies, in which the variable is defined.

8
Standardizing the test

In chapter 1 it was made clear that one of the advantages possessed by psychological tests in comparison with other forms of measurement is that tests are standardized. Hence it is possible to compare a subject's score with that of the general population or other relevant groups, thus enabling the tester to make meaningful interpretations of the score.

From this it follows that the standardization of tests is most important where scores of subjects are compared explicitly or implicitly – as in vocational guidance or educational selection. Norms may also be useful for mass-screening purposes. For the use of psychological tests in the scientific study of human attributes – the psychometrics of individual differences – norms are not as useful. For this the direct, raw test-scores are satisfactory. Thus norms meet the demand, in general, of the practical test user in applied psychology. Since norms are usually necessary for tests of ability, our discussion of how a test should be standardized will relate in the main to such tests.

Sampling

This is the crucial aspect of standardization: all depends upon the sample. In sampling there are two important variables: size and representativeness. The sample must accurately reflect the target population at which the test is aimed (of course, there may be several populations and consequently several samples), and it must be sufficiently large to reduce the standard errors of the normative data to negligible proportions.

Size

For the simple reduction of statistical error a sample size of 500 is certainly adequate. However, the representativeness of a sample is not independent of size. A general population norm, for example, of school-children would require in the region of 10,000 subjects. A sample from a limited population such as lion-tamers or fire-eaters would not have to be so large (indeed, the population would hardly be that large). Thus no statement about sample size can be made without relating it to the population from which it is derived. This discussion clarifies the point that more important than size is the representativeness of the sample. A small but representative normative sample is far superior to a large but biased sample. Some examples taken from actual tests will make this point obvious and will also indicate the best methods for test constructors of obtaining standardization samples.

Obtaining a representative normative sample

Clearly, the most heterogeneous population is the general population of which all others are subsets. For this reason, to obtain a sample of given quality from the general population is the most difficult sampling problem. Our first example shows a well-known attempt to do this – the standardization of the Lorge–Thorndike Intelligence Test (1957) for children, which is quoted in part by Jackson and Messick (1967).

EXAMPLE 1: GENERAL POPULATION SAMPLE FROM THE LORGE–
THORNDIKE TEST
Since ability norms must be related to age, we shall consider the samples of each age group.

Age groups. There were twelve age groups, from 6-year-olds to 17-year-olds. This is obviously a satisfactory division by age, although six-month or even three-month range groups would have been better. There was a total N of 136,000, that is more than 11,000 per age group. Obviously, statistical sampling error must be virtually nil.

Representativeness of sample. To eliminate bias, a stratified sample of communities was taken, the basis of stratification being the factors which are most related to intelligence: (1) percentage of adult literacy, (2) proportion of professional workers in the population, (3) percentage of home ownership, and (4) median home-rental value. Each community was then classified by these four variables into 'very high', 'high', 'average,' 'low' and 'very low'. All pupils at each grade in each community were then tested, and separate norms for each of these grades at each group were produced. In fact, the total N was drawn from forty-four communities in the USA.

It should be obvious that these sampling procedures should produce a sample that closely resembles the general population for each group.

However, it must be equally obvious that enormous resources are necessary to sample in this way. This Lorge–Thorndike study well illustrates the sheer size of sample necessary for adequate normalization and the huge administrative burden such extensive testing demands. It also illustrates clearly how fully adequate sampling needs to be done. Notice the basis of stratification: variables were taken relevant to the variable being measured. If establishing norms for a measure of anxiety, it could well be that the sample could be stratified on other variables. Note, too, that norms are produced not only for each age group as a total but for the sub-groups (high, low, etc.) on the social-class variables. These are useful and meaningful comparisons.

In brief, This first example illustrates well the full demands of sampling if a general population sample is required – huge numbers and proper stratification. The fact that even here sub-group scores are given shows clearly that such scores are useful. Indeed, in considering the individual case they are often more useful than a total group score. Within-stratifications sampling should be random.

EXAMPLE 2: GENERAL POPULATION SAMPLE FOR THE CATTELL 16 PF TEST

Cattell, Eber and Tatsuoka (1970) also argue that a properly stratified sample is more effective, size for size, than a random sample.

Basis of stratification. (a) Social status, (b) geographical area, (c) age and (d) urban or rural. The standardization sample reflected the proportions of these categories in the total population. In fact, eight areas of the USA were chosen, eight population densities, five age-groups and seven income-groups.

Total N: 977. This is a relatively small sample even though it has been accurately stratified. Its small size reflects the problems involved in obtaining the co-operation of adults who are not students, servicemen or prisoners, in filling up psychological tests. Although the total adult sample of 977 is, because of its stratification, probably adequate, some of the sub-groups seem too small to be useful. For example, there are only thirty mountain dwellers – this cannot be a good sample. Similarly, the different age-groups where there are only ninety-four under-25s are far too small.

Conclusions. This example indicates the necessity, if the total group is to be broken down, of having very large samples. Indeed, if the subsets of the total sample are not large enough to provide reliable information, the adequacy of the whole could be questioned. It does appear that when we compare the 16 PF test (which incidentally is one of the better personality tests in respect of normative data) with the Lorge–Thorndike test, there is no escaping the necessity for very large samples of several thousands.

Rules for general norms

From this a few general rules for the production of general population norms can be stated. (1) The sample must be stratified. It is usually adequate to use a fourfold stratification. Social status, age and sex are usually important stratification variables. (2) In each subsection there should be sufficient numbers to form an adequate sample, that is around 300 at minimum. This inevitably means that, with all the possible classifications, a very large N is required, for example (social status) $\times 2$ (sex) $\times 5$ (age) produces 40 categories which, with 300 subjects in each, yields a total of 12,000 subjects. There is little hope of avoiding so large an N (and this is a bare minimum), as the Lorge–Thorndike test indicates. Hence the provision of adequate general population norms requires huge resources. Norms on a lesser scale, as in the Cattell 16 PF test, are still useful but must be used with caution.

For the reason above, namely the need for huge resources, many test constructors put in more specific norms for groups, especially relevant to the nature and practical application of the test.

EXAMPLE 3: SPECIAL GROUP NORMS – THE CONSERVATISM SCALE
This scale (Wilson and Patterson, 1970) attempts to measure the dogmatism or rigidity that is regarded as an important social attitude affecting a wide variety of real-life behaviours, as is fully discussed in Rokeach (1960). For such a scale the scores of any distinctive group would be of interest. Thus a large number of different norms are supplied. For example, university students from four countries, college-of-education students, schoolgirls, New Zealand professionals, skilled workers, each have norms, as do heterogeneous males. However, examination of the N of each of these groups indicates that these figures are of little value. The largest sample is 340 for an occupational quota sample from New Zealand, and it is difficult to argue that this could be adequate to reflect accurately so diverse a sample. There are only fifty university students from the UK. Since there are approximately forty universities and taking into account the large number of subjects studied at university, this sample is worthless as normative data. Many of their samples are similarly valueless: twenty-two lab technicians, twenty-two clerical workers, thirty businessmen; none of these can be safely used as normative groups.

This example is a clear illustration of how norms, even of published tests, can be worthless. The choice of groups is revealing but unless large and stratified samples are used, no reliance can be put on the results. Notice that all the groups could not be meaningfully summated to form a general population norm. The use of specific group norms demands large representative sampling of the groups.

Sampling specific groups

To obtain adequate specific norm groups it is necessary to stratify the sample by the major variable affecting those groups. A few examples will show how this is to be done, in principle, although to choose the stratifying variables requires considerable study of the group.

SIXTH-FORM PUPILS

To obtain a proper sample of sixth-form pupils it is necessary to ensure that we have an adequate sample of sixth-forms. Thus the basis of the sampling would be to take all the sixth-formers in a sample of sixth-forms. For schools some of the main stratifying variables are:

(1) Finance: public, direct grant, aided, state. (It is realized that these categories are being swept away, but our aim is to exemplify sampling for norms.)
(2) Sex: boys, girls, mixed.
(3) Geographic location: inner city, town, rural.
(4) The state school system: grammar schools, comprehensive schools and sixth-form colleges.

It will be difficult to draw up a precisely balanced sample on all variables (for there are few inner-city public schools), but nevertheless, a sample reflecting the proportions of such schools in the total population, even if there were only two schools per category, would yield adequate norms. The present writer in his development of Ai3Q (Kline, 1971) used such a sample of northern sixth-forms which resulted in 1000 boys and 1000 girls from twenty-eight schools. Thus, even for this, very large resources are necessary. It is noteworthy that we were unable to provide any further normative groups. Resources of time, money and research assistance were not sufficient.

EXAMPLE 4: MYERS–BRIGGS TYPE INDICATOR – SPECIFIC NORMS

This test (Briggs and Myers, 1962) designed to allocate subjects into the Jungian system of classification has extensive normative groups, some of which meet the necessarily stringent criteria for adequate normalization, stringent because decisive interpretation is made on the strength of such norms. For example, there is a sample of Penna: eleventh- and twelfth-grade children which is well drawn – 3503 boys and 2511 girls from twenty-seven schools. These must constitute a sound normative group. There is similarly a sample of 4562 liberal-arts and engineering students, drawn from eight universities rated high on those lists describing the entrance qualifications of their students. Of such students this again is an excellent sample. There is little doubt that these two samples provide a good basis for norms. On the other hand, three samples of creative, less-creative and least creative architects (N's 40, 43 and 41) are hardly adequate for anything. Similarly, the sample of gifted children – thirty-four males and twenty-five females – is too small to be useful.

The Myers–Briggs indicator is evidence that good norms can be collected. It also shows clearly how difficult this is, and that usually investigators make do with less than perfection.

Rules for sampling special groups

(1) Find the most important variables relevant to the groups and use these as a basis for stratifying the sample.
(2) Build up the sample to as many as possible: 300 is a minimum. Norms usually involve the collection of data over a period of time.
(3) Remember that a small sample (as in Wilson and Patterson, 1970) is better than nothing at all. If small numbers have been used, explicitly warn test users not to use the norms except with the utmost caution.

Enough has now been written to make it clear that there is no intellectual problem in establishing norms. Rather, the difficulty is one of resources: time, money, subjects and assistance in administering and scoring tests. However, if a test is to be used for practical purposes of selection and guidance, it is essential that its norms do meet the high standards suggested here. Stratified and large samples are essential.

However, given that we have good normative groups, we must now turn to the second problem of standardization: how best to express the results.

The norms

It is usual to compare an individual's score with the relevant normative group by means of some transformation that reveals that individual's status relative to the group. There are various methods of doing this, the commonest of which I shall describe and evaluate.

Percentiles

The percentile rank of a score is defined by the percentage of subjects in the normative group who obtain a lower score. This is a type of norm easily understood even by the mathematically phobic. The fifteenth percentile means that 15 per cent of the population score below the score. The disadvantage of percentiles is really twofold.

(1) Percentiles are not capable of further statistical analysis, if we use the most powerful parametric statistics, simply because they are ordinal scores.
(2) Second, since the distribution of percentiles is rectangular, whereas the distribution of many tests approaches the normal, small differences around the mean become exaggerated by percentiles, whereas relatively large differences at the tails of the distribution become compressed. Percentiles can thus distort results, and for these reasons, together with their statistical limitations, their use is not recommended.

Various types of standard scores

A superior method of expressing norms is in terms of standard scores. There are various types of standard score, which, as we shall see, are generally similar. They are described below.

Z SCORES
A standard score is the deviation of the raw score from the mean divided by the standard deviation of the distribution:

$$Z = \frac{X - \bar{X}}{\sigma}$$

where Z = standard score, X = raw score, $\bar{X}$ = mean. Thus, if we have a set of raw scores with a mean of 50 and a s.d. of 10, the standard score conversions shown in table 8.1 can be made. From the example given in this table we can see that Z scores have a mean of 0 and therefore take negative and positive values. The larger the Z score, the further away from the mean it must be, positive Z scores being above, negative Z scores below the mean. Since the transformation of the raw scores into Z scores is linear, the distribution of Z scores reflects the distribution of raw scores. If the raw-score distribution is normal, then the Z scores will range from $+3$ to -3, and they will be particularly informative because the proportion within different segments of the normal curve are known. For example, approximately 68 per cent of the curve lies between the mean and one standard deviation. Hence a Z score of 1 can immediately be translated into percentage terms; that is, 16 per cent of the population have done better ($+1$) or worse (-1). The same can be done for any Z score by reading off from normal curve tables.

A computer program for converting to Z scores may be found in the appendices.

Table 8.1 Z scores and raw scores

Raw score	Computation		Z
60	$\dfrac{60-50}{10}$	=	1.0
65	$\dfrac{65-50}{10}$	=	1.5
50	$\dfrac{50-50}{10}$	=	0
40	$\dfrac{40-50}{10}$	=	−1.0
54	$\dfrac{54-50}{10}$	=	0.4

There are two disadvantages of Z scores:

(1) Since the main value of norms, as I have argued, is for applied psychology, and since in applied psychology it is often useful and necessary to discuss scores with clients and their relatives who may be unsophisticated numerically, Z scores have a major flaw, that the mean is 0 and that the highest possible score is 3. This has led test users to develop further transformations of Z scores.
(2) Since no obtained distribution is likely to be perfectly normal and very many distributions are by no means normal, one useful property of Z scores is lost, namely that we cannot infer or look up equivalent percentiles. Consequently, to restore this useful information, as well as for other reasons, some test constructors prefer to use normalized transformations.

Z-SCORE TRANSFORMATIONS

The standard transformation of Z scores is: $Z_t = A + BZ$, where Z_t = transformed Z score, A = the mean of the transformed distribution, B = the s.d. of the transformed distribution and Z = the Z score. An example (table 8.2) will clarify the point (we shall use the data of table 8.1).

A computer program for transformed Z scores may be found in the appendices.

Here are the computational steps for Z and Z_t scores:

(1) Compute mean and standard deviation of scores.
(2) Express each score as a deviation from the mean: $X - \bar{X}$.
(3) Divide (2) by s.d.: Z score.
(4) Multiply each Z score by desired s.d. of transformed distribution.
(5) Add (4) to desired mean: Z_t.

It is common practice in test construction to transform Z scores to

Table 8.2 Raw scores, Z scores and transformed Z scores

Raw score	Computation	Z	Computation	Zt
60	$\dfrac{60-50}{10}$ =	1.0	$Z_t = 100 + 1 \times 10$ =	110
65	$\dfrac{60-50}{10}$ =	1.5	$Z_t = 100 + 1.5 \times 10$ =	115
50	$\dfrac{50-50}{10}$ =	0	$Z_t = 100 + 0 \times 10$ =	100
40	$\dfrac{40-50}{10}$ =	-1.0	$Z_t = 100 - 1 \times 10$ =	90
54	$\dfrac{54-50}{10}$ =	0.4	$Z_t = 100 + 0.4 \times 10$ =	104

Raw score $\bar{X} = 50$, s.d. $= 10$
Transformed Z score $\bar{X} = 100$, s.d. $= 10$

distributions with means of 50 and s.d.s of 10. In this case, if the distribution approaches normality, then scores will run from around 80 to 20.

Thus, if we want norms of this kind for our tests, we transform our sets of normative scores to Z_t scores with means of 50 and s.d.s of 10. Test users, therefore, look up the raw scores of their subjects and can read off a Z_t score. Transformed Z scores of this kind are easy to understand, and in those cases where the distributions of the test scores approach normality, they are quickly interpreted in terms of percentiles. Such scores are of course suited to statistical analysis.

A further advantage of standard scores is that standard scores are always comparable; thus a Z score of 1 represents a performance on any test that is one standard deviation above the mean. Similarly, if a battery of tests uses a transformed standard score with the same means and standard deviations, scores across the battery are directly comparable. In my view, for tests where the distribution, if not normal, is at least symmetrical, *transformed Z scores with $\bar{X}$ of 50 and s.d.s of 10* are a sensible norm.

NORMALIZED STANDARD SCORES
Sometimes a normal distribution of norms is required (e.g. if it is expected on theoretical grounds, as in intelligence tests).

Here are the computations of normalized standard scores:

(1) Work out the cumulative proportion, *CP*, for each raw score. To do this follow (2) to (5), below.
(2) Prepare a frequency distribution of the scores.
(3) From this the cumulative frequency, *CF*, can be worked out. This

is the sum of all the frequencies below each raw score. For example, the CF for raw-score 5 is the number of subjects scoring below 5.

(4) Find the CF to the mid-point of each score interval. This is done by adding to the CF for each score half the number of subjects at each score. Thus, if the CF for raw-score 5 was 10 and four subjects scored 5, the CF to mid-point of 6 would be 12.

(5) Divide this mid-point cumulative frequency for each raw score by N. This gives the cumulative proportion (1).

(6) In statistical tables giving the areas under the normal curve find the Z score for each CP. Where the CP is >0.500 use the parts of the table indicating the area of the larger proportion; conversely, where the CP is <0.500 use the tables for the smaller proportion.

(7) This now gives us a set of normalized Z scores: Z_n.

(8) To transform Z_n scores to standard scores, the procedure is the same as for the computation of Z_t scores, and is as set out previously.

(9) Multiply each Z_n score by the desired S.D. of our transformed distribution.

(10) Add (9) to desired mean of transformed distribution.

In the American Psychological Association's guide to test constructors (e.g. Buros, 1972) it is suggested that the typical transformation, as with unnormalized standard scores, should be to a mean of 50 and a standard deviation of 10. These are known as *T* scores – normally distributed standard scores with standard deviations of 10.

A computer program for normalized *Z* scores may be found in the appendices.

The advantage of *T* scores over their unnormalized equivalents is that the scores are immediately transferable to percentiles, thus making interpretation simple, especially for the non-statistical. On the other hand, if the raw distribution were not normal in the first place, normalization would clearly be a distortion. In my view, normalized standard scores should only be used (1) where the original distribution resembles a normal distribution, (2) where we have some sound theoretical basis for expecting a normal distribution and, in either case, (3) where we are confident that our normalization group is sufficiently large and representative to be a true reflection of the population. Otherwise, I would argue that standard scores (transformed to a distribution with reasonable mean and s.d.) are better. They do not distort the distribution, and since each score reflects deviation from the mean, its interpretation is still clear.

As should be clear from our discussion and from the computational procedures, standard scores and normalized standard scores can be produced with any desired mean and standard deviation. One widely used transformation which is useful in applied psychology is the Stanine score.

STANINES

As the name suggests, these are standard scores which break up the normal distribution into nine categories. The highest category, 1, and lowest, 9, each contains 4 per cent of the distribution; categories 2 and 8 each contain 7 per cent; categories 3 and 7, each 12 per cent; categories 4 and 6, each 17 per cent; and category 5 contains 20 per cent.

A similar norm is favoured by Cattell and his colleagues, the normalized *Sten score*, which divides the normal distribution into ten categories.

SUMMARY

(1) Raw scores are only meaningful when they are related to scores of normative groups.
(2) The value of norms depends upon the quality of the sampling of normative groups; only if these are adequate can the norms be used with any confidence.
(3) There are various methods of expressing normative scores.
(4) Percentiles, though easy to understand, are not suitable for statistical analysis.
(5) Standard scores are therefore recommended, based on the deviation of scores from the mean.
(6) Transformed standard scores are always comparable: the same standard scores being the same distance from the mean.
(7) Normalized standard scores have the added property that they are readily translated into percentiles.

Presentation of norms

In constructing test norms, the following procedures should be carried out. This makes the test far more valuable and less misleading.

(1) The sample size, the basis of its stratification (if any), and its provenance must be clearly stated.
(2) The type of norm used must be set out.
(3) For each normative group the raw scores should be set out clearly against the standard scores. If desirable, percentiles can also be set out against the raw scores.

The reason for discussing norms and standardization was that meaning could be given to a score by relating it to the performance of a standard group. Again I must stress that norms are important for applied psychology. For the study of psychological variables *per se*, raw scores are sufficient – indeed, preferable, for they are the original data.

However, there are two other methods of interpreting test scores which some writers (e.g. Brown, 1976) regard as different from standardization and these must be briefly discussed.

The content criterion

In our discussion of content validity it was pointed out that if a test consists of items demanding subjects to expand certain algebraic expressions, then for that particular operation the test is *per se* a valid measure. Obviously, content validity can only be a useful concept where particular skills and behaviours can be specified. This can be done fairly easily, at the elementary level, for mathematics (the four rules, the use of 0, and so on) and for music (does the subject know notation, can he harmonize a simple tune?) and for the basic elements of most scientific subjects in which there is a factual corpus of knowledge. However, to specify content in this way at a more advanced level is exceedingly difficult. Clearly, content validity is most relevant for educational achievement tests.

The content criterion is applicable to scores on a test which has been designed as content valid. An example will clarify the point. A music test might be concerned with mastery of notation. Thus items would consist of crotchets, minims and so on at various pitches, and subjects would have to indicate what they were. In such a test a score of 100 per cent would represent complete mastery of music notation. A score of 90 per cent obviously would indicate that 90 per cent of the material was known. With such tests it is necessary to have prior evidence that some cut-off point is sufficient to allow a student to proceed to the next stage of the course. This requires evidence that students scoring above the point are successful, whereas those below it are not. Usually, however, such cut-off points are arbitrary, based upon the experience of those teaching the subject. With this type of test there is effectively only a two-point score: pass or fail. It must be noted parenthetically that our example is hypothetical. Musical notation is a simple affair when given time. The problem lies in responding immediately and correctly.

Problems with the content criterion

The concealed weakness of the content-criterion scores resides in the difficulty of sampling the subject which the test purports to measure.

What is the meaning of a 90 per cent score? Is it correct that an individual with such a score knows 90 per cent of the subject. It almost certainly cannot be the case, and even if it were so, two subjects with the same score may have got different items wrong so that the scores are not truly equivalent. This difficulty means that such tests should be restricted to subjects with precisely defined material and to levels where the knowledge is so fixed and determined that sampling becomes a viable possibility, as for example in the elementary arithmetic rules. Notice that those subjects where any set of test items is a tiny sample of the population are not therefore suited to tests using the content criterion.

CONCLUSIONS
The content criterion is useful for tests where mastery of some skill or a particular knowledge is required. This means that its value is only for achievement testing. At the lowest level at the primary school, where basic skills are important, it is worth considering as a test constructional technique. Schonell's (1951) reading tests are outstanding examples of content-criterion tests since these diagnostic tests indicate the precise source of difficulty; for example, confusion of p and b or d and b, and so on. However, it is to be noted that reference to the items 'correct' and 'wrong' would also indicate this fact. In summary, I would argue that the content criterion is not a highly useful method for evaluating test scores: in any case, it is limited only to achievement tests.

Criterion prediction

A second method other than using norms to interpret scores is to construct a series of expectancy tables setting out the probability of subjects at each score reaching a criterion score. There are several points here worthy of discussion. First, this method is only suitable where some clear criterion score is possible. This is most often the case in educational applications of testing, where examination scores and grades are available. Similar scores are possible in industry, where examinations or other rating procedures are used for selection. In industrial psychology, ratings of job success by supervisors can be used, although the reliability and validity of these criteria is open to doubt.

In the second place, these probabilities have to be discovered experimentally. To do this, large-scale studies have to be carried out with the relevant populations. This, of course, involves precisely the same sampling problems as I have discussed in our study of sampling for norms. In this sense the probabilities of expectancy tables are still normative data. Instead of presenting standard scores for a particular group or a group mean and standard deviation, probabilities of reaching a criterion score are presented.

Third, expectancy tables illustrate with especial clarity the dilemma of practical psychology: the difference between actuarial and individual prediction. If a particular score on a test yields a 0.38 probability of passing a particular examination, it means that 38 per cent of persons with such a score (in the normative group) passed the examination. The implication is that 38 per cent of persons with such a score will pass – but which 38 per cent? When faced with an individual in the practical application of psychology, such actuarial predictions are difficult. However, to reject such a scorer would mean in the long run that the selector would be more often right than wrong. In this sense the figures are useful, but only in this sense. This weakness of actuarial predictions in individual cases is true in most normative studies in psychometrics. However, it is immediately obvious in the case of expectancy tables, which appear to offer such clear predictions. Test constructors must be aware of this before deciding to construct such tables.

STEPS IN COMPUTING AN EXPECTANCY TABLE

(1) Obtain scores from sample on test and criterion.
(2) Divide criterion scores into meaningful groups; for example, pass, fail.
(3) Divide test scores into categories such that in each category there are large numbers. Equal numbers in the categories, except at the extremes, is often the best method.
(4) A table is then constructed showing frequencies in each category:

Table 8.3

Category	Criterion		Total
	Pass	Fail	
1	x	y	$x+y$
2	z	a	$z+a$
3	b	c	$b+c$

(5) For each category compute the proportion of cases that pass or fail the criterion; for example, for category 2 work out the proportion of z to $a+z$ and of a to $a+z$.
(6) An expectancy table can then be constructed with these proportions instead of frequencies in each cell. These represent the probability of people with any score passing or failing the criterion.

Note: It is obvious, when this method is used, that the value of expectancy tables depends on the quality and size of the sample. With poor sampling, the resulting inaccuracies make the method of little value.

ALTERNATIVE METHOD OF CONSTRUCTING EXPECTANCY TABLES

(1) to (3) are as above.
(4) For each category of test score, present the mean and S.D. on the criterion score. However, unless the correlation between test and criterion is high, there is likely to be so much overlap in the mean scores of the categories that its practical value is not high.

A computer program to print out expectancy tables may be found in the appendices.

THE REGRESSION EQUATION AS A METHOD OF COMPUTING EXPECTANCY TABLES

With this method a regression equation is used to predict the criterion score from the test scores. The computation in this approach is more complex but nevertheless can be carried out easily with an electronic calculator. A computer program is, of course, more rapid and simple.

Here are the computational steps in the regression equation method:

(1) Obtain scores on the test and the criterion.
(2) Compute the correlation between the two sets of scores.
(3) The regression line between the two sets of scores is computed by the equation $Y_{pred} = a + by \times X$, where Y_{pred} = the predicted criterion score (the average of those with a given predictor score); a = the intercept constant, allowing for differences in means; b = the slope or regression constant; X = the score on the predictor test.
(4) The regression equation can only be computed if a and b are known. $a = \bar{Y} - by \times \bar{X}$, where $\bar{Y}$ = the mean of the criterion score and $\bar{X}$ = the mean of the test score. $by = r_{xy}$ S.D.$_y$/S.D.$_x$, where r = the correlation of xy, S.D.$_y$ = the standard deviation of Y, and S.D.$_x$ = the standard deviation of X
(5) Thus by use of this equation we can set up a table of predicted criterion scores for each category of test scores.

As I have argued, the Y_{pred} is the predicted average score of subjects with a given test score. However, this is obviously subject to error, unless there is a perfect correlation between the criterion and test. Thus it is necessary to compute the *standard error of the estimated scores*. This is obtained from the formula $S_{est} = $ S.D.$_y$ $\sqrt{1 - r_{xy}^2}$, where S.D.$_y$ is the standard deviation of the obtained test scores and r_{xy} is the correlation between the test and criterion. As with the standard deviations and other standard errors, 68 per cent of criterion scores will fall within one standard error of the estimated scores and 95 per cent will fall between two standard errors.

COMPUTING STEPS FOR THE STANDARD ERROR OF THE ESTIMATE OF PREDICTED SCORES

(1) Square the correlation between criterion and test: r_{xy}^2.

(2) Subtract (1) from 1 and take its square root: $\sqrt{1 - r_{xy}^2}$.

(3) Multiply (2) by the standard deviation of the test score: S.D.$_y$ $\sqrt{1 - r_{xy}^2}$ This gives us the standard error of the estimated scores.

In the expectancy tables based upon regression equations, the predicted scores should be accompanied by their standard errors. This means that unwarranted conclusions will not be drawn. For example, suppose the standard error of estimate for predicting grades was 1. Thus, if a test score gave a grade prediction of 3, it would mean that 95 per cent of such scorers would get criterion scores between 1 and 5. In a five-point scale this means that almost any category could be obtained!

The expectancy tables, based upon scores predicted from a regression equation, can be illustrated graphically. If this is done, it is a simple matter to insert around the regression line the limits indicated by the standard error of the estimate.

If sampling is good, if the standard error of the estimate is low, and if the criterion scores are reliable and valid, then the regression-based expectancy tables are a useful method of interpreting test scores. Essentially, however, since the predictions depend upon the performance of a sample, such expectancy tables are another form of expressing norms rather than a different approach from standardization.

9

Other methods of test construction

In this chapter I shall describe how to construct tests by two other methods of test construction, both widely used but each with their own peculiar problems.

Criterion-keyed tests

This is a method of test construction which has produced some of the most used psychological tests, notably the Minnesota Multiphasic Personality Inventory, the MMPI (Hathaway and McKinley, 1951) and the Strong Interest Blank (Campbell, 1971), the former in clinical psychology, the latter in the field of vocational guidance.

In criterion-keyed tests, items are selected for scales if they can discriminate the relevant criterion groups from controls. Although the original item pool from which the MMPI was derived was written in the light of knowledge of neurotic symptoms so that the item writers attempted to describe abnormal behaviour, in some instances a more empirical approach is adopted. In the case of the original Strong test, for example, items were used with no obvious relevance to the particular criterion groups and were included in scales if they did in fact discriminate, even though there was no rationale, either theoretical or intuitive, for the item's success.

The basis of this method is simple and pragmatic in its effectiveness. Thus where discriminations between groups are necessary as in diagnosis and selection or guidance, criterion-keyed tests, if sufficiently developed so that enough efficient items can be found, will do the job. With tests of this type, the emphasis is on discriminating power; what is important is the fact that the test discriminates, not the reason it does so.

There are difficulties and objections to the rationale of this method which in my view contraindicate its use in many applications and fields of testing.

Selection of criterion groups

In many fields there is considerable difficulty in establishing criterion groups. Where this is so a test will perform far less efficiently than it did during the item trials. The MMPI, to take a concrete example, used groups defined by the Minnesota psychiatrists and psychologists. Since there are considerable problems in psychiatric diagnosis, there would be disagreement on classification with workers with a different theoretical orientation. Such objections obtain not only in clinical classifications but more generally in classifications of all kinds. This problem with the reliability of classification simply leads to an imperfect validity.

Lack of psychological meaning

However, even if such objections have been overcome, there is a far more severe defect in my view. This is related to the psychological inanity (in the literal sense) of the variables measured by criterion-keyed tests. Let us take the MMPI again. It is possible (indeed, highly likely) that obsessional neurotics differ from other groups and controls on more than one variable. Thus items selected simply because they can discriminate groups may well measure a variety of variables. Any scale thus constructed is unlikely to be homogeneous but will obviously be multivariate. Not only, therefore, could two apparently identical scores be psychologically different but, in addition, there is no *prima facie* way of knowing what the scale measures. Thus, that a test can discriminate X group from Y group tells us nothing about the nature of this test variable, unless it is known that the groups differ from each other on only one variable.

Lack of generality

There is a specificity about results from criterion-keyed tests which is also a serious limitation. For example, if a criterion-keyed test is used to select tank fitters, much will depend upon the nature of the tasks involved in fitting out the particular tanks. If these should be changed, the tasks would change, and a previously efficient criterion-keyed test would fail. Tests, on the other hand, which tapped the underlying abilities would still be useful. Thus even in their apparently effective role in selection, the tests have severe problems.

Despite these difficulties, it is sometimes useful to construct criterion-keyed tests, and how this is done will now be described. This utility derives from the ease with which criterion-keyed tests can be constructed. Thus I shall describe only simple methods. Elaborate statistical exercises in criterion-keyed test construction I do not consider worthwhile because of the problems of these tests. If good resources are available, it is preferable to construct a larger battery of factored tests which measure the important factors underlying the tasks, or behaviours to be examined in the criterion groups.

THE PROCEDURES IN CRITERION-KEYED TEST CONSTRUCTION

(1) Establish (a) clear criterion groups *or* (b) a criterion score. How this is done is best understood from examples. If we were attempting to devise a pilot selection-test, then into our criterion groups would go the highest passes in the group and the worst failures. If, as sometimes occurs, there is a relatively small group of failures, the two groups will consist of the passes and the failures. Another possibility would be to follow up the pilots who had passed their examinations a few years previously and get ratings by commanding officers of their flying ability. This would then establish a criterion score. In industrial psychology, for the development of selection tests, these techniques can be applied to any specific occupation.

(2) Obviously the establishment of our criterion groups constitutes the sample. The larger the numbers that can be used the better since this makes the findings more reliable. Since it is useful to know the P value of an item, it is in this respect an advantage to use the whole group rather than the extremes.

(3) The best coefficient for the dichotomous correlation between item and criterion groups, as was discussed in our section on item analysis (see p.138) is probably phi. The advantage of phi, that it is a true correlation coefficient, offsets the fact that it fluctuates with the level of difficulty. Compared with r_{tet}, it is less dependent on the distribution of the variables.

    (a) If we have a continuous-score criterion, then our item statistic is the r_{pbis} between each item and the criterion.

(4) Since in a criterion-keyed test we are interested in items solely because they discriminate the groups rather than on account of any psychological rationale, item selection is simplified. We take all items, regardless of content, that correlate significantly with the criterion (in the case of 3a above). If we have more than say thirty, we take up to this number. If less, we can try to rewrite items in the light of our knowledge of the items that were successful and try them out again.

(5) Collect the successful items together; compute K-R20 reliability and Ferguson's delta.
(6) Cross-validate items on the new sample. Unless this is done, thus showing that results are replicable, criterion-keyed tests are worthless, even for practical selection. It is always necessary to show that they will discriminate with a new sample.

COMPUTATIONAL STEPS
(1) Select groups, as discussed above.
(2) For each item compute phi with the pass/fail dichotomy (or group membership).
(3) Count the number putting keyed response to each item.
(4) Select items, rewrite any items that fail to reach the criteria and retry.
(5) Cross-validate all items.
(6) If there is a continuous-criterion score instead of (2)
(7) For each item compute the r_{pbis} with the continuous-criterion score.
(8) For these computations the two formulae are:

$$\phi: \quad \begin{array}{c} \quad P \quad F \\ \text{Criterion group} \end{array}$$

		P	F
Item 1	P	a	b
	F	c	d

$$\phi = \frac{ac - bd}{\sqrt{(a + b)(c + d)(b + c)(a + d)}}$$

Since $X^2 = N\phi^2$, the significance of ø can be tested by referring to the X^2 tables with one degree of freedom.

The usual formula for computing the point-biserial correlation is:

$$r_{pbi} = \frac{(\bar{X}_A - \bar{X}_B) \sqrt{N_A N_B}}{N\sigma_t}$$

where $\bar{X}_A$ and $\bar{X}_B$ = the means of groups A and B, N_A and N_B = the number of subjects in each group, $N = N_A + N_B$, and σ_t = the standard deviation in the combined groups.

A computer program for item/criterion correlations may be found in the appendices.

Factor-analytic tests

The aim of the factor-analytic test constructor is to develop a test that measures one factor only, and this the one intended by him – a qualification by no means tautologous since it can happen that tests measure factors unintended by their authors. First I shall describe the essentials of factor analysis.

The rationale, logic and description of factor analysis

DEFINITION OF A FACTOR

There have been many attempts to define a factor. Royce (1963) found that the most common explanations involved the following terms, that is factors were conceived as dimensions, determinants, functional unities, parameters, taxonomic categories and Eysenck's (1953) description – a condensed statement of (linear) relationships between a set of variables. In this review of all the meanings imputed to factors, Royce's own definition is one that seems to embrace all previous terms and to clarify, from the viewpoint of the test constructor, just what a factor is: *a construct operationally defined by its factor loadings* (which last are to be thought of as the correlations of variables with the factor).

So that the full significance of this definition of a factor for test construction may be seen, it is necessary to define first some of the other terms used in factor analysis. This will aid explanation.

FACTOR LOADINGS

These are the correlations of the variables with the factor. Thus in test construction we factor-analyse the correlations between items and select those items which load on the common factor, that is correlate with the common factor. This factor is then the construct defined by its factor loadings, that is by its correlations with the test items. This procedure ensures that the test measures only one variable and that each item is measuring that variable.

An example will clarify the point. If we factor mathematical items and obtain a factor loading on items relevant to all the mathematical procedures and techniques, it is reasonable to assume that the factor is one of mathematical ability, being defined by its loading items. However, it is not sufficient to identify factors just by their loadings, and further experimental evidence would be needed before such a factor could be identified as one of mathematical ability.

FIRST-ORDER FACTORS OR PRIMARY FACTORS

These are the factors that emerge from the first factor-analysis of the correlations between the variables. The factors account for or explain the variance of the variables.

TEST VARIANCE

The square of each factor loading tells us the proportion of variance explained by the factor. Thus, if an item loads 0.84 on a factor, this means that approximately 58 per cent of its variance is accounted for by that factor. Similarly, we can square the loadings of any item on all the factors on which it loads, to examine its variance. Thus in the example above, the item might load 0.84 on factor 1 and 0.43 on factor 2, with negligible loadings on the other factors. This would mean that approximately 68 per cent of the variance was explained by factor 1 and a further 17 per cent by factor 2, leaving approximately 15 per cent as error variance.

It is also possible to square the loadings of the items on each factor. If factor 1 has, say, ten items loading on it, the square of these loadings can indicate how much of the item variance is explained by the factor. If the test is a good test, one factor will account for most of the test variance.

SECOND-ORDER FACTORS

Just as variables, such as intelligence and verbal ability, may be correlated, so too may primary factors. It is possible to factor-analyse the correlations between primary factors, and the end result is second-order factors. These too may be correlated, and if these are factored, they yield third orders. It is to be noted that second-order factors load on primary factors and are thus constructs broader than primaries. Indeed, the higher factors are, in terms of order, the broader they are as constructs.

As we have seen, a factor may be regarded as a construct defined by its factor loadings and accounting for a proportion of the variance, contributed by each item, and explaining the intercorrelations. Factor analysis is, therefore, a method of simplifying a matrix of correlations. Royce (1963) conceives first-order factors as intervening descriptive variables – these summarize the intercorrelations. Higher order factors are regarded as hypothetical constructs – summarizing the intervening variables.

ROTATION

This is a major problem in factor analysis, the implications of which I shall discuss later in this chapter. Here I want simply to describe it as clearly as possible.

In factor analysis there is no *a priori* method for determining the position of the factors relative to each other. Consequently, it is possible to rotate the axes relative to each other and thus change the factor loadings. This, however, does not change the *total* variance, only the proportions of it explained by each factor.

SIMPLE STRUCTURE
Given the indeterminacy of factor positions and hence loadings, the obvious point arises of what position the factors should be in. Thurstone (1947) proposed that factors should be rotated to simple structure, defined essentially as the attainment of factors with mainly nil loadings, but with high loadings on the remaining few variables. The essential rationale for simple structure is, as Cattell and Kline (1977) have argued, that of the law of parsimony, Occam's razor – the principle that entities are not to be multiplied beyond necessity; in other words, of explanations that fit a certain set of facts, the most economic and simple is best.

Now, a factor-analytic solution can be considered as an explanation of the facts (the observed correlations). Each rotational position is an alternative explanation and simple structure is, by definition, the simplest in that each factor is deliberately rotated so that it is related, but highly, to a few variables. Although there is considerable agreement among factor analysts that simple structure is a solution to the indeterminacy of factor analysis (e.g. Harman, 1964), there is far less agreement about how this structure is to be obtained. However, this is a technical problem which need not concern us here. Suffice it to say at this point that by maximizing the zero loadings on factors, simple structure can be obtained (Cattell, 1966, has a full discussion of this point). My main reason for brevity of discussion of the techniques for obtaining simple structure is that actually, as we shall see, in test construction we do not always aim at simple structure. This is because the other solution to the indeterminacy of factors is to hypothesize (on the basis of theory) a factor structure and rotate the factors to fit that position as closely as possible. This is essentially what is done in test construction where we ensure that there is going to be a general factor and aim at a solution which creates one. A general or common factor is one that loads on a large number, if not all, variables, and such a solution is therefore antithetical to simple structure. All these points, where relevant to test construction, will be fully discussed below, where the practical techniques are out.

To summarize, simple structure is a factor solution where the factors each have a few high loadings while all the other loadings are as near zero as possible.

(1) *General factor*. This was defined above as a factor with loadings on all or almost all variables.

(2) *Specific factor*. This is a factor specific to a particular variable.
(3) *Group factor*. This is a factor with loadings on a group of variables.
(4) *Orthogonal factors*. These are factors which are uncorrelated. To obtain these the factor axes are rotated to be at right angles to each other. Since they are uncorrelated, if factors have been rotated to the orthogonal position, further second-order or higher order factors cannot be obtained.
(5) *Oblique factors*. These are correlated factors, that is the factor axes are oblique. The correlation between factors is the cosine of the angle between them. Normally, if simple structure as defined by Thurstone (1947) is to be attained, the oblique position is required.

Problems in factor analysis

If the definition of a factor as an operationally defined construct is accepted, it is clear why a number of psychometric authorities – Spearman (1927), Thurstone (1947), Burt (1940), Guilford (e.g. 1959), Cattell (e.g. 1957) and Eysenck (e.g. 1952) – have regarded factor analysis as a most important method for a scientific psychology. To take the complex field of personality as an example, it is possible to conceptualize it in terms of concepts almost defying measurement and hence rational evaluation, such as Eros and Thanatos (Freud, 1920), or instead we can utilize factors, demonstrated to account for certain proportions of variance and mathematically defined – constructs which explain observed correlations. Indeed, as Eysenck (1953) points out, factors are also parsimonious explanations, especially higher order factors.

In fact, an even more important attribute of factors lies in their claimed causal status. Cattell (1966) has argued that the mathematical model of factor analysis, especially when factors are rotated to simple structure, implies that factors are causal agencies. This, however, is an extreme view. On the other hand, there can be no doubt that factors can be causal agencies. Eysenck (1953) gives a nice example of this, arguing that if we were to factor tuberculosis symptoms, a factor would emerge loading on all these, and thus be interpretable as the tubercle causing the disease. However, despite this potential – to produce parsimonious, mathematically defined, constructs of sometimes at least causal status – factor analysis has not been widely adopted in psychology, on account of problems which I shall now briefly examine.

THE INDETERMINACY PROBLEM
This difficulty which we have discussed in our examination of simple structure has led many psychologists who have not worked with factor

analysis to abandon it as a method. Heim (1975) falls into this category. However, the notion of simple structure as the most parsimonious explanation, and the fact that most workers in the field insist that factors and factor structure be replicated (e.g. Cattell, 1973), have largely overcome this objection.

However, Guilford in his work on personality (1959) and more importantly in his work on human abilities (1967) has insisted that orthogonal solutions are in fact more simple. He argues that a set of complex but unrelated factors is a more simple and elegant account of a large set of data, than a set of simple but correlated factors. This argument ultimately is one of judgement, which we need not settle here – I only note it in that it is relevant to the arguments about simple structure. Guilford does not deny the force of simple structure in solving the indeterminacy problem, but his concept of simple structure does differ from the orthodox factorial position.

In brief, this first objection to the indeterminacy of factor analysis can be refuted by insisting on the attainment of simple structure and replicable factors.

THE CIRCULARITY PROBLEM

The circularity problem is stated, for example by Heim (1975) and Mischel (1968) in the form that factor analysis is not useful because you only get out what you put in. There are two points here that require discussion. First, as Eysenck's (1953) example showed, this claim is incorrect. The tuberculosis factor was never inserted into the analysis. The emerging construct was a new concept. Similarly, the general factor, g, underlying performance in several different ability tests was not put into the analysis. It is a construct to account for the observed correlations. On the other hand, if we fail to utilize any tests of ability X, then obviously no factor X can emerge. In this respect factor analysis is no different from any other psychological research method.

Heim (1975) also argues that factor analysis cannot tell us what a particular test measures or whether it measures anything other than the ability to take the test. This ignores the distinction between specific and group factors. A specific factor is one specific to that test alone. If in a factor analysis we find a test loading up with others, the ability cannot be specific to that test. Again, if we find a test that loads highly on those intelligence tests accepted even by Heim as measuring intelligence (her own tests AH5 and AH6, for example; Heim *et al.*, 1970), then *ipso facto* the test also measures intelligence. Heim is wrong here, as so often are critics of factor analysis who have never themselves used the technique.

In conclusion, then, it can be seen that the two fundamental objections to factor analysis as a method can be (and have been in the work of the best psychometrists) answered. Factors rotated to simple structure, replicated, and identified relative to external criteria cannot be criticized on either of the grounds mentioned. All this assumes, of course, that the technical criteria for good factoring (described below, p.186), such as adequate sampling of subject and variables, have been attained.

Special problems of factor analysis in test construction

As should now be clear, the rationale for the use of factor analysis in test construction is to produce items loading on a common factor that accounts for much of their variance. However, there are certain special problems over and above the general difficulties with the technique which were discussed above.

THE CHOICE OF CORRELATION COEFFICIENT

As discussed earlier in our section on item analysis (see p.138), there are three indices which are commonly used for the correlation of dichotomies, the tetrachoric correlation, r_{tet}, the phi coefficient and the G index (Holley, 1973). Phi is a short form of the product-moment correlation, and it yields the same coefficient as would be obtained if standard item scores were entered into the formula for r. This is important because its mathematical equivalence to the product-moment correlation means that the phi coefficient can meaningfully be used as a basis for further statistical analysis. However, as the item endorsement rate of the items in the phi correlation departs from the 50 per cent level, so phi, even if there is perfect correlation, cannot reach 1, the restriction reflecting the difference in the p value for each item. Furthermore, the phi correlation is affected by the polarity of the items (whether in a personality test the keyed response happens to be Yes or No). All these possible sources of fluctuation mean that the factoring of phi coefficients is bound to lead to unreliability of results.

R_{tet} is, if anything, worse, and I shall say little about it other than to argue that it should not be used as a basis for factor analysis. The reason for this is that it is not an algebraic equivalent of the Pearson product-moment correlation which means that the deductions concerning test variance cannot be made from it. In the past, tests were constructed in which tetrachoric correlations were factored (the work of Barnes, 1952, is an example of this), but this procedure was to reduce computation and can be otherwise defended only on the grounds that the tetrachoric correlation is an estimate of the product-moment correlation. Today there is no excuse for using r_{tet}.

Finally, the G index should be mentioned. Developed by Holley and

Guilford (1964), the *G* index has been fully examined and exemplified in a series of studies with the Rorschach test by Holley (1973). Hampson and Kline (1977) have also found it useful in a study of the projective-test scores of criminals. The *G* index has the advantage over phi that it is not affected by the differences in *P* values between items or by item polarity. However, as Levy (1966) points out, its value in item analysis is lessened because it tends to produce factors that are factors of item difficulty. Indeed, Holley himself (1973) recommends that the *G* index is best used in *Q* analysis, the factoring of people rather than items. In view of this it seems that the phi coefficient is the best, albeit not ideal solution. It has less problems than the other coefficient and is used by many of the leading test constructors. It is, of course, numerically equivalent to the product-moment correlation.

LACK OF VARIANCE AMONG THE INTERCORRELATIONS OF TEST ITEMS
Factor analysis yields the clearest results when there is a wide variance among the correlations between variables. It has been shown that simple structure is most easily obtained when there is a large number of zero correlations (Cattell, 1966) – hyperplane stuff – and it is certainly also helpful to the production of well-defined factors if there are some variables (items) in the analysis with high correlations. Now, as Nunnally (1978) points out, these conditions are not met in the item-correlation matrix. If dichotomous items are used, the average correlation is only around 0.2, and there is little variance, although this position is slightly improved if multi-point response items form the matrix. With such correlations clear factors are unlikely to occur.

ROTATIONAL PROBLEMS
The difficulty here is more basic. Simple structure demands, by definition, no general factor. Test construction seeks a general factor. Thus rotation to simple structure is manifestly not sensible. Ideally, a method is required which maximizes the general factor. Since the principal components (unrotated solution) always produces a first general factor followed by bipolars, some test constructors leave the factor matrix unrotated. How this can be resolved in practice is discussed later (see p.187).

IDENTIFYING THE FACTOR
When a set of items loading a common factor has been produced it is still necessary to identify the factor, and this becomes part of the study of the test's validity. Suffice it to say that response sets such as acquiescence (Cronbach, 1946 – the endorsement of the Yes response) and social desirability (Edwards, 1957 – the tendency to put the socially acceptable response) can both lower the validity of apparently unifactorial tests.

Solution to the problems

As a first step I shall set out the practical rules for technically correct factor analyses, to be found in Cattell (1973) and Cattell and Kline (1977), because in these are to be found some of the resolutions to our problems:

(1) Strategic choice of variables.
(2) Wide sampling of people.
(3) The decision of the number of factors should be based upon an objective test.
(4) Fixing communalities.
(5) Unique rotational solution.
(6) Test of significance for simple structure.
(7) Check on degree of invariance of factor pattern across research.
(8) Check on invariance of higher order structure.

These rules were devised as a set of criteria for evaluating factor analyses not simply of tests, and I shall comment on those relevant to test construction. The strategic choice of variables is critical in test construction. If, for example, we are attempting to develop a test of extraversion and by chance we include no items concerned with sociability, then necessarily any emerging factor cannot load on sociability. Our picture of extraversion would be inaccurate. Thus rule 1 *stresses the need for a strict rationale for item writing when constructing factored tests.* Without this the power of factor analysis to unearth basic constructs is set at nought. Factor analysis is antithetical to blind empiricism in test construction. In terms of our model of measurement error, rule 1 implies that we must sample properly from (which in turn involves accurate definition of) the universe of items.

One of the objections to the factor analysis of items, cited previously, was the inevitable lack of variance among the correlations of test items. The choice of subjects who are not homogeneous for the variable we are trying to measure minimizes this objection to some extent, for a heterogenous sample will ensure the maximum possible variance of inter-item correlations. This does not allow us, of course, to break the rule previously discussed under sampling in item analysis, namely that the subjects that we use to try out the test must reflect its intended population. Thus wide sampling will help to ensure an adequate factor analysis.

Rules 3 to 6 cannot be directly applied without great consideration to the factor analysis of items. This is because these are concerned with the attainment of simple structure, which almost inevitably in a broad area, such as ability, temperament or dynamics, will result in a few oblique factors.

However, as Harman (1976) shows, rotational programmes of almost all types, whether orthogonal or not, aim to produce factors with a few high loadings and many negligible loadings. However, the hypothesis underlying the factor analysis of items is that there is one general factor accounting for most of the variance. Since principal-components analysis automatically produces a general factor, followed by a series of bipolar factors in decreasing order of proportion of variance accounted for, in the case of item factor-analysis, it may be permissible to use the unrotated components as a solution. Certainly, rotation to simple structure is not to be undertaken automatically without careful consideration of the particular variable or variables which we are attempting to measure.

The final two rules, 7 and 8, are important because these stress the need for replication of factors before any attempt is made to identify them experimentally – and this concerns both the primary and second-order factors. Of course, if we wish to extract higher order factors, rotation to simple oblique structure is necessary. Obviously, higher orders cannot be obtained from orthogonal principal components.

This discussion of the practical rules for carrying out technically adequate factorial analysis sets the background to the procedures which I shall advocate for the construction of factor-analytic tests. To avoid repetition where the methods are identical to those described in the section on item analysis, I shall simply refer back to them.

Procedures in the construction of factor-analytic tests

ITEMS

All that was said previously applies here. The same items can be submitted to both item analysis and factor analysis. However, there is one further point. In factor-analytic item studies it is often convenient to study more than one variable simultaneously. So, if we needed to construct several tests, all the items could be analysed together. This aids rotation to simple structure since for each test factor the other test items, especially if uncorrelated, act as hyperplanes.

A warning must be given here. If too many items are administered to subjects, boredom and fatigue not to say hostility may produce poor item responses. This is more likely to occur if we are trying out several tests at once.

SAMPLING

All that was argued about sampling for item-analytic studies applies in the factor-analytic case. The only difference is in the size of sample.

According to Nunnally (1978) the ratio of subjects to items should be 10:1. For 100 items we need 1000 subjects. Since separate samples for males and females are necessary, this leads to considerable difficulties in sampling.

However, in my view Nunnally's claim for the need for so many subjects is not justified for the following reasons:

(1) This figure of ten times more subjects than items is certainly larger than that suggested by most other writers. Guilford (1956), for example, is content with a proportion of 2 : 1, as is Vernon (1964). Barrett and Kline (1980) showed in a study of the EPQ items that with a ratio of 2 : 1 the main factors emerged with clarity. A ratio of 3 : 1 gave loadings essentially identical to those with a ratio of 10 : 1. Although 2 : 1 is a minimum figure, studies cannot be impugned for a ratio of this size.

(2) Provided that – as our rules 7 and 8, above, suggest – item factor analyses are replicated the need for huge samples is minimized.

(3) Finally, to obtain replicable factor analyses, the standard errors of the correlations must be reduced as far as is possible. For this reason sample sizes of about 200 are required, even if relatively few items are tried out. The minimum sample size is certainly 100 subjects.

THE FACTOR ANALYSIS OF ITEMS

(1) Compute the number in each sample putting the keyed response to each item. This is identical to computing P in item analysis.

(2) Compute the inter-item phi coefficients.

Here is a possible alternative to phi coefficients. Because of the difficulty of obtaining a clear, simple structure from the intercorrelations between items, Cattell (1973) has advocated item parcelling where groups of items, homogeneous but not necessarily factor-homogeneous, are the basis of the correlation matrix. This is the procedure Cattell and Bolton (1969) adopted in their study of the 16 PF test and the MMPI. However, the problem here (although the parcels are more reliable and provide greater intercorrelations than do items) lies in the formation of the parcels. If the parcels are too long, they become no different from scales, and in any case, separate item analysis of the items within each homogeneous parcel would have to be carried out at a later stage, since no information is obtained on items within parcels. For these reasons, although item parcels seem to overcome the problems of individual items in factor analysis and clear results can be obtained, the loss of information concerning each item is too great to render the method valuable in test *construction*, although it is probably useful in the study of pre-existing scales.

CONCLUSIONS

Thus in the construction of factor-analytic tests it still remains the best policy to (a) compute the P for each item, and (b) compute phi coefficients between all items.

Factor analysis of the phi matrix

The difficulty here, as I have discussed, is that rotation tends to diminish the general factor which emerges from the first principal-components analysis. On the other hand, principal-components analysis is unlikely to yield replicable factors, and any first factor is artifactually general. However, most of the best-known investigators – Cattell, Eysenck and Guilford included – do rotate their factors, and it seems best, despite the difficulties, to attempt to reach simple structure. This is more likely to yield replicable results.

Where possible, construct several different scales at once. This will make rotation to simple structure a viable procedure. Even when only one scale is constructed there are usually enough minor factors to enable a meaningful simple structure to be obtained. As with item analyses, factor analyses should be cross-validated on new samples.

Selection of items after factor analysis

Once the items have been selected by factor analysis, the procedure is exactly as was the case after item analysis, the only difference being the statistical criterion: the factor loading of the item on the test factor should be greater than 0.3, and all other factor loadings of the item should be around zero. I do not use the term 'significance', for the statistical significance of a rotated factor loading remains a cause of disagreement among statisticians.

All other criteria, length, applicability of content, P value of items and the other procedures, computing the K–R20 reliability and Ferguson's delta, the rewriting of items in the light of the comparison of item analyses and the subsequent item retrials, and precisely the same as was the case with the item-analytic method previously discussed.

Failure to form a test

However, when the items have been subjected to factor analysis the causes of the failure to find sufficient adequate items (given that they have been properly rewritten and retried in the light of the first factor analysis) can usually be quickly diagnosed. Thus, if we examine the causes of failure noted in our previous discussion, we can argue as follows.

There is no such variable. If this is the case there will be no factor with clear loadings on a majority of items. Instead, on each factor, there will be a few items loading, and each item will load on several factors. Almost all loadings will be small, and no factor will be easy to interpret. If this occurs, the item pool is best abandoned and new items written. Probably it is more sensible to conclude that the variable has no proper basis and attempts to measure it should cease.

The items are factorially complex. This is immediately revealed by the factor analysis. Items should be selected which load on one factor only. If two factors account for the variance among the items, those items loading on one factor should be separated off and other similar items written. The same procedure should be followed with items loading on the second factor. On item retrial this should yield us two satisfactory tests. It is to be noted that since the factor-analytic results are available from the first computations, this fault can be diagnosed early on before the second item-trial and remedied at that early stage.

Insufficient good items. This is obvious when we have say twelve good items, while all the rest have low loadings on a number of factors. This is remedied by item rewriting in the light of the successful items. This, as with the preceding point can be done relatively early on in the test construction.

Bad items. As was previously discussed this is a last ditch explanation which logically cannot be rejected when items have failed. It can be demonstrated only by rewriting successful items.

Computational steps

It is not practicable even with electronic calculators to factor-analyse a matrix of any size by hand. I shall not therefore set out here the computation of rotated factor analysis. The algebraic procedures in any case are now standardized and are fully described in various textbooks. For a simple description readers are referred to Child (1971). Good accounts with full algebraic details are to be found in Harman (1976) and Tatsuoka (1971).

(1) All responses to each item are tabulated for each person: 1 if the keyed response to the item is given, otherwise 0. In a multi-point response, the score obtained by the subject on each item is given.

(2) These scores are then put into the factor-analysis computing program. This will usually give us correlations, principal components and some form of rotation.

ROTATION

In our discussion of simple structure I argued that simple structure, as defined by Thurstone (1947), ensured replicable results and yielded a parsimonious and hence scientific account of the data. On the other hand, the bias of simple structure against a general factor, the one underlying the test items, made this approach antithetical to the rationale of the test construction. The best method might appear to be one which aimed to produce a general factor (e.g. the Procrustes procedures of Guilford and his colleagues), by which any target factorization is approached as closely as the data allow. Unfortunately, the work of Horn and Knapp (1973) shows that such targeted rotational programmes can produce almost any result.

Wilson and Patterson (1970) in the construction of the conservatism scale left the factor analysis at the principal-components stage. However, this, although a general factor is obtained, relies on the arbitrary algebra of principal components.

In deciding to rotate to simple structure, I have chosen a solution which is very much *faute de mieux*. However, the results are likely to be replicable, and in terms of parsimony are superior to others. It is to be noted that although we want a general factor unless all our items are good (and this is by no means often the case), the general factor applies only to the finished test. Hence simple structure is not as illogical an approach to test construction as might be thought. I thus advocate both orthogonal and oblique rotation. The latter is necessary if higher order factors are required.

Orthogonal rotation. It seems generally agreed among factor analysts that Varimax (Kaiser, 1958) orthogonal rotation leaves little to be desired.

Oblique rotation. As for oblique rotation, there is now a plethora of programs and methods. Gorsuch (1974) and Hakstian (1971) have compared various methods empirically, as have Barrett and Kline (1982a). We found, working with EPQ items that Direct Oblimin gave excellent results and reached simple structure.

Thus I advocate in factor rotations of item factors Varimax if we are trying to construct one scale and Direct Oblimin if more than one scale is being tried out. Such an oblique rotation is, of course, essential if higher order factors are desired.

One further point needs to be mentioned. It is important to rotate only the significant factors. Barrett and Kline (1982a) examined a variety of methods, as Carroll (1983) has done. Cattell's (1966) Scree test seems quite effective, although it should be checked by other methods.

Conclusions

Factor-analytic test construction, as is now obvious, has the advantage over criterion-keyed methods that it produces a unifactorial test. In practice, however, unless huge samples are used, as Nunnally (1978) points out, it is often difficult to obtain clear-cut results. For this reason, Nunnally advocates item-analytic test construction followed by factor analysis of the short set of selected items. Certainly, Barrett and Kline (1982b), working with the EPQ, found a very high correlation between the two methods, so high that in practice the same items would have been selected. Nunnally's view seems the practical, sensible approach. Criterion-keyed methods are only recommended where quick screening or selection procedures are required and psychological meaning or insight is unimportant.

10
Computerized testing, tailored testing, Rasch scaling and cognitive process studies

Computerized testing

Computers, it has been said, have now penetrated into all aspects of society. Psychometrics is no exception, and many psychological tests are now presented and scored on micro-computer. The results, too, are often printed out almost immediately after subjects have taken the test.

There are several somewhat distinct issues here, which I shall treat separately.

The computer presentation of standard tests

In principle any test (virtually) can be presented on computer. Tests using complex visual stimuli such as hidden pictures involve the practical difficulty of having to program these stimuli accurately. Tests using three-dimensional objects cannot as yet be computer-presented.

Any test so presented must be shown to correlate as highly as possible with its original and to be valid, since computer presentation could change its validity.

ADVANTAGES OF COMPUTER PRESENTATION
There are few advantages in presenting a test by computer compared with the standard form. One is that the administration is essentially automatic given that subjects are familiar with computers. This, however, is offset by the fact that testing is individual. If large groups are to be tested at once, large numbers of computers, one per subject, are needed.

Indeed, the presentation of standard tests by computer *per se* has little to be said for it. The true advantage is that it allows automatic scoring and presentation of results and automatic storing of data in any form required, thus facilitating statistical analyses. In other words, it saves punching in the test results.

From the viewpoint of the test constructor therefore, it considerably eases the burden of item trials since all the necessary item and factor analyses can be carried out by program on the data already in the micro-computer, or if there are too many data, these can be easily transferred to mainframe computing facilities.

Indeed, it is possible, by the construction of electronic answer keys that are connected to micro-computers, to have subjects answer typed items on the keyboards, thus still obtaining automatic data collection and analysis without presenting the test on the computer. This allows (on the BBC computer) up to eight subjects to be tested at once. By providing nine answer keys a huge variety of item-formats can be accommodated.

Because computer presentation of test items allows automatic data analysis, it is useful for test construction if a large number of computers or terminals are available. If this is not the case, normal presentation of the items, followed by transfer of the data into a computer, will be quicker and thus more efficient.

Computer-specific test items

The real advantage, yet to be realized, of computerized testing lies in the possibility of using items that could not be presented in any other way. Yet a test can be no better than the sum of its items. Thus a computerized version of a standard test resembles, perhaps, a wonderfully bound edition of a book – but morocco binding would not improve Enid Blyton.

However, computer-specific tests allow the use of items that would be impossible without computers. Great care must be taken in developing computer-specific tests not to create items merely because the computer makes this possible. In other words, there must be a sound rationale for the item.

Some examples of computer-specific test-items together with their rationale are set out below.

(1) Present EPQ items and time-response latency. Rationale: latencies should be large to disturbing items. As a test of validity we might expect high N scorers to show high latency to N items.
(2) Reaction time to responding like me or unlike me to descriptive terms. Rationale: similar to above and related to the Jungian notion of complex.

(3) Reaction times to judging line-length similarity. Rationale: speed of information processing is a measure of g_f (Jensen, 1980).
(4) Choice-reaction time tasks. Rationale: Jensen's work on the relation of these to intelligence (Jensen, 1982).
(5) Rotated shapes – identification. Rationale: obvious measures of spatial ability.
(6) Hidden figures embedded in matrix of dots. Rationale: computer method of producing hidden figures as in embedded-figures test.
(7) Counting dots task with false feedback (negative). Rationale: persistent subjects will continue longer under conditions of being allowed to stop at will.

These are simply examples of how the computer's facilities, especially as a response timer, can be used to develop genuinely new tests and items. Example 7 constitutes an objective computer-test of persistence.

These examples indicate that a range of items beyond the dreams of older psychometrists is now available at the keyboard of the micro-computer. All that is required, as with standard item-writing, is imagination, creativity and a mastery of the technical procedures described in this book.

Although this ability to produce amazing items is a feature of computer testing, this is not the main advantage of computerizing testing. The true power of computerized testing lies in *tailored testing*.

Tailored testing

As the name suggests, tailored testing may be defined as producing tests successfully fitted for each individual taking those tests. Experienced intelligence testers do not have to give all the items in the scales to all subjects. Usually they can gauge the difficulty level and thus give a few items before the subject begins to fail. All the earlier items in the scale can be assumed to be correct. Thus the skill and insight of the tester has enabled him, in these cases, to produce a tailored test of intelligence.

In the case of tailored testing on micro-computer a similar procedure is introduced into the test presentation program. The essence of tailored testing can be described in a series of steps:

(1) Item difficulties (P values from item analyses) are stored together with each item.
(2) These values can be different for different groups – for example, P values for policemen, and for students; different P values for males and females.
(3) These difficulty indices can be Rasch-scaled, in which case they are population-free.

(4) A subject punches in his name, age, sex and profession (any or all of these).

(5) In the simplest tailored testing, the subject is presented with an item of the 50 per cent difficulty level.

(6) If he gets it right, a more difficult item is presented; if wrong, an easier item.

(7) Proceeding in this way, a very brief test can quickly determine his difficulty level.

(8) A more sophisticated program can take into account age, sex and occupation before presenting the first item – utilizing the information in (2).

(9) Alternatively, a brief set of Rasch-scaled items can be presented, thus allowing item and population-free measurement.

Advantages

(1) A relatively short test can accurately assess a subject's ability.

(2) This means subsets of items can be used from the total pool. This is ideal when retesting (as in developmental research) is required.

(3) The brevity is good in applied psychology (where time is at a premium). It is also useful for keeping the interest and attention of subjects, which may wane if tests are too long.

Disadvantages

(1) The main problem with tailored testing lies in the importance placed on the P value or difficulty level. In the sphere of abilities and educational attainment this makes sense. There is a genuine dimension of difficulty underlying maths problems, for example. In other fields such as personality and motivation this is by no means the case, and even if tailored tests of personality could be constructed based on P values, it is possible that their validity would be thereby impaired compared with a normal psychometric test with a large number of items. Research on this point is urgently required.

(2) The final problem concerns the need for highly accurate P values and thus large samples for the normative work, if tailored testing is to be valid. Obviously, if the item statistics are poor, then tailored testing will be inaccurate. For this reason Rasch scaling is often preferred where the item indices are population-free.

Rasch scaling

In chapter 1, I described Rasch scaling and other methods of test construction which used item-characteristic curves. I also described their advantages over normal test construction methods and discussed some of their problems and limitations. Suffice it to repeat here that for some purposes, especially where retesting is important and where there is a well-defined universe of items, Rasch scaling could be useful. I shall now set out the computational steps involved in Rasch scaling test items. I shall describe what is involved using only the simplest form of the Rasch model – simply to enable readers to grasp the essentials. More elaborate methods are left for specialists who may wish to use them for some specific purpose.

Description of the Rasch model

The Rasch model has been described, and we shall not repeat it here. The probability of response in the Rasch model was shown to depend on two parameters: t, a subject's status on the trait, and k, the facility value of an item on eliciting this trait. It is considered essential to carry out Rasch analysis by computer.

Computational steps in Rasch scaling

(1) Give items to subjects.
(2) Sample: Although exponents of Rasch scaling claim that the item analysis is sample-free, Lord (1980) has shown this to be an exaggeration. The first item calibration must be carried out on a representative sample or the calibrations will be inaccurate. Furthermore, to satisfy the statistical demands of maximum likelihood estimations, at least 1000 subjects are necessary. Once the initial calibration has been done, then Rasch scaling is sample-free, but all depends on a large and representative initial sample. This must be, therefore, a minimum of 1000 subjects.
(3) Split the sample into a high-scoring and a low-scoring group – all the former scoring higher than the latter.
(4) Set out the scores for each item for each member of the groups: 1 = correct, 0 = wrong.
(5) Compute the Rasch parameters.
(6) Since a number of different results emerge, these will be examined separately.
(7) The Rasch computer program yields item-difficulty figures

together with their standard errors, for each item separately in the two groups. Items are held to conform to the Rasch model if their difficulty indices are the same (within the boundaries of the standard error) for both groups. It must be remembered that these groups are quite separate (by selection, see step 3) in respect of ability in the latent trait. Normal item indices of difficulty levels would show no overlap for the two groups.

(8) Select those items which show the same level of item difficulty in the two groups.

(9) If insufficient items are available, write others in the light of the successful Rasch items. Unsuccessful items should be studied for purposes of possible correction and to see whether it becomes clear why items failed and thus avoid these item-writing pitfalls.

(10) The item-free measurement of persons. The first nine steps are concerned with Rasch item analyses which yield items showing the same difficulty level in two quite separate samples. However, a second check (and a far more important one, for it is the *raison d'être* of the Rasch model) can now be made. Do different subsets of Rasch items yield the same scores for individuals or not?

(11) To test the item-free measurement: (a) split the Rasch items into two groups, one group containing the easiest items, the other the hardest items. Obviously, the mean score of subjects on two such tests will be different.

(12) By means of the computer program, for each subject find the trait score on each test and its associated standard error of measurement. If the items fit the Rasch model, each subject within the limits of the standard error will receive the same score from each group of items. If subjects do not receive the same score, items will require removal or rewriting.

(13) These items should be cross-validated. The items previously selected by the Rasch analysis should be given to a new sample to test their fit. The test can only be regarded as completed when the items continue to work with new samples.

(14) If subjects fall outside the limits of equivalence on the two tests, this may be due to guessing, which is a major difficulty with the Rasch model (Nunnally, 1978). The remedy here is to improve the quality of the distractors, which will help eliminate it. Actually, a three-parameter model which includes guessing has been developed by Birnbaum (1968), although Wood (1976) has argued that this destroys the dimensionality of the model.

(15) Finally, it is possible to scale the trait-level measurements from Rasch scales which range from +4 to −4, to scores which resemble more closely those from conventional tests. This is important, especially since the main application of the model is in the

educational sphere, and teachers quite rightly are suspicious of scores apparently implying negative ability. The item difficulty estimates and the trait estimates are both probabilities, since the Rasch is a probability model.

The scale used in (15) is the W scale or Wits (Chopin, 1976). From the Rasch equations it can be seen that when the trait ability estimate of an individual exceeds the difficulty level of an item by one unit, the probability of a correct response increases by 2.178. As Wilmott and Fowles (1974) point out, the Wits scale has an arbitrary reference point of 50, reached by the transformation $D = 50 + 4.55 = d$, where D is the new item difficulty and d is the difficulty level computed by the Rasch equation when the mean difficulty level is set at zero.

This scale was chosen because it links subjects' performance and item difficulty in a relatively clear way. For every five points' difference between an individual's trait score and item difficulty, the probability of success increases or decreases three times. This is highly useful in selecting suitable items for item banks for groups of pupils and constitutes a method of tailoring tests to individual needs and still obtaining comparable measures of those individual's abilities.

Evaluation of the Rasch-scaling procedures

I shall go no further into the construction of Rasch scales because there are a number of problems with the method which makes its use, except in certain cases, of limited value. In general, in the twenty years since the model was developed, it has not been widely used despite the apparently considerable advantages it enjoys over tests based on the classical model of error measurement. Certainly, a few enthusiasts – for example, Wright (1967) and Andrich (1978) – continue to support it, but until the points discussed below are satisfactorily answered, Rasch scaling should not replace the classical model.

Are the item statistics sample-free?

In my view the claim that item statistics derived from the Rasch model are item-free is not entirely true. Certainly, items can be found that in the top and bottom scorers showed the same Rasch difficulty-level. However, two issues have to be discussed: first, those items that do not give the same results and, second, the results with other samples.

First, what does it mean when items do not give the same result in the two samples, and thus do not fit the model and are rejected? In some cases guessing can distort the parameters, and certain features of the item writing (perhaps a need for comprehension) can affect behaviour in good compared with less able groups. Often, however, there is no apparent reason for an item's failure.

Second, items are rejected as not fitting the model if they perform differently in the two groups. However, this item calibration might go on for ever if we kept on trying them out on new groups. Chopin (1976), who has considerable experience working with item banks, actually argues that 'no item fits the model exactly'; if you test enough times, all items have to be rejected.

Wood (1976) also points out that item calibration is a major problem in the Rasch-scaling method and that items fitting the model are not easily found, that is, they do vary from sample to sample, and thus are not sample-free.

Take our example – Andrich and Kline (1981) – where personality tests were studied in two populations, Australian and British students. It was therefore argued that Rasch scaling by obtaining item-free person measurement would be useful for cross-cultural study. Certainly, items were found which fitted the model both among the Australian and the British. However, does this mean that we could use them to compare the Eskimos and the Chinese? Clearly, new item calibrations would have to be undertaken. Thus the results are not sample-free.

To demonstrate truly the sample-freeness of Rasch scales, test items from various banks would have to be given to clearly distinctive populations, with item statistics remaining the same. The remarks of Chopin (1976) and Wood (1976) indicate that this cannot be done. If this cannot be done one of the great advantages of the Rasch method disappears. Of course, if sample-free item-measurement is a chimera, so too is its converse, item-free person-measurement, for if the item calibrations are not trustworthy, neither are the trait measurements taking these into account. Thus 'sample-free' is not an accurate description of Rasch scaling. As Wood (1976) argues, following Lord (1980), calibration is best done on properly stratified samples.

Further objections to Rasch scaling

Nunnally (1978) summarizes some further objections to the Rasch model and other similar models based on item-characteristic scores, as discussed in Lord and Novick (1968). Broadly, it is the assumptions underlying these models which are probably not true, a point strongly emphasized by Levy (1973), who argues that to construct psychological tests on the basis of any of these models actually runs counter to the psychological nature of the variables which they are attempting to measure. For example, these models assume that all items have the same discriminating power (given by the steepness of the curve). It is assumed too in latent-trait theory that only one factor accounts for item responses, an assumption which the factor analyses of even those tests which load most clearly on one factor, such as tests of *g*, shows to be wrong. In addition, the influence of guessing remains untreated in the simple two-parameter model.

As the work on item banking by Wood and Skurnick (1969) and Chopin (1976), discussed in that report, indicates most Rasch calibrated tests have dealt with factorially simple tests where the single latent-trait concept is probably not a gross distortion. Even here, however, as we have argued, items do not always fit the model; this alone makes us doubt its value.

A final objection to tests based upon these models is that when conventional tests are administered to subjects and then the same items are subjected to Rasch analysis and scoring, the correlation between the two tests is extremely high, often beyond 0.9. This was certainly the case in the study of the oral personality test carried out by Andrich and Kline (1981), where there was little difference in the results of the two scales.

Uses of Rasch scaling

Despite these objections, Rasch scaling is probably valuable in assembling item pools, for the calibration of items by this method is simpler than carrying it out by constant standardization on large samples. As I have argued, Rasch scales are useful in developmental studies where retesting is required. As I hope is now obvious, it is possible to use Rasch-scaled items presented on a computer. Here, in place of tailored testing based upon item difficulties, a random subset of Rasch scaled items could be presented.

In brief, Rasch scaling may be a useful method of test construction where there is a clearly defined item pool, as in educational testing. However, for reasons that have been fully discussed, I would not support its use in a general procedure for test construction.

Cognitive-processing approach to human abilities

Finally, there is one further approach to the understanding and assessment of human abilities which must be discussed. This is the attempt to link psychometric studies and experimental cognitive psychology. It came into being because of the dissatisfaction with the factorial model on the grounds that a factor, *per se*, fails to explain the nature of the ability. Even if, for example, fluid ability, g_f, regularly appears, its factor loadings do not make manifest the cognitive processes which presumably go on when subjects are displaying their fluid ability in problem solving.

Indeed, this approach to the study of human abilities now dominates the field, as any issue of *Intelligence* makes clear. However, its impact on testing is limited, because, as shall be seen, it is applicable to testing only where the variables are somewhat circumscribed.

Carroll (1980) has listed and classified all the experimental tasks which have been used in cognitive psychology and which might prove to be useful (and in some instances have been shown to be useful) in the elucidation of psychometric ability factors. The essence of the method advocated by Carroll is to attempt to predict performance on factors from performance on these elementary cognitive tasks (ECTs). Since these ECTs are each indicants of mental processing, such work elucidates the nature of the psychometric factors. Hunt (e.g. 1982) and his colleagues, Snow at Stanford and Carroll at Chappel Hill, are leading American exponents of this method.

Before describing it further, an essentially similar experimental analysis of human abilities has been developed by Sternberg and his colleagues in numerous publications, the first text of which (Sternberg, 1977) puts the position in most detail. This is the componential analysis of abilities. In this work, which was originally concerned with the solution of verbal analogies, a model of the performance was drawn up in terms of component processes, and by ingenious experimental presentations of the analogies these components (times to complete certain processes) were measured and the model was put to the test. One of Sternberg's models can predict an individual's performance on verbal analogies to a high degree, and these components are held by Sternberg to be important in a variety of problems. These components are encoding, mapping, application, inference and response.

Kline (1985) has argued that ultimately it may be the case that primary factors could emerge which are essentially processes, and that components and processes as measured by ECTs should not be seen as radically different from each other. The problem with this rapprochement lies in the linearity of the factor model, since it seems clear that processes are not thus combined in performance (Kyllonen *et al.* 1984) nor that individuals necessarily combine their processes in the same way in solving apparently similar problems.

I do not want to discuss further the information-processing approach to the study of human abilities other than to give an indication of some typical ECTs, which are set out below. Most of these ECTs are computer-presented and the measure obtained is a subject's latency of response or some transformation of it.

Some typical ECTs

(1) Perceptual closure tasks. Subjects are required to recognize degraded stimuli.
(2) Auditory form of the visual task above.
(3) Choice reaction time. A subject is primed to respond. His reaction time is compared with a condition where there is no priming.
(4) Lexical decision task. Is a word a real word or not? Is a word a member of a category or not?
(5) Lexical decision task. Is a sentence meaningful?
(6) Name identity and physical identity. Stimuli are judged same or different. Variations in shape and in shape name are played, thus giving access to scoring codes.

I hope that this description is sufficient for readers to understand the essentials of the cognitive-processing approach to human abilities. I shall now turn to the question of how these methods can influence test construction.

Implications for test construction

One consequence of this cognitive-processing approach is, as Carroll (1980) argues, that it might be possible to substitute ECTs for tests, if they could be shown to be reliable and valid. If, for example, access to long-term memory is important in verbal ability, a reliable and discriminatory ECT to measure this would be useful. However, this is not the most important aspect of ECTs, as yet, for test construction as substitutes for tests, although at Exeter we have got so far as to demonstrate that a number of ECTs are reliable (Cooper *et al.*, in press).

Far more important from the viewpoint of test construction is the fact that a good understanding of the cognitive processes involved in abilities allows test constructors to write items with precisely known characteristics, almost by algorithm. I shall take an example from spatial ability because this illustrates both the strengths and weaknesses of the method.

Kyllonen *et al.* (1984) investigated the effects of training and aptitude, *inter alia*, on spatial problem solving. One of the factors studied was item facets, or the characteristics of items – in this case paper-folding items, as used in the paper-folding test (French, Ekstrom and Price, 1963). Studies of performance in this task had revealed that there are three dimensions of item difficulty and that these are important determinants of individual differences in performance. The three facets are: number of folds in an item, number of fold edges obscured from view by subsequent folds, and the number of asymmetric folds (i.e. those that do not bisect a symmetric figure).

The point is, for test construction, that a knowledge of the dimensions of item difficulty (and the strategies used by subjects to solve the problems for these two are related) enables test constructors to write items of precise difficulty level – varying the number of folds, their obscurity and their symmetry. In this way items that are truly measuring the variable, and of given difficulty, can be constructed more or less automatically, by rule. There is little of the *art* of item writing involved here.

It is interesting to note that item difficulty interacts with strategies used by subjects and with the aptitude of the subjects in spatial ability. It is noteworthy that difficulty in this sense is not *normative*, as is the difficulty level of items ascertained by item analysis. It is objective depending upon the complexity of the item facets.

The advantages of this method of item writing, its objectivity and its algorithmic quality are obvious. Usually, however, such item facets can only be developed for relatively narrow and specific variables. A more general or broad factor, such as, say, flexibility, would be difficult to analyse in this way.

Sternberg's work with non-verbal analogies is similar to what has been discussed above in that in his People Pieces Test, analogies were used in which, again, from a knowledge of the model underlying analogy solution, the difficulty level of items can be precisely specified. Thus Sternberg presents schematic figures which can differ on four bivalent features – height, width, sex and clothing colour. According to Sternberg's model, difficulty level of analogies can be precisely manipulated by using varying numbers of feature changes between the terms of the analogy. As with the facet analysis above, difficulty level is objectively defined by the characteristics of the item and is not a normative concept.

I shall conclude this section by arguing that where good models of abilities exist (and as yet these are for rather 'narrow' tasks, such as non-verbal or geometric analogies and spatial-ability items) the facet analysis of items can enable items to be written at precise difficulty levels. However, for many kinds of ability this is not possible, and our own studies of flexibility suggest that there is a long way to go with this kind of variable (May *et al.*, 1986). Nevertheless, for certain ability variables it is possible that facet analysis will be a useful method of item analysis. However, some caution is needed. Since it has been shown that individuals do not always use the same strategies, and that strategies differ among individuals, facet-analytic-developed items will still vary in *obtained* difficulty level, so that for practical test construction, item difficulties will have to be observed and sampled. Nevertheless, it is true that when cognitive-process studies have finally explicated the processing underlying all factors, then facet analysis for items will become possible and item writing will become entirely algorithmic. Until that time the art of item writing discussed in this book is still essential.

A final point should be made. I do not think it is a sensible strategy for a test constructor to attempt to develop a cognitive model of a human ability so that item facets can be used in item writing. This is because such research is bound to be lengthy and there is no guarantee that models can be produced sufficient for the task. Test constructors can use models that have already been shown to work. As has been argued, less precise, more intuitive item-writing is necessary for most abilities. For other test variables, such process-models are indeed remote.

11

Summary and conclusions

In this brief summary I want to lay out the essence of test construction as it has been explicated in this book. It will, I hope, form a guide and an *aide memoir*.

The steps in test construction are:

(1) Consider and set accurate bounds to item content.
(2) Write as many and as varied items, relevant to this content, as is possible.
(3) Try out the items on as large a sample of subjects as is possible.
(4) Item-analyse the test – selecting out good items.
(5) Cross-validate the items on a new sample. Check items for adequate coverage of context.
(6) Compute alpha coefficient.
(7) Validate the test.
(8) Construct norms for the test.
(9) Factor-analyse the items and compare with item analysis.
(10) If that seems successful and useful, write up results into the test handbook.

Other possible methods of test construction are:

(11) Construct a test using criterion groups.
(12) Construct a test using factor analysis rather than item analysis.
(13) Present and automatically score tests on micro-computers.
(14) Present a tailored test on a micro-computer.
(15) Rasch-scale a set of test items.
(16) Tests constructed by these five methods require evidence of validity and reliability. Standardization other than for the Rasch-scale tests is also required.

If these procedures are carried out as described in the relevant chapters of the book, the production of valid and reliable tests is virtually guaranteed. However, a note of caution will end this book.

Simple as good psychometrics are, it remains an unfortunate fact that a huge majority of psychological tests are both invalid and unreliable. Let our tests join the élite minority.

Appendix 1: Item-analysis programs

by Colin Cooper, Department of Psychology, University of Ulster

Program P. MENU

```
 10 REM this version 6/12/85
 20 REM*********************************
 30 REM * ITEM ANALYSIS *
 40 REM (c) Colin Cooper
 50 REM Department of Psychology
 60 REM University of Ulster
 70 REM No responsibility of any kind is
 80 REM accepted for any consequences of
 90 REM using these programs, which are
100 REM offered in good faith but without
110 REM guarantee.
120 REM*********************************
130 missingcode%=999
140 maxitems%=70
150 PROCinitialise(maxitems%)
160 REPEAT
170 VDU3
180 MODE 7
190 PRINT CHR$141;CHR$131;"Item analysis programs"
200 PRINT CHR$141;CHR$131;"Item analysis programs"
210 PRINT CHR$141;CHR$130;"*********************"
220 PRINT CHR$131"Select one of the following options:"'
230 PRINT"(1)  Type in a new data file"
240 IF T%=FALSE PRINT"    or edit an existing data file"
250 PRINT'"(2)  Read an existing data file"
260 PRINT "    for item analysis"'
270 PRINT"(3)  Scale the scores"'
```

```
280 PRINT"(4)  Examine means, s.d.s & "
290 PRINT"     correlations between items"'
300 PRINT"(5)  Examine item-total correlations"
310 PRINT"     & perform classical item analysis"'
320 PRINT"(6)  Correlate items with a criterion"
330 PRINT"     & construct expectancy tables"'
340 PRINT"(7)  Output an r-matrix in SPSS format"
350 REPEAT
360 a$=GET$
370 choice=INSTR("1234567",a$)
380 UNTIL choice>0
390 IF choice=1 CHAIN "P.INPUT"
400 IF choice=2 A%=0:PROCread
410 IF choice=3 CHAIN "P.scaling"
420 IF choice=4 PROCsimplestats
430 IF choice=5 PROCitem_analysis
440 IF choice=6 CHAIN "P.crit"
450 IF choice=7 PROCmatrix_output
460 UNTIL FALSE
470 REM
480 REM
490 REM-------------
500 DEF PROCreadraw
510 REM-------------
520 LOCAL delta,total,a$,a
530 delta=1E-10
540 in=OPENIN("D."+name$)
550 INPUT #in,title$
560 PRINT "This file holds.."'title$
570 INPUT #in,a$
580 N%=VAL(a$): REM No. of variables=N%
590 PRINTCHR$131;"Reading data & computing correlations."
600 IF N%>12 PRINTCHR$129;"This procedure will take a"'CHR$(129)
    ;"considerable time."'
610 PROCset_offsets
620 M%=0:REM no. of subjects
630 REPEAT
640 PRINT
650 M%=M%+1
660 total=0
670 FOR I%=1 TO N%
680 INPUT #in,a$
690 PRINT a$;" ";
700 a=VAL(a$)
```

```
710 mean(I%)=(mean(I%)*(M%-1)+a)/M%
720 sd(I%)=(sd(I%)*(M%-1)+a^2)/M%
730 total=total+a
740 temp(I%)=a
750 NEXT
760 temp(0)=total
770 mean(0)=(mean(0)*(M%-1)+total)/M%
780 sd(0)=(sd(0)*(M%-1)+total^2)/M%
790 FOR I%=0 TO N%
800 FOR J%=I% TO N%
810 PROCsetr(I%,J%,((M%-1)*FNr(J%,I%)+temp(I%)*temp(J%))/M%)
820 NEXT
830 NEXT
840 UNTIL EOF #in
850 CLOSE #in
860 FOR I%=0 TO N%
870 sd(I%)=SQR(sd(I%)-mean(I%)*mean(I%))
880 IF sd(I%)<delta sd(I%)=-delta
890 NEXT
900 FOR J%=0 TO N%: REM rows
910 FOR K%=J% TO N% : REM columns
920 IF FNvalid(K%)=TRUE AND FNvalid(J%)=TRUE PROCsetr(J%,K%,(FNr
    (K%,J%)-mean(K%)*mean(J%))/(sd(K%)*sd(J%))) ELSE PROCsetr
    (J%,K%,missingcode%)
930 NEXT
940 NEXT
950 A%=1: REM shows that a file is loaded
960 x=OPENIN("R."+name$)
970 CLOSE #x
980 IF x=0 THEN PROCwritematrices
990 REM i.e. if "R"+name$ does not exist.
1000 ENDPROC
1010 REM---------------
1020 DEF PROCsimplestats
1030 REM---------------
1040 LOCAL a$,print
1050 CLS
1060 IF A%<>1 THEN PROCread
1070 print=FNyesorno("Do you want the output printed ")
1080 CLS
1090 IF print=TRUE THEN VDU2,14 ELSE VDU3,14
1100 PRINT"MEANS AND STANDARD DEVIATIONS"
1110 PRINT"from a data file called "'title$
    1120 PRINT"holding ";N%; " variables,"
```

```
1130 PRINT"and based on ";M%;" cases."
1140 VDU3
1150 PRINTCHR$136"PRESS SHIFT to continue"''
1160 IF print=TRUE VDU2
1170 PRINT"Item no.      Mean      s.d."
1180 PRINT"_____"
1190 @%=&2030A: REM set field width/2 decimal places
1200 FOR I%=1 TO N%
1210 PRINT I%,mean(I%),SQR(M%/(M%-1))*sd(I%)
1220 NEXT I%
1230 PRINT''"Total",mean(0),SQR((M%/(M%-1)))*sd(0)
1240 PROCprintcorrs
1250 *FX 15,1
1260 REM *FX15,1 clears keyboard buffer
1270 PRINT''"PRESS THE SPACEBAR TO CONTINUE"
1280 REPEAT
1290 a$=GET$
1300 UNTIL a$=" "
1310 @%=10
1320 ENDPROC
1330 REM
1340 REM------------
1350 DEF FNyesorno(a$)
1360 REM------------
1370 LOCAL a%,b$
1380 REPEAT
1390 PRINTa$;
1400 INPUT b$
1410 a%=INSTR("YyNn",LEFT$(b$,1))
1420 IF ASC(b$)<ASC("0") THEN a%=0
1430 IF a%<=0 THEN PRINTCHR$7
1440 UNTIL a%>0
1450 IF a%<3 THEN=TRUE ELSE=FALSE
1460 REM--------------
1470 DEF FNr(i%,j%)
1480 REM--------------
1490 IF i%>j% THEN temp%=i%:i%=j%:j%=temp%
1500 =ray(offset%(i%)+j%-i%)
1510 REM-----------
1520 DEF PROCsetr(i%,j%,val)
1530 REM-----------
1540 IF i%>j% THEN temp%=i%:i%=j%:j%=temp%
1550 ray(offset%(i%)+j%-i%)=val
1560 ENDPROC
```

```
1570 REM------------
1580 DEF PROCinitialise(maxitems%)
1590 REM------------
1600 *FX229,1
1610 DIM mean(maxitems%),sd(maxitems%),
     ray((maxitems%^2+maxitems%)/2)
1620 DIM temp(maxitems%),offset%(maxitems%)
1630 A%=0 :REM shows no file in memory
1640 a=1
1650 T%=FALSE
1660 REM T%=TRUE if tape based.
1670 ans=0:ans2=0
1680 ENDPROC
1690 REM----------
1700  DEF FNvalid(i%)
1710 REM----------
1720 IF sd(i%)<0 THEN =FALSE ELSE =TRUE
1730 REM---------------
1740 DEF FNsd(i%)
1750 REM---------------
1760 =ABS(sd(i%))
1770 REM-----------
1780 DEF PROCprintcorrs
1790 REM-----------
1800 @%=&00020206: REM field width 6, 2 d.p.
1810 width%=6:end%=0
1820 count%=0
1830 REPEAT
1840 start%=end%+1
1850 end%=end%+width%-1
1860 count%=count%+1
1870 PRINT''"Correlations between items"
1880 PRINT"         :::: Section ";count%'
1890 IF N%<end% THEN end%=N%
1900 PRINTTAB(width%);" |";
1910 FOR J%=start% TO end%
1920 PRINTJ%;
1930 NEXT
1940 PRINT'"_____        "
1950 FOR I%=1 TO N%
1960 PRINTI%;" |";
1970 FOR J%=start% TO end%
1980 r=FNr(I%,J%)
1990 IF r <> missingcode% THEN PRINT r; ELSE PRINT "  ????";
```

```
2000 NEXT
2010 PRINT
2020 NEXT
2030 UNTIL end%=N%
2040 ENDPROC
2050 REM----------------
2060 DEF PROCitem_analysis
2070 REM----------------
2080 CLS
2090 LOCAL print,var_of_sum
2100 IF A%<>1 PROCread
2110 PRINT
2120 print=FNyesorno("Print the results")
2130 IF print=TRUE THEN VDU2
2140 PRINT'"Item-total correlations"
2150 PRINT"_____"
2160 VDU14
2170 var_of_sum=sd(0)^2
2180 PROCitem_stats
2190 REPEAT
2200 PRINT"Do you want to remove the item with the"
2210 ans=FNyesorno("lowest correlation with the total")
2220 IF ans=TRUE THEN PROCeliminate(lowest%) ELSE
     ans2=FNyesorno(".. or remove any OTHER item")
2230 IF ans2=TRUE THEN PROCremove_some_item
2240  UNTIL n_items%<3 OR (ans2=FALSE AND ans=FALSE)
2250 VDU3,15
2260 ENDPROC
2270 REM-----------------
2280 DEF PROCeliminate(item%)
2290 REM-----------------
2300 ans=9:ans2=9
2310 PRINT"Item ";item%;" is to be removed at this step."'
2320 sd(item%)=-ABS(sd(item%)): REM flags item as being eliminated
2330 PROCcompute_total_sd(item%)
2340 PROCpartialout(item%)
2350 PROCitem_stats:REM re-compute i/t corrs, alpha, etc.
2360 ENDPROC
2370 REM----------------
2380 DEF PROCitem_stats
2390 REM----------------
2400 LOCAL alpha
2410  n_items%=0
2420 total_var=0
```

```
2430 lowest_r=999
2440 PRINT"Item no.   r with      corrected r"
2450 PRINT"             total      with total"
2460 PRINT"_____"
2470 FOR I%=1 TO N%
2480 IF FNvalid(I%)=TRUE AND FNr(I%,I%)<>missingcode% THEN
     PROCupdate
2490 NEXT
2500 alpha=(n_items%/(n_items%-1))*(1-total_var/sd(0)^2)
2510 @%=&0002030A
2520 PRINT '"Coefficient alpha= ";alpha''
2530 @%=10
2540 ENDPROC
2550 REM----------------
2560 DEF PROCupdate
2570 REM----------------
2580 n_items%=n_items%+1
2590 total_var=total_var+sd(I%)^2
2600 REM now compute item-total corrs corrected for overlap
2610 it_corr=(FNr(I%,0)*FNsd(0)-FNsd(I%))/SQR(FNsd(0)^2+FNsd
     (I%)^2-2*FNr(I%,0)*FNsd(0)*FNsd(I%))
2620 IF it_corr < lowest_r THEN lowest_r=it_corr:lowest%=I%
2630 @%=&00020308
2640 PRINT I%,FNr(I%,0),it_corr
2650 @%=10
2660  ENDPROC
2670 REM--------------
2680 DEF PROCpartialout(item%)
2690 REM--------------
2700 FOR I%=1 TO N%
2710 REM r(xi,tot_excluding_xp)=(r(xi,tot)*s(tot)-r(xi,xp)
     *s(xp))/(sd of total exluding xp)
2720 new_r=(FNr(I%,0)*FNsd(0)-FNr(I%,item%)*FNsd(item%))/sd_of_sum
2730 PROCsetr(I%,0,new_r)
2740 NEXT
2750 sd(0)=sd_of_sum :REM replace the sd with the updated value
2760 ENDPROC
2770 REM------------
2780  DEF PROCcompute_total_sd(item%)
2790 REM------------
2800 LOCAL I%
2810 var_of_sum=var_of_sum - FNsd(item%)*FNsd(item%)
2820 FOR I%=1 TO N%
2830 IF I%<>item% AND FNvalid(I%)=TRUE THEN var_of_sum=var_of
```

```
     _sum-2*FNr(I%,item%)*FNsd(I%)*FNsd(item%)
2840 NEXT
2850 sd_of_sum=SQR(var_of_sum)
2860 REM sd_of_sum=the sd of the sum of the remaining n_items%-1
     items.
2870 ENDPROC
2880 REM--------
2890 DEF PROCwritematrices
2900 REM--------
2910 VDU7
2920 out=OPENOUT("R."+name$)
2930 PRINT#out,title$
2940 PRINT#out,N%
2950 PRINT#out,M%
2960 FOR I%=0 TO N%
2970 PRINT#out,mean(I%)
2980 PRINT#out,ABS(sd(I%))
2990 NEXT
3000  FOR I%=0 TO (N%+1)*(N%+2)/2
3010 PRINT#out,ray(I%)
3020 NEXT
3030 CLOSE #out
3040 ENDPROC
3050 REM--------
3060 DEF PROCread
3070 REM--------
3080 REPEAT
3090 REPEAT
3100 INPUT "Name of data file "name$
3110 UNTIL FNgood_filename(name$)=TRUE
3120 in=OPENIN("D."+name$)
3130 IF in=0 PRINT "File not found."
3140 UNTIL in>0
3150 A%=1: REM shows that data has been read.
3160 a=OPENIN("R."+name$)
3170 IF a<>0 THEN CLOSE#a:PROCreadmatrices ELSE PROCreadraw
3180 ENDPROC
3190 REM--------------
3200 DEF PROCreadmatrices
3210 REM--------------
3220 in=OPENIN("R."+name$)
3230 INPUT #in,title$
3240 INPUT #in,N%
3250 INPUT #in,M%
```

```
3260 PROCset_offsets
3270 FOR I%=0 TO N%
3280 INPUT#in,mean(I%)
3290 INPUT#in,sd(I%)
3300 NEXT
3310  FOR I%=0 TO (N%+1)*(N%+2)/2
3320 INPUT #in,ray(I%)
3330 NEXT
3340 CLOSE #in
3350 ENDPROC
3360 REM------------
3370 DEF PROCset_offsets
3380 REM------------
3390 offset%(0)=0
3400 tot%=0
3410 FOR I%=1 TO N%
3420 offset%(I%)=offset%(I%-1)+N%+2-I%
3430 NEXT
3440 ENDPROC
3450 REM--------------
3460 DEF PROCmatrix_output
3470 REM--------------
3480 LOCAL a,out
3490 CLS
3500 @%=&0102070A :REM "F10.7"
3510 IF A%=0 PROCread
3520 a=FNyesorno("File ""S."+name$+""" is to be written out. OK")
3530 IF a=FALSE PROCread
3540 out=OPENOUT("S."+name$)
3550 FOR I%=1 TO N%
3560 FOR J%=1 TO N%
3570 a$=STR$(FNr(I%,J%))
3580 IF LEN(a$)<10 REPEAT:a$=" "+a$:UNTIL LEN(a$)=10
3590 FOR K%=1 TO LEN(a$)
3600 BPUT #out,ASC(MID$(a$,K%,1))
3610 NEXT
3620 IF J% MOD 8=0 OR J%=N% BPUT#out,13
3630 NEXT
3650 CLOSE #out
3660 ENDPROC
3670 REM------------------
3680  DEF PROCremove_some_item
3690 REM------------------
3700 REPEAT
```

```
3710 REPEAT
3720 INPUT "Remove which item" it%
3730 UNTIL it%<=N% AND it%>0
3740 UNTIL FNvalid(it%)=TRUE
3750 PROCeliminate(it%)
3760 ENDPROC
3770 REM---------------
3780 DEF FNgood_filename(name$)
3790 REM---------------
3800 IF LEN(name$)<8 AND LEN(name$)>0 AND INSTR(name$,".")=0
     THEN =TRUE
3810 PRINTCHR$7;CHR$129;"File name too long, null, or"
3820 PRINTCHR$129;"contains a "".""". Try another name."
3830 =FALSE
```

Program P. SCALING

```
 10 REM**********************************
 20 REM***ITEM  SCALING  ROUTINES*********
 30 REM*** Colin Cooper 31/8/85  *********
 40 REM**********************************
 50 A%=0: REM SHOWS NO DATA FILE LOADED.
 60 MODE 7
 70 @%=10
 80 max_subs%=2000
 90 DIM mean(1),sd(1),temp(1),score(max_subs%)
100 REM MODE 7
110 REPEAT
120 PROCmenu
130 UNTIL FALSE
140 REM
150 REM-------------
160 DEF PROCread
170 REM-------------
180 CLS
190 REPEAT
200 REPEAT
210 PRINTCHR$130;
220 INPUT "Name of data file "name$
230 UNTIL FNgood_filename(name$)=TRUE
240 in=OPENIN("D."+name$)
250 IF in=0 PRINT"File not found."
260 UNTIL in>0
```

```
270 PRINT'CHR$(131);"Reading ::: please wait"'
280 REM
290 INPUT #in,title$
300 PRINT "This file holds.."'title$''
310 INPUT #in,a$
320 N%=VAL(a$): REM No. of variables=N%
330 M%=0:REM no. of subjects
340 REPEAT
350 M%=M%+1
360 total=0
370 FOR I%=1 TO N%
380 INPUT #in,a$
390 total=total+VAL(a$)
400 NEXT
410 score(M%)=total
420 mean(0)=(mean(0)*(M%-1)+total)/M%
430 sd(0)=(sd(0)*(M%-1)+total^2)/M%
440 UNTIL EOF #in
450 CLOSE #in
460 sd(0)=SQR(sd(0)-mean(0)*mean(0))
470 IF sd(0)<0.000001 sd(0)=1E12
480 PROCsort_scores
490 A%=1
500 ENDPROC
510 REM
520 REM------------
530 DEF FNyesorno(a$)
540 REM------------
550 LOCAL a%,b$
560 REPEAT
570 PRINTa$;
580 INPUT b$
590 a%=INSTR("YyNn",LEFT$(b$,1))
600 IF ASC(b$)<ASC("O") THEN a%=0:PRINTCHR$(7)
610 UNTIL a%>0
620 IF a%<3 THEN=TRUE ELSE =FALSE
630 REM------------
640 DEF PROCsort_scores
650 REM------------
660 PRINT'"Sorting ::: please wait"'
670 REM Shell sort.
680 G%=M%
690 REPEAT
700 G%=INT(G%/2)
```

```
710 FOR I%=1 TO M%-G%
720 FOR J%=I% TO 1 STEP -G%
730 J1%=J%+G%
740 IF score(J%)>score(J1%) THEN W=score(J%):score(J%)=score
    (J1%):score(J1%)=W ELSE J%=0
750 NEXT
760 NEXT
770 UNTIL G%=0 OR G%=1
780 ENDPROC
790 REM
800 REM----------
810 DEF PROCprint_centiles
820 REM----------
830 IF A%<>1 PROCread
840 print=FNyesorno("Print the centiles")
850 CLS
860 PRINTCHR$131;CHR$141;"CENTILE SCORES"
870 PRINTCHR$131;CHR$141;"CENTILE SCORES"
880 PRINTCHR$131" **************"''
890 IF print=TRUE THEN VDU2,14 ELSE VDU3,14
900 PRINTCHR$131"Computed from a file called ";name$;";"'title$'
910 @%=&0002020A
920 VDU3
930 IF print=TRUE VDU2
940 PRINTCHR$131"Raw scores range from ";score(1);" to"
950 PRINTCHR$131score(M%);" with a mean of ";mean(0)
960 PRINTCHR$131"and an s.d. of ";sd(0);"."''
970 PRINTCHR$136;CHR$131;"(press SHIFT to continue)"''
980 PRINTCHR$130" Centile      Corresponding raw score"
990 PRINTCHR$130" _____"''
1000 FOR I=5 TO 100 STEP 5
1010 PRINTI,FNcum_pct(I)
1020 NEXT
1030 @%=10
1040 PRINT'CHR$131;"(remember that the median is the"
1050 PRINTCHR$131;" the 50 centile)"'
1060 VDU3,15
1070 PROCspacebar
1080 CLS
1090 ENDPROC
1100 REM
1110 REM-----------
1120 DEF PROCzscores
1130 REM-----------
```

```
1140 IF A%<>1 PROCread
1150  LOCAL z,print,newmean,newsd
1160 @%=&0002030A
1170 print=FNyesorno("Print transformed z-scores")
1180 REPEAT
1190 CLS
1200 IF print=TRUE VDU2,14 ELSE VDU3,14
1210 PRINTCHR$141;CHR$134;"Z-scores"
1220 PRINTCHR$141;CHR$134;"Z-scores"
1230 PRINTCHR$134;" ********"''
1240 PRINTCHR$134"Computed from a file called ";name$;";"'title$''
1250 PRINTCHR$134;"These scores originally had a"
1260 PRINTCHR$134;"mean of ";mean(0);" & a s.d. of ";sd(0);"."''
     ;CHR$134
1270 INPUT "Rescale them to have which mean";newmean
1280 REPEAT
1290 PRINTCHR$134;
1300 INPUT "..and which (sample) s.d.",newsd
1310 UNTIL newsd>0
1320 VDU3
1330 PRINT''CHR$(136)"Press SHIFT to continue"''
1340 IF print=TRUE VDU2
1350 PRINTCHR$134;"Original    z-score   transformed"
1360 PRINTCHR$134;" score                z-score"
1370 PRINTCHR$134;"_____"
1380 FOR I%=1 TO M%
1390 z=(score(I%)-mean(0))/sd(0)
1400 PRINTscore(I%),z,z*newsd+newmean
1410 NEXT
1420 PRINT''
1430 UNTIL FNyesorno("Rescale again")=FALSE
1440 @%=10
1450 VDU3,15
1460 CLS
1470 ENDPROC
1480 REM------------
1490 DEF PROCT_scores
1500 REM------------
1510 LOCAL print,tscore,last_tscore
1520 IF A%<>1 PROCread
1530 print=FNyesorno("Print T-scores ")
1540 CLS
1550 IF print=TRUE THEN VDU2,14 ELSE VDU3,14
1560 PRINTCHR$130;CHR$141;"T - SCORES"
```

```
1570 PRINTCHR$130;CHR$141;"T - SCORES"
1580 PRINTCHR$132;" **********"''
1590 PRINTCHR$134"Computed from a file called ";name$;";"'title$''
1600 PRINTCHR$134;CHR$136;"Press SHIFT when the"
1610 PRINTCHR$134;CHR$136;"screen is full."''
1620 PRINTCHR$134;"Raw score    T-equivalent"
1630 PRINTCHR$134;"_____"
1640 @%=&0002020A
1650 last_tscore=-4
1660 FOR I%=1 TO M%
1670 tscore=-4:diff=last_tscore-tscore
1680 IF score(I%+1)<> score(I%) THEN tscore=FNinverse_normal
     (I%/(M%+1)):PRINT score(I%),tscore*10+50
1690 NEXT
1700 @%=10
1710 VDU3,15
1720 PROCspacebar
1730 ENDPROC
1740 REM-----------
1750 DEF PROCmenu
1760 REM-----------
1770 CLS
1780 PRINTCHR$134;CHR$141;"Item scaling"
1790 PRINTCHR$134;CHR$141;"Item scaling"
1800 PRINTCHR$134;CHR$141;"*************"'''
1810 PRINTCHR$131;"(1)";CHR$130;"  Read a data file"'
1820 PRINTCHR$131;"(2)";CHR$130;"  Examine z-scores"'
1830 PRINTCHR$131;"(3)";CHR$130;"  Examine centile scores"'
1840 PRINTCHR$131;"(4)";CHR$130;"  Examine T-scores"'
1850 PRINTCHR$131;"(5)";CHR$130;"  Return to main menu"'''
1860 PRINTCHR$134;"Select which option?"
1870 REPEAT
1880 a$=GET$
1890 a%=INSTR("12345",a$)
1900 UNTIL a%>0
1910 IF a%=1 PROCread
1920 IF a%=2 PROCzscores
1930 IF a%=3 PROCprint_centiles
1940 IF a%=4 PROCT_scores
1950 IF a%=5 A%=0:CHAIN"P.MENU"
1960 ENDPROC
1970 REM--------------
1980 DEF FNinverse_normal(prob)
1990 REM--------------
```

```
2000 Q=0.5-ABS(prob-0.5)
2010 t=SQR(-2*LN(Q))
2020 top=2.30753+0.27061*t
2030 bottom=1+0.99229*t+0.04481*t^2
2040 =(t-top/bottom)*SGN(prob-0.5)
2050 REM---------
2060 DEF FNcum_pct(I)
2070 REM---------
2080 =score(INT(I*M%/100))
2090 REM-------------
2100 DEF PROCspacebar
2110 REM-------------
2120 LOCAL a$
2130 *FX15,1
2140 REM clear keyboard buffer
2150 PRINT"Press the spacebar to continue..";
2160 REPEAT
2170 a$=GET$
2180 UNTIL a$=" "
2190 ENDPROC
2200 REM---------------
2210 DEF FNgood_filename(a$)
2220 REM---------------
2230 IF LEN(a$)>0 AND LEN(a$)<8 AND INSTR(a$,".")=0 THEN =TRUE
2240 PRINTCHR$(7);CHR$(129);"File name too long, null, or contains"
2250 PRINTCHR$(129);"a ""."".   Try another name."
2260 =FALSE
```

Program P. INPUT

```
 10 REM********************
 20 REM**DATA ENTRY*******
 30 REM**CC 29/11/85 *****
 40 REM********************
 50 maxitems%=250
 60 DIM score$(maxitems%),work%(maxitems%)
 70 DIM cat 5
 80 MODE 7
 90 REPEAT
100 PROCmenu
110 UNTIL FALSE
120 STOP
130 REM----------
```

```
140 DEF PROCinput
150 REM----------
160 LOCAL outfile$,present,N$
170 PRINTCHR$134;"These data will be stored in a file."''
180 PRINTCHR$134;"What do you want to call this"
190 PRINTCHR$134;"file?";CHR$130;
200 REPEAT
210 REPEAT
220 INPUT ""outfile$
230 UNTIL FNgood_filename(outfile$)=TRUE
240 UNTIL FNoutexists(outfile$)=FALSE
250 out=OPENOUT("D."+outfile$)
260 PRINT''CHR$134;"Now briefly describe what these data"
270 PRINTCHR$134;"are ";CHR$130;
280 INPUT title$
290 REPEAT
300 PRINTCHR$134;"How many items?";CHR$130;
310 INPUT ""N$
320 IF VAL(N$)<=maxitems% THEN N%=VAL(N$) ELSE VDU7:N%=0:PRINT
    "Too big!"
330 UNTIL N%>0 AND N%<=maxitems%
340 DIM data$(N%)
350 PRINTCHR$134;"Now type in the ";N%;"variables for"
360 PRINTCHR$134;"each person."''
370 PRINT #out,title$
380 PRINT #out,STR$(N%)
390 person%=0
400 end_of_file=FALSE
410 REPEAT
420 person%=person%+1
430 PRINT''CHR$131;"Subject no. ";person%
440 SOUND 1,-7,200,5
450 I%=0
460 REPEAT
470 PROCprint_reminder
480 I%=I%+1
490 PRINT CHR$134;"Score on item ";I%;" = ";CHR$130;
500 INPUT a$
510 IF LEFT$(a$,3)="END" OR LEFT$(a$,3)="end"
    THEN end_of_file=TRUE
520 number=FNcheck_if_number(a$)
530 IF end_of_file=FALSE AND number=FALSE THEN PROCerror
540 IF number=TRUE THEN data$(I%)=a$
550 UNTIL I%=N% OR end_of_file=TRUE
```

```
560 IF end_of_file=FALSE THEN FOR J%=1 TO N%:PRINT#out,data$(J%)
    :NEXT
570 UNTIL end_of_file=TRUE
580 CLOSE #out
590 CHAIN "P.MENU"
600 REM
610 REM------------
620 DEF FNoutexists(title$)
630 REM------------
640 LOCAL dummy
650 IF T%=TRUE THEN =FALSE : REM if a tape based system
660 dummy=OPENUP("D."+title$)
670 IF dummy=0 THEN =FALSE
680 CLOSE #dummy
690 PRINTCHR$129;"This file already exists."
700 PRINTCHR$129;"Try another name"
710 =TRUE
720 REM---------
730 DEF PROCmenu
740 REM---------
750 LOCAL a$
760 CLS
770  PRINTCHR$134;CHR$141;"Data entry/editing"
780 PRINTCHR$134;CHR$141;"Data entry/editing"
790 PRINTCHR$134;CHR$141;"*******************"''
800 PRINTCHR$134;"(1)   Type in a new file"'
810 PRINTCHR$134;"(2)   Edit an existing file"'
820 PRINTCHR$134;"(3)   See which data files are"
830 PRINTCHR$134;"         on this disc"'
840 PRINTCHR$134;"(4)   Return to main menu"''
850 REPEAT
860 a$=GET$
870 UNTIL INSTR("1234",a$)>0
880 IF a$="1" PROCinput
890 IF a$="2" PROCedit
900 IF a$="3" PROCcat
910 IF a$="4" CHAIN "P.MENU"
920 ENDPROC
930 REM----------
940 DEF PROCedit
950 REM----------
960 LOCAL a$
970 CLS
980 IF T%=TRUE THEN PRINTCHR$(7):ENDPROC
```

```
 990 PRINTCHR$131;CHR$141;"Editing options"
1000 PRINTCHR$131;CHR$141;"Editing options"
1010 PRINTCHR$131;CHR$141;"***************"''
1020 PRINT CHR$131;"(1)    Inspect data file case by case"'
1030 PRINTCHR$131;"(2)    Search for values"'CHR$131;"
     above a given maximum"'
1040 PRINTCHR$131;"(3)    As (2) but on only"'CHR$131;"
     some variables"'
1050 REPEAT
1060 a$=GET$
1070 UNTIL INSTR("123",a$)>0
1080 PROCopen_files
1090 IF a$="1" PROCcasewise
1100 IF a$="2" PROCsearchformax(0)
1110 IF a$="3" PROCsearchformax(1)
1120 ENDPROC
1130 REM-------------
1140 DEF PROCopen_files
1150 REM-------------
1160 CLS
1170 REPEAT
1180 REPEAT
1190 INPUT "Name of existing file",infile$
1200 UNTIL FNgood_filename(infile$)=TRUE
1210 UNTIL OPENIN("D."+infile$)>0
1220 in=OPENIN("D."+infile$)
1230 INPUT #in,title$
1240 INPUT #in,N$
1250 N%=VAL(N$)+1E-6
1260 PRINT''
1270 REPEAT
1280 REPEAT
1290 REPEAT
1300 INPUT "Name of file to hold edited data",outfile$
1310 UNTIL FNgood_filename(outfile$)=TRUE
1320 UNTIL outfile$<>infile$
1330 UNTIL FNoutexists("D."+outfile$)=FALSE
1340 out=OPENOUT("D."+outfile$)
1350 PRINT#out,title$
1360 PRINT#out,STR$(N%)
1370 ENDPROC
1380 REM
1390 REM-----------
1400 DEF PROCcasewise
```

```
1410 REM----------
1420 LOCAL case%,a
1430 case%=0
1440 REPEAT
1450 case%=case%+1
1460 FOR I%=1 TO N%
1470 INPUT #in,score$(I%)
1480 NEXT
1490 REPEAT
1500 CLS
1510 PRINTCHR$134;"Case no. ";case%
1520 FOR I%=1 TO (N% DIV 4)+1
1530 PRINT
1540 FOR J%=1 TO 4
1550 K%=(I%-1)*4+J%
1560 IF K%<=N% PRINT TAB((J%-1)*10)CHR$130"V";STR$(K%)"=";
     CHR$131;score$(K%);
1570 NEXT
1580 NEXT
1590 PRINT''
1600 a=FNyesorno("Alter any value")
1610 IF a=TRUE THEN PROCalter
1620 UNTIL a=FALSE
1630 FOR I%=1 TO N%
1640 PRINT #out,score$(I%)
1650 NEXT
1660 UNTIL EOF #in
1670 CLOSE #in
1680 CLOSE #out
1690 ENDPROC
1700 REM------------
1710 DEF PROCalter
1720 REM----------
1730 LOCAL v%,a$,v$
1740 REPEAT
1750 REPEAT
1760 INPUT "No. of variable to alter"v$
1770 v%=VAL(v$)
1780 UNTIL FNcheck_if_number(v$)=TRUE
1790 UNTIL v%>0 AND v%<=N%
1800 PRINTCHR$129;"Var. ";v%;"=";score$(v%);" ::: New value =";
1810 REPEAT
1820 INPUT a$
1830 score$(v%)=a$
```

```
1840 UNTIL FNcheck_if_number(a$)=TRUE
1850 ENDPROC
1860 REM-----------
1870 DEF FNyesorno(A$)
1880 REM-----------
1890 LOCAL a%,b$
1900 REPEAT
1910 PRINT A$;
1920 INPUT b$
1930 a%=INSTR("YyNn",LEFT$(b$,1))
1940 IF ASC(b$)<ASC("0") THEN a%=0
1950 UNTIL a%>0
1960 IF a%<3 THEN =TRUE ELSE =FALSE
1970 REM-----------
1980  DEF FNcheck_if_number(a$)
1990 REM-----------
2000 LOCAL number,J%,b
2010 number=TRUE
2020 FOR J%=1 TO LEN(a$)
2030 b=ASC(MID$(a$,J%,1))
2040 IF b<ASC("-") OR b>ASC("9") OR b=ASC("/") THEN number=FALSE
2050 NEXT
2060 =number
2070 REM----------------
2080 DEF PROCsearchformax(n%)
2090 REM----------------
2100 LOCAL person%
2110  IF n%>0 PROCaskformax ELSE PROCset_array
2120 person%=0
2130 REPEAT
2140 person%=person%+1
2150 FOR I%=1 TO N%
2160 INPUT #in,score$(I%)
2170 NEXT
2180 FOR I%=1 TO N%
2190 IF work%(I%)<VAL(score$(I%)) PROCshow
2200 NEXT
2210 FOR I%=1 TO N%
2220 PRINT#out,score$(I%)
2230 NEXT
2240 UNTIL EOF#in
2250 CLOSE #in
2260 CLOSE #out
2270 ENDPROC
```

```
2280 REM----------------
2290 DEF PROCaskformax
2300 REM----------------
2310 LOCAL I,A$,a
2320 CLS
2330 FOR I=1 TO N%
2340 PRINT"Item ";I;
2350 REPEAT
2360 INPUT " ::: max. allowable score = "A$
2370 UNTIL FNcheck_if_number(A$)=TRUE
2380 a=VAL(A$)
2390 work%(I)=a
2400 NEXT
2410 ENDPROC
2420 REM------------
2430 DEF PROCshow
2440 REM------------
2450 LOCAL A$
2460 PRINTCHR$129;"Case ";person%;" item ";I%;"=";score$(I%);":
     ";CHR$131;
2470 REPEAT
2480 INPUT "Correct value=" A$
2490 UNTIL FNcheck_if_number(A$)=TRUE
2500 score$(I%)=A$
2510 ENDPROC
2520 REM-----------
2530 DEF PROCset_array
2540 REM-----------
2550 LOCAL a$
2560 REPEAT
2570 INPUT "What is the max. score" a$
2580 UNTIL FNcheck_if_number(a$)=TRUE
2590 FOR I%=1 TO N%
2600 work%(I%)=VAL(a$)
2610 NEXT
2620 ENDPROC
2630 REM-------------
2640 DEF FNgood_filename(A$)
2650 REM-------------
2660 IF INSTR(A$,".")=0 AND LEN(A$)<8 AND LEN(A$)>0 THEN =TRUE
2670 PRINTCHR$(7);CHR$(129);"File name too long or"
2680 PRINTCHR$(129);"contains a "".""".  Try another"
2690 =FALSE
2700 REM------------------
```

```
2710 DEF PROCprint_reminder
2720 REM-----------------
2730 LOCAL xpos,ypos
2740 xpos=POS
2750 ypos=VPOS
2760 PRINT TAB(0,0)STRING$(40," ")
2770 PRINT TAB(0,1)STRING$(40," ")
2780  PRINT TAB(0,0);CHR$133;CHR$136;"Type  END  to finish"
2790 PRINT TAB(xpos,ypos);
2800 ENDPROC
2810 REM-------------
2820 DEF PROCerror
2830 REM-------------
2840 VDU7
2850 I%=I%-1
2860 PRINT'CHR$(129);CHR$(136);"***INVALID DATA***"
2870 PRINT'CHR$(129);"Re-enter this score."
2880 ENDPROC
2890 REM------------
2900 DEF PROCcat
2910 REM------------
2915 IF T%=TRUE ENDPROC
2920 ?cat=ASC"."
2930 cat?1=&0D
2940 X%=cat MOD 256
2950 Y%=cat DIV 256
2960 CALL &FFF7
2970 CLS
2980 PRINTCHR$131;"Data files on this disc are :"'
2990 FOR I%=&0EOF TO &0EFF STEP 8
3000 IF FNgetbyte(I%)=ASC("D") THEN PROCprint_title
3010 NEXT
3020 PRINT''CHR$133;"Press the spacebar to continue.."
3030 REPEAT
3040 A$=GET$
3050 UNTIL A$=" "
3060 ENDPROC
3070 REM----------------
3080 DEF PROCprint_title
3090 REM----------------
3100 PRINTCHR$(130)
3110 FOR J%=I%-7 TO I%-1
3120 PRINT CHR$(FNgetbyte(J%));
3130 NEXT
```

```
3140 ENDPROC
3150 REM------------
3160 DEF FNgetbyte(a%)
3170 REM------------
3180 oldA%=A%:oldX%=X%:oldY%=Y%
3190 cat?2=&FF
3200 cat?3=&FF
3210 cat?1=a% DIV 256
3220 ?cat=a% MOD 256
3230 A%=5
3240 X%=cat MOD 256
3250 Y%=cat DIV 256
3260 CALL &FFF1
3270 A%=oldA%:X%=oldX%:Y%=oldY%
3280 =cat?4
```

Program P. CRIT

```
 10 REM****************
 20 REM**ITEM-CRIT R **
 30 REM**CC 08/12/85
 40 REM****************
 50 REM
 60 criteria_read=FALSE
 70 nitems%=100
 80 maxcases%=270
 90 max_crit_level%=6
100  max_item_level%=12
110 DIM mean(nitems%),sd(nitems%),r(nitems%),work(maxcases%),
    criterion(maxcases%)
120 DIM prob_table(max_item_level%,max_crit_level%)
130 MODE 7
140 A%=0: REM NO data file loaded
150 print=FALSE
160 REPEAT
170 PROCmenu
180 UNTIL FALSE
190 REM
200 REM---------
210 DEF PROCmenu
220 REM---------
230 CLS
240 PRINTCHR$131;CHR$141;"Criterion keying & Contingency Tables"
```

```
250 PRINTCHR$131;CHR$141;"Criterion keying & Contingency Tables"
260 PRINTCHR$131;CHR$141;"***********************************"
270 PRINT''"(1)  Correlate items with a criterion"''
280 PRINT"(2)   Display expectancy tables"''
290 PRINT"(3)   Return to main menu"''
300 REPEAT
310 A$=GET$
320 UNTIL INSTR("123",A$)>0
330 IF A$="3" THEN CHAIN"P.MENU"
340  IF criteria_read=FALSE THEN PROCfind_file :
    PROCread_criteria_etc
350 IF A$="1" THEN PROCcrit_corr
360 IF A$="2" THEN PROCexpectancy
370 ENDPROC
380 REM
390 REM------------
400 DEF PROCcrit_corr
410 REM------------
420 PROCprint_corrs
430 PROCselect_items
440 ENDPROC
450 REM
460 REM-------------
470 DEF PROCfind_file
480 REM------------
490 criteria_read=TRUE
500 REM shows that data have been read
510 REPEAT
520 INPUT "Read data from which file" in$
530  IF FNvalidname(in$)=TRUE THEN in=OPENUP("D."+in$) ELSE in=0
540 IF in=0 PRINTCHR$129;"File not found."
550 UNTIL in>0
560 INPUT #in,title$
570 INPUT #in,N$
580  N%=VAL(N$)+0.5
590 ENDPROC
600 REM-------------------
610 DEF PROCoutputitems
620 REM-------------------
630 REPEAT
640 REPEAT
650 PRINT"Write out these items into"'"which file ";
660 INPUT out$
670 UNTIL FNvalidname(out$)=TRUE
```

```
 680 out=OPENIN("D."+out$)
 690 IF out>0 CLOSE #out:PRINTCHR$129;CHR$7;"File exists.
     Try another title"'
 700 UNTIL out=0
 710 out=OPENOUT("D."+out$)
 720 outtitle$="<Subset of "+in$+" holding only items "
 730 PROCwrite_data
 740 ENDPROC
 750 REM
 760 REM-------------
 770 DEF PROCread_criteria_etc
 780 REM-------------
 790 LOCAL item%
 800 CLS
 810 PROCprint("criteria")
 820 biggest_criterion=-1E20
 830 smallest_criterion=1E20
 840 M%=0
 850 REPEAT
 860 M%=M%+1
 870 REPEAT
 880 PRINTCHR$131;"Criterion score of subject ";M%;"=";CHR$130;
 890 INPUT a$
 900 UNTIL FNcheck_if_number(a$)=TRUE
 910 crit=VAL(a$)
 920 criterion(M%)=crit
 930 IF crit<smallest_criterion THEN smallest_criterion=crit
 940 IF crit>biggest_criterion THEN biggest_criterion=crit
 950 mean(0)=(mean(0)*(M%-1)+crit)/M%
 960 sd(0)=(sd(0)*(M%-1)+crit*crit)/M%
 970 FOR item%=1 TO N%
 980 INPUT #in,a$
 990 a=VAL(a$)
1000 mean(item%)=(mean(item%)*(M%-1)+a)/M%
1010 sd(item%)=(sd(item%)*(M%-1)+a*a)/M%
1020 r(item%)=(r(item%)*(M%-1)+a*crit)/M%
1030 NEXT item%
1040 UNTIL EOF #in
1050 CLOSE #in
1060 FOR I%=0 TO N%
1070 sd(I%)=SQR(sd(I%)-mean(I%)^2)
1080 IF sd(0)ANDsd(I%)>0 r(I%)=(r(I%)-mean(I%)*mean(0))/(sd(0)
     *sd(I%)) ELSE r(I%)=0
1090 NEXT
```

```
1100 VDU3
1110 ENDPROC
1120 REM---------------
1130 DEF FNcheck_if_number(a$)
1140 REM---------------
1150 LOCAL number,J%,b
1160 number=TRUE
1170 FOR J%=1 TO LEN(a$)
1180 b=ASC(MID$(a$,J%,1))
1190 IF b<ASC("-") OR b>ASC"9" OR b=ASC"/" THEN number=FALSE
1200 NEXT
1210 IF number=FALSE VDU7
1220 =number
1230 REM
1240 REM-------------
1250 DEF PROCprint_corrs
1260 REM---------------
1270 PROCprint("correlations")
1280 VDU3
1290 CLS
1300 IF print=TRUE VDU2
1310 PRINTtitle$'
1320 PRINT"Correlations between items & criterion"
1330 PRINT"_____        "
1340 delta=0.01
1350 FOR J%=0 TO (N% DIV 4)
1360 PRINT
1370   FOR I%=1 TO 4
1380 item%=J%*4+I%
1390 IF item%<=N% PRINT TAB((I%-1)*10)"("+STR$(item%)+")";
1400 @%=&01020205
1410 IF ABS(r(item%))<delta THEN temp=0 ELSE temp=r(item%)
1420 IF item%<= N% THEN PRINT temp;
1430 @%=10
1440 NEXT
1450 PRINT
1460 NEXT
1470 PRINT
1480 VDU3
1490 PRINT"Press the spacebar to continue":REPEAT:A$=GET$:UNTIL
     A$=" "
1500 PROCprint("details of item selection")
1510 ENDPROC
1520 REM-------------
```

```
1530 DEF PROCselect_items
1540 REM-------------
1550 LOCAL n%,I%
1560 FOR I%=1 TO N%
1570 work(I%)=r(I%)
1580 NEXT
1590 PROCsort_scores(N%)
1600  PRINT''"Now to select the best of these items"'"for
     cross-validation."
1610 REPEAT
1620 REPEAT
1630 PRINT"How many items should be retained?";CHR$131;
1640 INPUT n%
1650 UNTIL n%>0 AND n%<=N%
1660 PROCsummarise_correlations(n%)
1670 CLS
1680 PRINT"File name is ";in$;"..."
1690 PRINTCHR$(131);title$''
1700 PRINTCHR$132;"Item-criterion correlations"
1710 PRINTCHR$132;"=========================="
1720 PRINT'"If the best ";n%;" items are retained,"'
     "correlations with the criterion range"
1730 @%=&00020205
1740 PRINT"from ";r_lowest;" to ";r_highest;" with a mean of
     ";mean_r;"."''
1750 PRINT"The non-conservative, 1-tailed"'"probabilities of the
     lowest & the"
1760 PRINT"highest correlations are"
1770 PRINTp_r_lowest;" and ";p_r_highest;"."''
1780 @%=10
1790 ans=FNyesorno("Try a different number of items")
1800 UNTIL ans=FALSE
1810 IF FNyesorno("Write these items out to a file")=TRUE
     PROCoutputitems
1820 VDU3
1830 ENDPROC
1840 REM-------------
1850 DEF PROCsummarise_correlations(m%)
1860 REM-------------
1870 r_lowest=work(N%-m%+1)
1880 r_highest=work(N%)
1890 tot=0
1900 FOR I%=N%-m%+1 TO N%
1910 tot=tot+work(I%)
```

```
1920 NEXT
1930 mean_r=tot/m%
1940 p_r_lowest=FNsig_r(work(N%-m%+1),M%)
1950 p_r_highest=FNsig_r(work(N%),M%)
1960 ENDPROC
1970 REM
1980 REM-----------
1990 DEF FNsig_r(r,m%)
2000 REM-----------
2010 LOCAL mean,sd,z
2020 z=0.5*LN((1+r)/(1-r))
2030 mean=0
2040 sd=SQR(1/(m%-3))
2050 =1-FNnormal_integral((z-mean)/sd)
2060 REM--------------
2070 DEF FNnormal_integral(x)
2080 REM--------------
2090 REM Simpson's rule.
2100 LOCAL lowest,n_strips,h,x1,x2,x3,x4,x5,x6,x7,x8
2110 lowest=0
2120 n_strips=8
2130 h=(x-lowest)/n_strips
2140 x1=lowest:x2=x1+h:x3=x2+h:x4=x3+h
2150 x5=x4+h:x6=x5+h:x7=x6+h:x8=x7+h
2160 area=(FN_ord(x1)+FN_ord(x)+4*(FN_ord(x2)+FN_ord(x4)+FN_ord
     (x6)+FN_ord(x8))+2*(FN_ord(x3)+FN_ord(x5)+FN_ord(x7)))*h/3
2170 IF x<-4 THEN =0
2180 IF x>4 THEN =1
2190 =0.5+area
2200 REM---------
2210 DEF FN_ord(z)
2220 REM---------
2230 =EXP(-z*z/2)/SQR(2*PI)
2240 REM-------------
2250 DEF PROCsort_scores(n_elements%)
2260 REM-------------
2270 REM Shell sort.
2280 G%=n_elements%
2290 REPEAT
2300 G%=INT(G%/2)
2310 FOR I%=1 TO N%-G%
2320 FOR J%=I% TO 1 STEP -G%
2330 J1%=J%+G%
2340 IF work(J%)<=work(J1%) THEN J%=0 ELSE W=work(J%):work(J%)
```

```
       =work(Jl%):work(Jl%)=W
2350 NEXT
2360 NEXT
2370 UNTIL G%<2
2380 ENDPROC
2390 REM
2400 REM-----------
2410 DEF PROCwrite_data
2420 REM-----------
2430 LOCAL delta
2440 CLS
2450 PRINTCHR$131;"Writing items... please wait"
2460 new_n%=0
2470 FOR I%=1 TO N%
2480 IF r(I%)>=r_lowest THEN outtitle$=outtitle$+STR$(I%)+"
     ":r(I%)=TRUE: new_n%=new_n%+1 ELSE r(I%)=FALSE
2490 NEXT
2500 outtitle$=outtitle$+">"
2510 in=OPENIN("D."+in$)
2520 INPUT #in,dummy$
2530 INPUT #in,dummy$
2540 PRINT #out,outtitle$
2550 PRINT #out,STR$(INT(new_n%+0.5))
2560 REPEAT
2570 FOR I%=1 TO N%
2580 INPUT #in,dummy$
2590 IF r(I%)=TRUE PRINT#out,dummy$
2600 NEXT
2610 UNTIL EOF #in
2620 CLOSE #in
2630 CLOSE #out
2640 PRINT"File """out$;""" has been saved."
2650 PRINT''"This file holds:"'outtitle$''
2660 PRINT''"Press the spacebar to continue"
2670 REPEAT
2680 A$=GET$
2690 UNTIL A$=" "
2700 ENDPROC
2710 REM
2720 REM-----------------
2730 DEF FNvalidname(a$)
2740 REM-----------------
2750 LOCAL ok
2760 IF LEN(a$)>7 OR ASC(a$)<0 OR INSTR(a$,".")>0 THEN ok=FALSE
```

```
     ELSE ok=TRUE
2770 IF ok=FALSE PRINTCHR$(129);"File name too long or contains
     a "".""."
2780 =ok
2790 REM------------
2800 DEF PROCprint(c$)
2810 REM------------
2820 print=FNyesorno("Print the "+c$)
2830 IF print=TRUE THEN VDU2 ELSE VDU3
2840 ENDPROC
2850 REM-------------
2860 DEF FNyesorno(a$)
2870 REM-------------
2880 LOCAL a%,b$
2890 REPEAT
2900 PRINT a$;
2910 INPUT b$
2920 a%=INSTR("YyNn",LEFT$(b$,1))
2930 IF ASC(b$)<ASC("O") THEN a%=0
2940  UNTIL a%>0
2950 IF a%<3 THEN =TRUE ELSE =FALSE
2960 REM
2970 REM----------------
2980 DEF PROCexpectancy
2990 REM----------------
3000 REM
3010 IF T%=TRUE PRINT"UNSUITABLE FOR TAPE-BASED SYSTEMS"'"Press a
     key to continue..";:A$=GET$
3020  PROCdetermine_criterion_levels
3030 IF crit_level%>max_crit_level% PRINT"Criterion has too many
     possible values"'"Press a key to continue":A$=GET$:ENDPROC
3040 PROCprint("expectancy tables")
3050 FOR item%=1 TO N%
3060 PROCread_item(item%)
3070 PROCshow_table
3080 NEXT item%
3090 VDU3
3100 ENDPROC
3110 REM------------
3120 DEF PROCdetermine_criterion_levels
3130 REM------------
3140 CLS
3150 FOR I%=1 TO N%
3160 work(I%)=criterion(I%)
```

```
3170 NEXT
3180 PROCsort_scores(N%)
3190 PRINT"Criteria range from ";work(1);" to ";work(N%);"."
3200 @%=&00020205
3210 work(0)=-1E20
3220 crit_level%=0
3230 FOR crit%=1 TO N%
3240 IF work(crit%)>work(crit%-1) THEN crit_level%=crit_level%+1
3250 IF crit_level%<=max_crit_level% THEN prob_table
     (0,crit_level%)=work(crit%)
3260 NEXT
3270 @%=10
3280 ENDPROC
3290 REM--------------------
3300 DEF PROCread_item(item%)
3310 REM--------------------
3320 in=OPENUP("D."+in$) :REM data file, defined above.
3330 INPUT #in,dummy$: REM title
3340 REM Next in the file is the no of items (already known: N%)
3350 REM & the data. Now to perform dummy reads up to item "item%"
3360 FOR reads%=1 TO item%
3370 INPUT #in,dummy$
3380 NEXT
3390 INPUT #in,a$
3400 work(1)=VAL(a$)
3410 n_read=1
3420 REPEAT
3430 IF N%>1 THEN FOR J%=1 TO N%-1:INPUT#in,dummy$:NEXT
3440 INPUT #in,a$
3450 n_read=n_read+1
3460 work(n_read)=VAL(a$)
3470 UNTIL n_read=M%
3480 CLOSE #in
3490 cutoff=-1E20
3500 item_level%=0
3510 REPEAT
3520 min=1E20
3530 higher_found=FALSE
3540 FOR I%=1 TO M%
3550 IF work(I%)<min AND work(I%)>cutoff THEN min=work(I%):
     higher_found=TRUE
3560 NEXT
3570 cutoff=min
3580 IF higher_found=TRUE item_level%=item_level%+1
```

```
3590 IF higher_found=TRUE AND item_level%<= max_item_level% THEN
     prob_table(item_level%,0)=cutoff
3600 UNTIL higher_found=FALSE
3610 ENDPROC
3620 REM--------------------
3630 DEF PROCshow_table
3640 REM--------------------
3650 IF print=TRUE THEN PRINT''':VDU3:CLS:VDU2 ELSE CLS
3660 IF item_level%>max_item_level% PRINT"Item ";item%;" has too
     many levels!":ENDPROC
3670 @%=&00020005
3680  PRINTCHR$131;"Cross-tabulation of item scores"'CHR$131;"and
     criterion scores - ";M%;" Ss."
3690 @%=&00020005
3700 PRINTCHR$130;"Item ";item%
3710  PRINT'"Item  | Criterion values"
3720  PRINT"value | ";
3730 FOR I%=1 TO crit_level%
3740 PRINTprob_table(0,I%);
3750 NEXT I%
3760 @%=&00020205
3770 PRINT';STRING$(40,"=")
3780 FOR I%=1 TO item_level%
3790 FOR J%=1 TO crit_level%
3800 prob_table(I%,J%)=0
3810 NEXT
3820 NEXT
3830 FOR case%=1 TO M%
3840 i_level%=FNdetermine_item_level(case%)
3850 c_level%=FNdetermine_crit_level(case%)
3860 prob_table(i_level%,c_level%)=prob_table(i_level%,c_level%)+1
3870 NEXT
3880 FOR I%=1 TO item_level%
3890 PRINTprob_table(I%,0);" ] ";
3900 FOR J%=1 TO crit_level%
3910 PRINTprob_table(I%,J%)/M%;
3920 NEXT
3930 PRINT
3940 NEXT
3950 VDU3
3960  PRINT'CHR$131;CHR$136;"Press the spacebar to continue.."
3970 IF print=TRUE VDU2
3980 REPEAT
3990 A$=GET$
```

```
4000 UNTIL A$=" "
4010 @%=10
4020 ENDPROC
4030 REM----------------------
4040 DEF FNdetermine_item_level(case%)
4050 REM----------------------
4060 LOCAL level%
4070 level%=0
4080 REPEAT
4090 level%=level%+1
4100 UNTIL work(case%)=prob_table(level%,0)
4110 =level%
4120 REM----------------------
4130 DEF FNdetermine_crit_level(case%)
4140 REM----------------------
4150 LOCAL level%
4160 level%=0
4170 REPEAT
4180 level%=level%+1
4190 UNTIL criterion(case%)=prob_table(0,level%)
4200 =level%
```

Appendix 2: Using the programs

Colin Cooper

General considerations

The set of four item-analysis programs listed above are written in BBC BASIC–2 and were designed to run on an Acorn BBC model B micro-computer with a single disc-drive, though some will also work with a tape-based system. They are compatible with the Acorn 6502 second processor, which increases both the capacity and execution speed. The amount of free memory in a BBC system depends on the degree to which it has been expanded: the figures given below assume that a disc interface has been fitted but that no other expansion has been attempted.

BBC BASIC

The programs are structured and should prove comprehensible to those without formal knowledge of this dialect – but because of the structuring it would probably be easier to translate them into a language such as PASCAL rather than into unenhanced BASIC. Some features of BBC BASIC are however non-obvious, and we shall now consider these briefly.

Variable names. These can be up to 255 characters long; all are significant. Real values (e.g. 'var 1') are stored in five bytes, integers (e.g. 'var 1%') in four.

$A\%$–$Z\%$. The 'resident integers' $A\%$–$Z\%$ remain unchanged by loading and running another program. They are therefore used to pass data between programs – $T\%$ should be set TRUE in P.MENU if the system used is tape-based rather than disc-based. $A\%$ is set

TRUE in a program if a data file has been read. N% is sometimes used to hold the number of items in a data file, and M% the number of subjects.

@%. Defines the print format. This four-byte number operates as follows (note the use of '&' to denote a quantity expressed in hex). The most significant byte determines whether the function STR$, which converts from real or integer to character type, pays heed to the setting of @%. If Byte 3 = &00, it does not; if & 01, it does. Byte 2 selects general (G) format (&00) or fixed format (&02). When fixed format is selected, Byte 1 specifies the number of digits which follow the decimal point, whilst Byte 0 sets the overall field width (including any sign). Thus to select floating-point display with a field width of five and three digits after the decimal point set @%=&00020305 any time before the PRINT statement. The default is (decimal) 10.

*VDUx.*This is similar to PRINT CHR$(x) in other dialects: VDU2 enables the printer whilst VDU3 disables it.

PRINT CHR$(x) where x> 128. Used for special graphics effects such as colour, flashing text, double-height text.

PROCedures & FuNctions. All variables are global unless they are declared otherwise inside a procedure with the LOCAL variable-list command or used as an argument when calling a procedure or function.

*GET, GET$* wait for a key to be pressed, either numeric (GET) or alphanumeric (GET$), and return its ASCII code.

INSTR(A$,B$) returns the position of the second string inside the first, the left-most character being '1'. Returns zero if no match found; for example, INSTR('PROGRAM','RA') would return 5.

DEF PROCfred, DEF FNfred. DEFines a procedure or function called 'fred'.

EOFLx. Determines whether or not end of the file previously assigned to channel x (e.g. for reading by x=OPENIN ['Fred']) has been reached: TRUE or FALSE.

*FXn. *FX commands are calls to the operating system and cannot be summarized here in any useful manner.

File structure

Files prefixed 'P.' are program files, 'D.' are data files, and 'S.' files are correlation matrices in SPSS (8F 10.7) format. 'R.' files hold intermediate results in a manner which is transparent to the user: these can save enormous amounts of time when item-analysing large data sets. Data ('D.') files are in string format, holding a title, the number of variables and then the data case by case. The number of cases is calculated by testing for end of file whilst reading the data. No provision is made for missing values.

Program P.MENU

This program is the most computationally complex of those in the package. Apart from showing the main menu, it evaluates inter-item correlations, item means and standard deviations, correlations between items and the sum of all items, correlations between each item and the sum of all *other* items (the 'Guilford correction factor' discussed by Cooper, 1982), and the reliability (internal consistency) coefficient, Cronbach's alpha. It additionally allows items to be dropped at will, following which the item-total correlations and coefficient alpha are recomputed. It is also possible to output a correlation matrix (in SPSS format) for further analyses.

Option 2 of the menu reads in an existing data file for item analysis and computes the inter-item and item-total correlations, means and standard deviations. To find out which data files are on the disc, scan the catalogue by first choosing option 1.

The data are stored in a manner which sacrifices speed for compactness and relative freedom from rounding errors, hence this option can be very slow with large data-sets. To circumvent this difficulty, a file of intermediate results is automatically written out to disc when this routine is first used on a given data file. If such a file exists, it is automatically used in preference to the raw-data file, with enormous savings in speed. All this is totally transparent to the user: it does however mean that second or subsequent analyses of a given set of data will be much faster than the first. In extreme cases it may be wise to perform the initial reading of the data overnight, or with the machine unattended.

Option 4 prints the means and standard deviations of the items and their total, and displays the correlations between the items. If an item has a zero standard deviation, its correlation with other items is shown as '???'.

Option 5 prints the correlations between each item and the total of all items, and between the items and also the correlation obtained after applying Guilford's correction factor, as described above. Coefficient alpha is also shown. It is then possible repeatedly to drop items with low item-total correlations – or, indeed, any other items – in order to produce a more homogeneous scale. However, this will inevitably tend to capitalize on chance and may well produce a 'bloated specific' – a set of items that are essentially synonymous. This facility should be used with caution, and any resulting scale cross-validated on a different sample.

Option 7 is provided as a simple means of transferring the correlation matrix to other programs.

Technical notes

If the programs are to be run on a tape-based system, line 1650 should be altered so that T%=TRUE. Whilst the use of arrays for mean () and sd() is obvious (mean and sd for the total score being stored in the zeroth element of such arrays), to economize on space the correlations are stored in a vector, 'ray()', which is read by FNr(row,col) and written to by PROCsetr(row,col,value). To flag an item as having been dropped from an analysis its standard deviation is set negative – hence FNvalid (which checks the sign of the sd) and the use of FNsd(). The formula for computing item-total correlations after eliminating an item was derived for this application and is shown on line 2710.

P.SCALING

This program contains three routines, all of which act on the *sum* of an individual's scores to the $N\%$ test items. There are routines to compute Z-scores (and optionally rescale the data to a given mean and standard deviation), to show the centile scores and to compute T-scores (called normalized scores by Gulliksen). All should be self-explanatory in use. It should, however, be mentioned that, as the T-scaling is performed on ungrouped raw scores, when the normal ordinates are computed it is assumed that the sample was based on $M\%+1$ rather than $M\%$ cases, to avoid all scores showing the same maximum. This should not be a problem with any but the most trivial sets of data.

Program P.INPUT

This program allows data files to be entered from the keyboard, and for simple alterations to be made to the data contained in such files. It also allows the disc-user to examine the names of the data files on the currently selected disc drive, a feature which may be of use in several other contexts. The program is self-explanatory, and little additional guidance should be needed.

The routines which display the names of the data files on the disc (PROCcat et seq) are machine specific, and are therefore offered without explanation. They may not work for disc-filing systems other than the standard Acorn implementation.

Program P.CRIT

This program allows the relationship between test items and a criterion to be examined in two ways: by correlating items directly with the criterion, and by tabulating item-scores against criterion-scores. It additionally allows those items which best correlate with the criterion to be written out as a separate data file for further analysis (e.g. item-total correlations, *T*-scaling).

The selection of either item-total correlations (option 1) or expectancy tables (option 2) from the initial menu leads to the data being read, the items from a previously created file and the criteria from the keyboard. Note that no facility is provided for grouping the data in any way, and that for the expectancy tables option only seven discreet criterion values are possible. These need not be integers, nor be adjacent. In addition, any item may take one of up to only twelve values if expectancy tables are to be constructed. These restrictions are unlikely to prove disadvantageous in practice, for unless very large samples are being used, some cell frequencies will otherwise tend to be very small. No such restrictions apply to the item-total correlations.

Assuming that option 1 has been selected and the data input as described above, the product-moment correlations between each item and the criterion are displayed on the screen and optionally dumped to the printer. It is then possible to examine subsets of the 'best' items – that is those with the highest correlations with the criterion – the highest and lowest correlation and its one-tailed probability being shown. These items may then be saved, as described above. Note that writing the best items to disc destroys the item-criterion correlations. Thus no attempt should be made to reanalyse these correlations after doing so: it is however possible to draw up expectancy tables after writing these items to disc.

Option 2 draws up expectancy tables as described above: these tables show for each level of each item in turn the proportion of cases which fall in each criterion category. The number of cases upon which the analysis was based is also shown. As repeated reads of the data file are necessary for each item, this option is unsuitable for tape-based systems.

Bibliography

Abraham, K. (1921) 'Contributions to the theory of the anal character', in *Selected Papers of Karl Abraham*, London, Hogarth Press and The Institute of Psychoanalysis, 1965.

Adler, A. (1927) *Understanding Human Nature*, New York, Chilton.

Adorno, T. W., Frenkel-Brunswick, E., Levinson, D. J. and Sanford, R. N. (1950) *The Authoritarian Personality*, New York, Harper.

Allport, G. W. (1937) *Personality: A Psychological Interpretation*, New York, Holt, Rinehart & Winston.

Andrich, D. (1978) 'Relationships between the Thurstone and the Rasch approaches to item scaling', *Applied Psychological Measurement* 2, 449–60.

——and Kline, P. (1981) 'Within and among population item fit with the simple logistic model', *Educational and Psychological Measurement* (in press).

Anstey, E. (1966) *Psychological Tests*, London, Nelson.

Bannister, D. and Bott, M. (1973) 'Evaluating the person', in Kline, P. (ed.) *New Approaches in Psychological Measurement*, Chichester, Wiley.

——and Fransella, F. (1966), 'A grid test of schizophrenia thought disorder', *British Journal of Social and Clinical Psychology*, 5, 95.

Barnes, C. A. (1952) 'A statistical study of the Freudian theory of levels of psychosexual development', *Genetic Psychology Monographs*, 45, 109–74.

Barrett, P. T. and Kline, P. (1980) 'The observation to variable ratio in factor analysis', *Personality Study and Group Behaviour*, 1, 23–33.

——(1982a) 'Factor extraction: an examination of three methods' *Personality Study and Group Behaviour*, 3, 135–44.

——(1982b) 'The itemetric properties of the EPQ – a reply to Helmes', *Journal of Personality and Individual Differences*, 3, 259–70.

——(1984) 'A Rasch analysis of the EPQ', *Journal of Personality and Group Psychology* (in press).

Beck, A. T. (1962) 'Reliability of psychiatric diagnoses: a critique of systematic studies', *American Journal of Psychiatry*, 119, 210–15.

Bendig, A. W. (1959) 'Score reliability of dichotomous and trichotomous item responses in the MPI', *Journal of Consulting Psychology*, 23, 181–5.

Bennet, G. K., Seashore, H. G. and Wesman, A. G. (1962) *Differential Aptitude Tests*, 2nd edn, New York, New York Psychological Corporation.

Berk, R. A. (1980) *Criterion Reference Measurement: The State of the Art*, Baltimore, Johns Hopkins University Press.

Berry, J. W. and Dasen, P. R. (eds) (1974) *Culture and Cognition: Readings on Cross-Cultural Psychology*, London, Methuen.

Birnbaum, A. (1968) 'Some latent trait models and their use in inferring an examinee's ability', in Lord F. M. and Novick, M. R. (eds) *Statistical Theories of Mental Test Scores*, New York, Addison-Wesley.

Bloom, B. (1956) *Taxonomy of Educational Objectives Handbook: Cognitive Domain*, New York, Longmans Green.

Blum, G. S. (1949) 'A study of the psychoanalytic theory of psychosexual development', *Genetic Psychology Monographs*, 39, 3–99.

Briggs, K.C. and Myers, I.B. (1962) *The Myers–Briggs Type Indicator: Manual*, Princeton, Educational Testing Service.

Brown, F. G. (1976) *Principles of Educational and Psychological Testing*, 2nd edn, New York, Holt, Rinehart & Winston.

Brown, G. W. (1974) 'Meaning, measurement and stress of life events', in Dohrenirend, B. S. and Dohrenirend, B. P. (eds) *Stressful Life Events: Their Nature and Effects*, Chichester, Wiley.

Browne, J. A. and Howarth, E. (1977) 'A comprehensive factor analysis of personality questionnaire items: a test of twenty putative factor hypotheses', *Multivariate Behavioural Research*, 12, 399–427.

Buck, J. N. (1948) 'The HTP test', *Journal of Clinical Psychology*, 4, 151–9.

——(1970) *The House Tree Person Technique: Revised Manual*, Los Angeles, WPS.

Buros, O. K. (1978) *The VIIIth Mental Measurement Year Book*, Highland Park, NJ, Gryphon Press.

——(ed.) (1959) *The Vth Mental Measurement Year Book*, Highland Park, NJ, Gryphon Press.

——(ed.) (1972) *VIIth Mental Measurement Year Book*, Highland Park, NJ, Gryphon Press.

Burt, C. (1940) *The Factors of the Mind*, London, University of London Press.

Campbell, D. P. (1971) *Handbook for the Strong Vocational Interest Blank*, Stanford, Stanford University Press.

Carroll, B. J. (1971) 'Plasma cortisol levels in depression', in Dames, B., Carroll, B. J. and Mowbray, R. M. (eds) *Depressive Illness*, Springfield, C. Thomas.

Carroll, J. B. (1980) *Individual Difference Relations in Psychometric and Experimental Cognitive Tasks*, Report No. 163, L. L. Thurstone Psychometric Laboratory, Chapel Hill, University of North Carolina.

——(1983) 'Studying individual differences in cognitive abilities: implications for cross-cultural studies', in Irvine, S. H. and Berry, J. W. (eds) *Human Assessment and Cultural Factors*, New York, Plenum Press.

Cattell, R. B. (1946) *Description and Measurement of Personality*, London, Harrap.

——(1952) 'The three basic factor-analytic research designs, their inter-relations and derivatives', in Jackson, D. N. and Messick, S. (eds) *Problems in Human Assessment*, New York, McGraw Hill, 1967.

——(1957) *Personality and Motivation Structure and Measurement*, New York, Yonkers.

——(1966) *Handbook of Multivariate Experimental Psychology*, Chicago, Rand McNally.

——(1971) *Abilities: Their Structure, Growth and Action*, New York, Houghton-Mifflin.

——(1973) *Personality and Mood by Questionnaire*, San Francisco, Jossey-Bass.

——and Bolton, L. S. (1969) 'What pathological dimensions lie beyond the normal dimensions of the 16 PF? A comparison of MMPI and 16 PF factor domains', *Journal of Consulting and Clinical Psychology*, 33, 18–29.

——and Butcher, H. J. (1968) *The Prediction of Achievement and Creativity*, New York, Bobbs Merrill.

——and Cattell, A. K. S. (1960) *The Culture Fair Intelligence Test: Scales 2 and 3* Champaign, Ill., IPAT.

——and Child, D. (1975) *Motivation and Dynamic Structure*, London, Holt, Rhinehart & Winston.

——and Kline, P. (1977) *The Scientific Analysis of Personality and Motivation*, London, Academic Press.

——and Muerle, J. L. (1960) 'The "Maxplane" program for factor rotation to oblique simple structure', *Educational and Psychological Measurement*, 20, 569–90.

——and Warburton, F. W. (1967) *Objective Personality and Motivation Tests* Urbana, Ill., University of Illinois Press.

——, Eber, H. W. and Tatsuoka, M. M. (1970) *The 16 PF Test*, Champaign, Ill., IPAT.

——, Horn, J. L. and Sweney, A. B. (1970) *Motivation Analysis Test*, Champaign, Ill., IPAT.

Child, D. (1971) *Essentials of Factor Analysis*, London, Holt, Rinehart & Winston.

Chopin, B. H. (1976) 'Recent developments in item banking', in De Gruitjer, P. N. M. and Van Der Kamp, L. J. T. (eds) *Advances in Psychological and Educational Measurement*, Chichester, Wiley.

Comrey, A. L. (1970) *The Comrey Personality Scales*, San Diego, Educational and Industrial Testing Service

Cooper, C. (1982) 'Correlation measures in item analysis', *British Journal of Mathematical and Statistical Psychology*, 35, 102–5.

——, May, J. and Kline, P. (in press) 'The reliability of some elementary cognitive tasks', *British Journal of Educational Psychology*.

Corah, N. L., Feldman, M. J., Cohen, I. S., Green, W., Meadow, A. and Rugwall, E. A. (1958) 'Social desirability as a variable in the Edwards Personal Preference Schedule', *Journal of Consulting Psychology*, 22, 70–2.

Corman, L. (1969) 'Le test PN Manuel', Paris, Presses Universitaires de France.

Crisp, A. H. and Crown, S. (1970) *The Middlesex Hospital Questionnaire*, Barnstaple, Psychological Test Publications.

Cronbach, L. J. (1946) 'Response sets and test validity', *Educational and Psychology Measurement*, 6, 475–94.

——(1951) 'Coefficient alpha and the internal structure of tests', *Psychometrika*, 16, 297–334.

——(1970) *Essentials of Psychological Testing*, New York, Harper & Row.

——and Meehl, P. E. (1955) 'Construct validity in psychological tests', *Psychological Bulletin*, 52, 177–94.

Crowne, D. P. and Marlowe, D. (1964) *The Approval Motive*, New York, Wiley.

De Gruitjer, P. N. M. and Van Der Kamp, L. J. T. (eds) (1976) *Advances in Psychological and Educational Measurement*, Chichester, Wiley.

Dohrenirend, B. S. and Dohrenirend, B. P. (eds) (1974) *Stressful Life Events: Their Nature and Effects*, Chichester, Wiley.

Edwards, A. L. (1957) *The Social Desirability Variable in Personality Research*, New York, Dryden Press.

——(1959) *The Edwards Personal Preference Schedule*, rev. edn, New York, Psychological Corporation.

——(1967) *Edwards' Personality Inventory*, Chicago, Science Research Associates.

——, Wright, C. E. and Lunneborg, C. E. (1959) 'A note on social desirability as a variable in the Edwards Personal Preference Schedule', *Journal of Consulting Psychology*, 23, 598.

Educational Testing Service (1963) *Multiple-choice Questions: A New Look*, Princeton, Educational Testing Service.

Elliott, C. D. (1983) *British Ability Scales Manual 1*, Windsor, NFER-Nelson.

——,Murray, D. J. and Pearson, L. S. (1978) *British Ability Scales*, Slough, NFER.

Eysenck, H. J. (1952) *The Scientific Study of Personality*, London, Routledge & Kegan Paul.

——(1953) 'The logical basis of factor analysis', in Jackson, D. N. and Messick, S. (eds) *Problems in Human Assessment*, New York, McGraw Hill, 1967.

——(1959) 'The Rorschach Test', in Buros, O. K. (ed.) *The Vth Mental Measurement Year Book*, Highland Park, NJ, Gryphon Press.

——(1967) *The Biological Basis of Personality*, Springfield, C. C. Thomas.

——(1970) *Readings In Introversion–Extraversion*, London, Staples Press.

——(1971) *Readings in Introversion–Extraversion II*, London, Staples Press.

——and Eysenck, S. B. G. (1969) *Personality Structure and Measurement*, London, Routledge & Kegan Paul.

——(1975) *The EPQ*, London, University of London Press.

——(1976) *Psychoticism as a Dimension of Personality*, London, Hodder & Stoughton.

Fan, Chung-Teh (1952) *Item Analysis Tables*, Princeton, Educational Testing Service.

Fenichel, O. (1945) *The Psychoanalytic Theory of Neurosis*, New York, Norton.

Ferguson, G. A. (1949) 'On the theory of test development', *Psychometrika* 14, 61–8.

Fisher, S. and Greenberg, R. P. (1977) *The Scientific Credibility of Freud's Theories and Therapy*, Brighton, Harvester Press.

Foulds, G. A. (1976) *The Hierarchical Nature of Personal Illness*, London, Academic Press.

French, J. W., Ekstrom, R. B. and Price, L. A. (1963) *Kit of Reference Tests for Cognitive Factors*, Princeton, Educational Testing Service.

Freud, S. (1900) *The Interpretation of Dreams*, Standard Edition of the Complete Psychological Works of Sigmund Freud, vols 4 and 5, London, Hogarth Press and The Institute of Psychoanalysis.

——(1905) *Three Essays on the Theory of Sexuality*, Standard Edition, vol. 7.

——(1908) *Character and Anal Erotism*, Standard Edition, vol. 9.

——(1911) 'Psychoanalytic notes on an autobiographical account of a case of paranoia (dementia paranoides)', Standard Edition, vol. 12.

——(1920) *Beyond the Pleasure Principle*, Standard Edition, vol. 18.

——(1933) *New Introductory Lectures in Psychoanalysis*, Standard Edition, vol. 22.

——(1940) *An Outline of Psychoanalysis*, Standard Edition, vol. 23.

Gagne, R. M. (ed.) (1965) *Psychological Principles in System Development*, New York, Holt, Rinehart & Winston.

Gilmer, B. V. H. (1966) *Industrial Psychology*, New York, McGraw-Hill.

Glaser, R. (1963) 'Instructional technology and the measurement of learning outcomes', *American Psychologist*, 18, 519–21.

Gorsuch, H. L. (1974) *Factor Analysis*, Philadelphia, W.B. Saunders.

Gottheil, E. (1965) 'An empirical analysis of orality and anality', *Journal of Nervous and Mental Diseases*, 141, 308–17.

Grygier, T. G. (1961) *The Dynamic Personality Inventory*, Windsor, NFER.

——and Grygier, P. (1976) *Manual to the Dynamic Personality Inventory*, Windsor, NFER.

Guilford, J. P. (1956) *Psychometric Methods*, 2nd edn, New York, McGraw-Hill.

——(1959) *Personality*, New York, McGraw-Hill.

——(1967) *The Nature of Human Intelligence*, New York, McGraw-Hill.

——,Zimmerman, W. S. and Guilford, J. P. (1976) *The Guilford–Zimmerman Temperament Survey Handbook*, San Diego, Sheridan.

Guttman, L. (1950) 'The basis for scalogram analysis', in Stoufer, S. A. (ed.) *Studies on Social Psychology in World War II, Volume 4: Measurement and Prediction*, Princeton, Princeton University Press.

Hakstian, A. R. (1971) 'A comparative evaluation of several prominent factor transformation methods', *Psychometrika*, 36, 175–93.

——and Cattell, R. B. (1974) 'The checking of primary ability structure on a broader basis of performance', *British Journal of Educational Psychology*, 44, 140–54.

Hampson, S. and Kline, P. (1977) 'Personality dimensions differentiating certain groups of abnormal offenders from non-offenders', *British Journal of Criminology*, 17, 310–31.

Harman, H. H. (1964) *Modern Factor Analysis*, Chicago, University of Chicago Press.

——(1976) *Modern Factor Analysis*, 3rd edn, Chicago, University of Chicago Press.

Hartog, P. and Rhodes, E. C. (1935) *An Examination of Examinations*, London, Macmillan.

Hathaway, S. R. and McKinley, J. C. (1951) *The Minnesota Multiphasic Personality Inventory Manual (Revised)*, New York, Psychological Corporation.

Heim, A. W. (1975) *Psychological Testing*, London, Oxford University Press.

——and Watts, K. P. (1966) 'The Brook Reaction Test of Interests', *British Journal of Psychology*, 57, 178–85.

——and Simmonds, V. (1969) *Brook Reaction Test*, Windsor, NFER.

——(1970) *AH4, AH5 and AH6 Tests*, Windsor, NFER.

Holley, J. W. (1973) *Rorschach Analysis*, in Kline, P. (ed.) *New Approaches in Psychological Measurement*, Chichester, Wiley.

——and Guilford, J. P. (1964) 'A note on the G Index of agreement', *Educational and Psychological Measurement*, 24, 749–53.

Holtzman, W. H., Thorpe, J. S., Swartz, J. D. and Heron, E. W. (1961) *Inkblot Perception and Personality: Holtzman Inkblot Technique*, Austin, Texas, University of Texas.

Horn, J. L. and Knapp, J. R. (1973) 'On the subjective character of the empirical base of Guilford's Structure-of-Intellect Model', *Psychological Bulletin*, 80, 33–43.

Howarth, E. (1976) 'Were Cattell's "Personality Sphere" factors correctly identified in the first instance? *British Journal of Psychology*, 67 (2), 213–30.

Hoyt, C. (1941) 'Test reliability obtained by analysis of variance', *Psychometrika*, 6, 153–60.

Hsu, F. L. H. (ed.) (1972) *Psychological Anthropology*, Cambridge, Mass., Schenkmann.

Hudson, W. (1960) 'Pictorial depth perception in sub-cultural groups in Africa', *Journal of Social Psychology*, 52, 183–208.

Hudson, W. (1967) 'The study of the problem of pictorial perception among unacculturated groups', *International Journal of Psychology*, 2, 89–107.

Hull, C. L. (1943) *Principles of Behaviour*, New York, Appleton-Century-Crofts.

Hunt, E. (1982) 'Towards new ways of assessing intelligence', *Intelligence*, 6, 231–40.

Jackson, D. N. (1967) *Personality Research Form*, New York, Research Psychologists Press.

——and Messick, S. (eds) (1967) *Problems in Human Assessment*, New York, McGraw-Hill.

Jensen, A. R. (1980) *Bias in Mental Testing*, New York, Free Press.

——(1982) 'Reaction time and psychometric g', in Eysenck, H. J. (ed.) *A Model for Intelligence*, Berlin, Springer-Verlag.

Jinks, J. L. and Eaves, L. J. (1974) 'IQ and Inequality', *Nature*, 248, 287–89

Jones, E. (1923) 'Anal erotic character traits', *Papers on Psychoanalysis*, London, Bailliere, Tindall & Cox.

Jung, C. G. (1978) 'The Tavistock Lectures', in *Collected Works of C. Jung*, London, Routledge & Kegan Paul, vol. 25.

Kaiser, H. F. (1958) 'The Varimax Criterion for analytic rotation in factor analysis, *Psychometrika*, 23, 187–200.

Kelly, G. A. (1955) *The Psychology of Personal Constructs*, New York, Norton, vols 1 and 2.

Kilbride, P. L. and Robbins, M. C. (1969) 'Pictorial depth perception and acculturation among the Baganda', *American Anthropologist*, 71, 293–301.

Kline, P. (1968) 'Obsessional traits, obsessional symptoms and anal erotism', *British Journal of Medical Psychology*, 41, 299–305.

——(1971) *Ai3Q Test*, Windsor, NFER.

——(1972) *Fact and Fantasy in Freudian Theory*, London, Methuen.

——(1973a) 'Assessment in psychodynamic psychology', in Kline, P. (ed.) (1973).

——(1973b) *New Approaches in Psychological Measurement*, Chichester, Wiley.

——(1975) *The Psychology of Vocational Guidance*, London, Batsford.

——(1976) *Psychological Testing*, London, Malaby Press.

——(1977) 'Cross-cultural studies and Freudian theory', in Warren, N. (ed.) *Studies in Social Psychology*, London, Academic Press.

——(1978) 'The status of the anal character: a reply to Hill', *British Journal of Psychology*, 51, 87–90.

——(1978) *OOQ and OPQ Personality Tests*, Windsor, NFER.

——(1979) *Psychometrics and Psychology*, London, Academic Press.

——(1985) 'Factors, components and processes', in Roskam, E. E. (ed.) *Measurement and Testing in Psychology*, Amsterdam, Elsevier Science.

——and Cooper, C. (1977) 'A percept-genetic study of some defence mechanisms in the test PN, *Scandinavian Journal of Psychology*, 18, 148–52

——and Gale, M. A. (1969) 'An objective method of administering a projective technique: the Blacky Pictures', *British Journal of Projective Psychology*, 15, 12–16.

——and Grindley, J. (1974) 'A 28-day case study with the MAT', *Journal of Multivariate Experimental Personality Clinical Psychology*, 1, 13–32.

——and Mohan, J. (1974) 'Item endorsements of a personality test – Ai3Q – in three cultures', *Journal of Social Psychology*, 94, 137–8.

——and Storey, R. (1978) 'A factor analytic study of the oral character', *British Journal of Social and Clinical Psychology*, 16, 317–28.

——(1980) 'The aetiology of the oral character', *Journal of Genetic Psychology*, 136, 85–94.

Knowles, J. B. (1963) 'Acquiescence response set and the questionnaire measurement of personality', *British Journal of Social and Clinical Psychology*, 2, 131–7.

Kragh, V. (1955) *The Actual Genetic Model of Perception Personality*, Lund, Gleerup.

——(1969) *The Defence Mechanism Test*, Stockholm, Testforlaget.

——and Smith, G. (1970) *Percept-Genetic Analysis*, Lund, Gleerup.

Kraepelin, E. (1907) *Clinical Psychiatry*, New York, Collier-Macmillan.

Krout, M. H. and Tabin, J. K. (1954) 'Measuring personality in developmental terms', *Genetic Psychology Monographs*, 50, 289–335.

Kyllonen, P. C., Lohman, D. F. and Snow, R. E. (1984) 'Effects of aptitudes, strategy training and task facets on spatial task performance', *Journal of Educational Psychology*, 76, 130–45.

Lazarsfeld, P. F. (1950) 'The logical and mathematical foundation of latent structure analysis', in Stoufer, S. (ed.) *Studies on Social Psychology in World War II, Volume 4: Measurement and Prediction*, Princeton, Princeton University Press.

Lee, S. G. (1953) *Manual of a Thematic Apperception Test for African Subjects*, Pietermantzburg, University of Natal Press.

Levy, P. (1960) 'Properties of the Holley-Guilford G index of agreement in R and Q factor analysis', *Scandinavian Journal of Psychology*, 7, 239–43.

——(1973) 'On the relation between test theory and psychology', in Kline, P. (ed.) *New Approaches in Psychological Measurement*, Chichester, Wiley.

Likert, R. A. (1932) 'A technique for the measurement of attitudes', *Archives of Psychology*, 40–52.

Lindzey, G. (1961) *Projective Techniques and Cross-Cultural Research*, New York, Appleton-Century-Crofts.

Lord, F. M. (1952a) 'The relation of the reliability of multiple choice tests to the distribution of item difficulties', *Psychometrika*, 17, 181–94.

——(1952b) 'A theory of test scores', *Psychometric Monograph 7*.

——(1974) *Individualised Testing and Item Characteristic Curve Theory*, Princeton, Educational Testing Service.

——(1980) *Applications of Item Response Theory to Practical Testing Problems*, New Jersey, Hillsdale.

——and Novick, M. R. (1968) *Statistical Theories of Mental Test Scores*, New York, Addison-Wesley.

Lorenz, K. (1966) *On Aggression*, London, Methuen.

Lorge, I. and Thorndike, R. L. (1957) *Technical Manual, Lorge–Thorndike Intelligence Tests*, Boston, Houghton-Mifflin.

Lynn, D. B. and Lynn, R. (1959) 'The structured doll play test as a projective technique for use with children', *Journal of Projective Techniques and Personality Assessment*, 23, 335–44.

McArthur, C. C. (1972) 'The Rorschach Test', in Buros, O. K. (ed.) *VIIth Mental Measurement Year Book*, Highland Park, NJ, Gryphon Press.

McDougall, W. (1932) *Energies of Men*, London, Methuen.

Masling, J. (1960) 'The influence of situational and interpersonal variables in projective testing, *Psychological Bulletin*, 57, 65–85.

May, J., Cooper, C. and Kline, P. (1986) 'The cognitive analysis of flexible thinking and some other ability factors', Report to APRE, Farnborough.

Mellenbergh, G. J. (1983) 'Conditional item bias methods', in Irvine, S. H. and Berry, J. W. (eds) *Human Assessment and Cultural Factors*, New York, Plenum Press.

Menninger, W. C. (1943) 'Characterologic and symptomatic expressions related to the anal phase of psychosexual development', *Psychoanalytic Quarterly*, 12, 161–93

Messick, S. (1960) 'Dimensions of social desirability', *Journal of Consulting Psychology*, 24, 379–87.

——(1962) 'Response style and content measures from personality inventories', *Educational and Psychological Measurement*, 22, 1–17.

Miller, K. M. (1968) *The Rothwell–Miller Interest Blank*, Windsor, NFER.

Miller, R. B. (1965) 'Task description and analysis', in Gagne, R. M. (ed.) *Psychological Principles in System Development*, New York, Holt, Rinehart & Winston.

——(1966) 'Human factors in systems', in Gilmer, B. V. H. (ed.) *Industrial Psychology*, New York, McGraw-Hill.

Miller, W. S. (1970) *Miller Analogies Test*, New York, Psychological Corporation.

Mischel, W. (1968) *Personality and Assessment*, New York, Wiley.

——(1973) 'Towards a cognitive social learning reconceptualization of personality', *Psychological Review*, 80 (4), 252–83.

——(1977) 'On the future of personality measurement', *American Psychologist*, 32 (4), 246–54.

Murray, H. A. (1938) *Explorations in Personality*, New York, Oxford University Press.

Murstein, B. I. (1963) *Theory and Research in Projective Techniques*, New York, Wiley.

Nisbet, J. D. (1972) 'AH4, AH5 and AH6 tests', in Buros, O. K. (ed.) *VIIth Mental Measurement Year Book*, Highland Park, NJ, Gryphon Press.

Nunnally, J. C. (1978) *Psychometric Theory*, New York, McGraw-Hill.

Phillips, H. P. (1965) *Thai Peasant Personality*, Berkeley, University of California Press.

Pike, K. L. (1966) *Language in Relation to a Unified Theory of the Structure of Human Behaviour*, The Hague, Mouton.

Price-Williams, P. R. (1965) *Journal of Social Psychology*, 65, 1–15.

Rasch, G. (1960) *Probabilistic Models for Some Intelligence and Attainment Tests*, Copenhagen, Denmark Institute of Education.

——(1961) 'On general laws and the meaning of measurement in psychology', in *Proceedings of the Fourth Berkeley Symposium on Mathematical Statistics and Probability*, Berkeley, University of California Press, vol. 4.

——(1966) 'An item-analysis which takes individual differences into account', *British Journal of Mathematical and Statistical Psychology*, 19, 49–57.

Raven, J. C. (1965) *Progressive Matrices*, London, H. K. Lewis.

Richardson, M. W. and Kuder, G. F. (1939) 'The calculation of test reliability coefficients based on the method of rational equivalence', *Journal of Educational Psychology*, 30, 681–7.

Rodger, A. (1952) *The Seven Point Plan*, London, NIIP.

Rokeach, M. (1960) *The Open and Closed Mind*, New York, Basic Books.

Rorschach, H. (1921) *Psychodiagnostics*, Berne, Hans Huber.

Rosenzweig, S. (1951) 'Idiodynamics in personality theory with special reference to projective methods', *Psychological Review*, 58, 213–23.

Royce, J. R. (1963) 'Factors as theoretical constructs', in Jackson, D. N. and Messick, S. (eds) *Problems in Human Assessment*, New York, McGraw-Hill.

Sandler, J. (1954) 'Studies in psychopathology using a self-assessment inventory', *British Journal of Medical Psychology*, 27, 142–5

Schneider, K. (1958) *Psychopathic Personalities*, London, Cassell.

Schonell, F. J. (1951) *The Schonell Reading Tests*, Edinburgh, Oliver and Boyd.

Schubo, W., Hentschel, V., Zerssen, D. V. and Mombour, W. (1975) 'Psychiatric classification by means of a discriminatory application of Q factor-analysis' *Archiv fuer Psychiatrie und Nervenkrankheiten*, 220, 187–200.

Semeonoff, B. (1973) 'New developments in projective testing', in Kline, P. (ed.) *New Approaches in Psychological Measurement*, Chichester, Wiley.

——(1977) *Projective Tests*, Chichester, Wiley.

Sjobring, H. (1963) *La Personalité: structure et development*, Paris, Doin.

Skinner, B. F. (1953) *Science and Human Behaviour*, New York, Macmillan.

Slater, P. (ed.) (1976) *The Measurement of Intrapersonal Space by Grid Technique: Explorations of Intrapersonal Space*, Chichester, Wiley.

Slukin, W. (1974) 'Imprinting reconsidered', *British Psychological Society Bulletin*, 27, 447–51.

Spain, D. H. (1972) 'On the use of projective tests for research in psychological anthropology', in Hsu, F. L. K. (ed.) *Psychological Anthropology*, Cambridge, Mass., Schenkmann.

Spearman, C. (1927) *The Abilities of Man*, London, Macmillan.

Spindler, L. G. (1975) 'Researching the psychology of culture-change', in Williams, T. R. (ed.) *Psychological Anthropology*, The Hague, Mouton.

Spiro, M. E. (1972) 'An overview and suggested reorientation', in Hsu, F. L. K. (ed.) *Psychological Anthropology*, Cambridge, Mass., Schenkmann.

Sternberg, R. J. (1977) *Intelligence, Information-processing and Analogical Reasoning*, New Jersey, Erlbaum.

Stoufer, S. (ed.) (1950) *Studies on social psychology in World War II, Volume 4: Measurement and Prediction*, Princeton, Princeton University Press.

Summerwell, H. C., Campbell, M. M. and Sarason, I. G. (1958) 'The effects of differential motivating instructions on the emotional tone and outcome of TAT stories', *Journal of Consulting Psychology*, 22, 385–8.

Tatsuoka, M. M. (1971) *Multivariate Analysis*, New York, Wiley.

Thorndike, R. L. and Hagen, E. P. (1977) *Measurement and Evaluation in Psychology and Education*, 4th edn, New York, Wiley.

Thurstone, L. L. (1947) *Multiple Factor Analysis: A Development and Expansion of the Vectors of the Mind*, Chicago, University of Chicago Press.

Thomson, G. (1904) 'General intelligence objectively determined and measured', *American Journal of Psychology*, 115, 201–92.

Vegelius, J. (1976) 'On various G Index generalisations and their applicability within the clinical domain', *Acta Universitatis Uppsaliensis* 4.

Vernon, P. E. (1950) *The Measurement of Abilities*, London, University of London Press.

——(1964) *Personality Assessment*, London, Methuen.

——(1969) *Intelligence and Cultural Environment*, London, Methuen.

——and Parry, J. B. (1949) *Personnel Selection in the British Forces*, London, University of London Press.

Warren, N. (ed.) (1977) *Studies in Cross-Cultural Psychology*, London, Academic Press.

Wechsler, D. (1958) *The Measurement and Appraisal of Adult Intelligence*, Baltimore, Williams and Wilkins.

Wenig, P. (1952) 'The relative role of naive, artistic, cognitive and press compatibility misperceptions and ego-defence operations in tests of mis-perception', unpublished Masters thesis, University of Illinois.

Westerlund, B. (1976) *Aggression, Anxiety and Defence*, Lund, Gleerup.

Williams, T. R. (ed.) (1975) *Psychological Anthropology*, The Hague, Mouton.

Wilmott, A. S. and Fowles, D. E. (1974) *The Objective Interpretation of Test Performance: The Rasch Model Applied*, Windsor, NFER.

Wilson, G. D. and Patterson, J. R. (1970) *The Conservatism Scale*, Windsor, NFER.

Wober, M. (1966) 'Sensotypes', *Journal of Social Psychology*, 70, 181–9.

Wood, R. (1976) 'Trait measurement and item banks', in De Gruitjer, P. N. M. and Van Der Kamp, L. J. T. (eds) *Advances in Psychological and Educational Measurement*, Chichester, Wiley.

——(1978) 'Fitting the Rasch model: a heady tale', *British Journal of Mathematical and Statistical Psychology*, 31, 27–32.

——and Skurnik, L. S. (1969) *Item Banking: A Method for Producing School-Based Examinations and Nationally Comparable Grades*, Slough, NFER.

Wright, B. D. (1968) 'Sample-free test calibration and person measurement', in *Proceedings of the 1967 Invitational Conference on Testing Problems*, Princeton, Educational Testing Service.

——and Douglas, G. A. (1975) 'Better procedures for sample-free item analysis', *Research Memo 20*, Statistical Laboratory Department of Education, University of Chicago.

——and Panchepakesan, N. (1969) 'A procedure for sample-free item analysis, *Educational and Psychological Measurement*, 29, 23–48.

Zubin, J., Eron, L. D. and Schumer, F. (1966) *An Experimental Approach to Projective Techniques*, Chichester, Wiley.

Name index

Subject index

DATE DUE

DATE DUE			
DEC 5 1991			
DEC 11 1992			
MAY 7 1993			
AUG -7 1996			
ILL			
5-17-98			
DEC 12 1998			
JAN 13 2000			
MAY 1 6 2002			
GAYLORD			PRINTED IN U.S.A.